ENEAS

A TWELFTH-CENTURY FRENCH ROMANCE

NUMBER XCIII

RECORDS OF CIVILIZATION

SOURCES AND STUDIES

ENEAS

A Twelfth-Century French Romance

TRANSLATED
WITH AN INTRODUCTION
AND NOTES BY

JOHN A. YUNCK

New York and London 1974
Columbia University Press

Library of Congress Cataloging in Publication Data

Énéas (Romance) English.
  Eneas; a twelfth-century French romance.

  (Records of civilization: sources and studies, no. 93)
  Bibliography: p. [267] – 272
  I. Yunck, John A., ed.   II. Title.   III. Series.
  PQ1459.E35E5 1974 841′.1   74-8543
ISBN 0-231-03823-2

TO THE MEMORY OF

JOHN ABBOT CLARK

1903-1965

οὕνεκ ἐπητής ἐσσι καὶ ἀγχίνοος καὶ ἐχέφρων

PREFACE

The translation which follows originated in practical academic exigencies. *Eneas* is a document so obviously crucial to the establishment of the romance genre that a knowledge of its style and content is almost indispensable to an understanding of romance origins. Though its language is not especially difficult, yet even those relatively few graduate students who approach it with an adequate knowledge of Old French lack the leisure, in a demanding graduate program, to study in the original a medieval narrative poem of over ten thousand lines, whose significance is admittedly more historical than intrinsic. I have made the translation and designed the accompanying notes primarily for these students, though I believe that the work will be of some convenience to mature scholars in the field. I have attempted to make the translation literal enough to be read in conjunction with Salverda de Grave's later edition of *Eneas*.

I am indebted to the Research Fund and the Humanities Research Committee of Michigan State University for providing funds and released time which enabled me to bring the work to a conclusion, and to the reference staff of the Michigan State University Library for their helpfulness in obtaining materials unavailable locally. Professor W. T. H. Jackson of the Department of Germanic Languages at Columbia University, the editor of this series, has been unfailingly patient in his reading of the text, and has offered valuable sugges-

[viii]

tions, especially concerning the introduction and the style of the translation, which have improved the final readings. Professor Lawton P. G. Peckham of the Department of French at Columbia University has read parts of the manuscript, and has rescued me from a number of blunders in translation. Mr. Henry H. Wiggins and Mr. William F. Bernhardt of Columbia University Press, and their staff, have been most gracious and helpful throughout the process of publication. I am especially grateful to Professor Ursula Karsten Franklin of the Department of Foreign Languages at Grand Valley State College for the many hours she has spent in reading, criticizing, and offering suggestions about the manuscript. The errors and infelicities which remain are of my own commission.

Michigan State University   *John A. Yunck*
January, 1974

CONTENTS

INTRODUCTION

I

In rare instances literary historians are fortunate enough to possess a document which exhibits some literary genre in its nascent state, a work in which we can see the form come to birth and establish itself as a distinct literary type. We can thereby obtain a peculiarly fruitful insight into the creative process of its author and into the literary, cultural, and intellectual forces which contributed to the new genre, which made it a socially viable artistic medium. The twelfth-century French romance of *Eneas* is such a document. It is not the first extant work which can justifiably be called a medieval romance, nor can it lay claim to any considerable literary distinction; yet, in it for the first time the constituent elements of the romance of love and adventure fall into place and assume a characteristic pattern. The feudal battles, single combats, and councils of barons—these essentials of the *chanson de geste*—remain, but are newly embellished by sumptuous descriptions of buildings and fortified cities, fine clothes, and rich armor, marvels of flora, fauna, and architecture, sorcery and enchantment, by a new concern with finesse in manners, by a sense of the exotic which the medieval writers found in the classical past. All of this is conveyed in relatively unemotional language, through highly contrived but sprightly, flexible, and swift octosyllabics, often graceful and sometimes moving, which replace the more staid and sonorous assonanced *laisses* of the older heroic narrative.

But, most important, love—the passionate and sentimental love between the sexes—makes its appearance as the supreme moving force in the hearts of the characters. With passionate love appear, rather crudely and obtrusively, its physiological symptoms: the swooning, the sighing, the weeping and groaning, changes of color, loss of appetite, chills and fever, sleepless nights or deluding dreams. And with love also comes—for the first time in a long vernacular narrative—introspection. The lovers probe their own psyches in interminable monologues analyzing the desires, the sentiments, the psychology, the principles, the powers, the observances, and the doctrines of love. This sort of introspective exposition became, as readers of the early work of Chrétien know, an essential part of the romance genre. Much of the credit for its essential character must be given to the author of *Eneas*. "We can say," Gustave Cohen remarked,

> that it is from him that all the romancers of the second half of the twelfth century learned to write the preface to love, to avoid hastening it too abruptly to a conclusion, a resolution, or a dissolution, that they learned to pose a psychological problem, to give variety to love's hesitations, to study its origins, to initiate discussions between the invalid *(amor est quaedam mentis insania,* says a thirteenth century poem) and the doctor or the nurse—in short, to practice that casuistry of passion of which the French, from Chrétien to Stendhal, are past masters, and which has made them, if we may so speak, the professors of love for Europe.[1]

A growing recognition of this centrality of *Eneas* in the development of romance—indeed of Western narrative in general—has precipitated a striking increase in *Eneas* scholarship during the past decade, most of which strongly seconds the judgment of Cohen. Recent discussions[2] are gratifyingly

[1] G. Cohen *Un grand romancier d'amour et d'aventure au XII siècle: Chrétien de Troyes et son oeuvre,* new ed. (Paris, 1948), p. 43.

[2] Recorded in the bibliography to this volume. Unfortunately, much of the newer

less concerned with the necessary dry bones of scholarship—
sources, influence, manuscript problems, dating, provenance —than with reading the romance as a courtly work
of art, or as an attractive and influential representative of
the humanistic intellectual and artistic explosion in
twelfth-century France. We are now in an excellent position to understand the true significance, historical and intrinsic, of *Eneas,* and to recognize with some clarity its relations to the great intellectual and artistic movements of its
century.

II

Eneas was written by an unknown Norman poet,[3] probably between 1155 and 1160. Although the problems of literary chronology in the period are yet unsolved—perhaps
unsolvable—we may conclude that the work certainly appeared after the *Roman de Thèbes,* and probably shortly
before Benoit's *Roman de Troie.*[4] It was probably written
somewhat later than the brief, influential *Piramus et Tisbé*

scholarship has reached me too late for use in the preparation of this introduction,
to parts of which it contributes valuable additions and modifications. Though most
of it has appeared since 1966, it had its beginnings in the appearance of Adler's
"Eneas and Lavine: *Puer et Puella Senes," Romanische Forschungen,* LXXI (1959),
73–91, and received further impetus from the publication of the Acts of the important
Strasbourg Colloquy of 1962, *L'Humanisme médiéval dans les littératures romanes
du XII au XIV siècle,* ed A. Fourrier (Paris, 1964). For a thorough and very useful
bibliographical survey see R. Cormier, "The Present State of Studies on the *Roman
d'Eneas," Cultura Neolatina,* XXXI (1971), 7–39.

[3] On language and provenance cf. *Eneas,* ed. J. J. Salverda de Grave (2 vols., Cfmâ,
Paris, 1925–29), pp. vii-xxi. Salverda de Grave (p. xix) finds that the language differs
little in fundamentals from that of *Thèbes, Troie,* and Marie de France, and that all
four show signs of a deliberately archaic pronunciation.

[4] This relative order of the three "romans antiques" was first suggested by G. Paris,
rev. of *Eneas, Texte critique, Romania,* XXI (1892), 285. Paris' view was cogently
supported by E. Langlois, "Chronologie des romans de *Thèbes, d'Eneas,* et de *Troie,"
Bibl. de l'Ecole des Chartes,* LXVI (1905), 107–20; and was confirmed, with addition-
al evidence, by E. Faral, *Recherches sur les sources latines des contes et romans
courtois du moyen âge* (Paris, 1913), pp. 169–87. It is the most widely accepted order,
and I think firmly established.

and Wace's Roman de Brut,[5] certainly before some of the
lais of Marie de France, and before the extant works of
Chrétien de Troyes.[6] *Eneas* has survived in virtually complete form in seven manuscripts and with rather large *lacunae*
in two others. J.-J. Salverda de Grave, its only editor, has
identified the manuscripts as follows:[7]

A: Bibl. Laurent., Florence, Plut. XLI, cod. 44 (end of XII
century or beginning of XIII century).

B: Brit. Mus. Add. 14100 (XIV century). Small lacuna at
end from a missing leaf.

C: Brit. Mus. Add. 34114 (end of XIV century).

D: Bibl. Nat. f. fr. 60 (end of XIV century).

E: Bibl. Nat. f. fr. 12603 (XIV century). Two large lacunae,
totaling over 4000 lines, from missing leaves.

F: Bibl. Nat. f. fr. 1416 (XIII century).

G: Bibl. Nat. f. fr. 1450 (XIII century).

H: Bibl. École de Médecine, Montpellier, No. 251 (middle of
XIII century).

I: Bibl. Nat. f. fr. 784 (end of XIII century or beginning of
XIV century). Large lacuna from lost leaves.

[5] On the probable influence of *Piramus et Tisbé* on *Eneas* see Faral, *Recherches,*
pp. 16–21. On the apparent influence of Wace's *Brut* see E. Hoepffner, "L'Eneas et
Wace," *Archivum romanicum,* XV (1931), 248–69; XVI (1932), 162–66. Hoepffner's
conclusions have been denied in a carefully reasoned argument by E. Frederick, "The
Date of the *Eneas,*" *PMLA,* L (1935), 984–96, but the weight of evidence appears to
support Hoepffner's view.

[6] On the influence of *Eneas* on Marie de France see esp. E. Hoepffner, "Marie de
France et l'Eneas," *Studi medievali,* n.s., V (1932), 272–308. The bold thesis of E.
Levi, "Marie de France e il romanzo di *Eneas,*" *Atti del Reale Instituto Veneto di
Scienze, Lettere ed Arti,* LXXXI (1921–22), parte 2a, 645–86, that Marie de France
was the author of *Eneas,* has found virtually no acceptance. On the influence of
Eneas on Chrétien see A. Dressler, *Der Einfluss des altfranzösischen Eneas-Ro-
manes auf die altfranzösische Literatur* (Leipzig, 1907), esp. pp. 117–27, and A.
Micha, "Eneas et Cliges," in *Mélanges. . . Ernest Hoepffner* (Paris, 1949), pp.
237–43.

[7] Salverda de Grave discusses the manuscript tradition at length in *Eneas, texte
critique* (Bibl. Normannica, IV, Halle, 1891), pp. iii-xiv, and more concisely in *Eneas,*
Cfmâ, I iv-xii. In the latter edition he abandons the effort to diagram the complex
relations between the manuscripts which he had made earlier.

In most of these manuscripts, *Eneas* is associated with Wace's *Brut* or with other of the *romans antiques.* (The significance of this regular association will be discussed later in the introduction.)

Salverda de Grave considers the earliest of these manuscripts, *A,* to be closest to the author's text. It is certainly not the author's holograph, nor an immediate copy of it, but rather, as the editor remarks, "a mediocre copy," with numerous faults, "of an excellent model." It is very closely connected with *B,* though the later manuscript is clearly not a copy of the earlier. *Manuscript C* belongs to the same group as *A* and *B,* but has been altered in numerous places to conform to the readings of the group represented by *D,* and hence has significant relations with both groups.

The readings of *D* represent a very interesting state of the text, in places almost an independent rehandling. Many of its readings bring the narrative closer to that of Vergil's *Aeneid* and may suggest that *D,* especially for the first half of the romance, is more authentic than *A.* Salverda de Grave rejects this conclusion on the basis of numerous readings, especially in the latter half of the manuscript, which indicate later revisions. The most notable of these is an entirely different ending of 300 lines which *D* provides for the romance, and which Salverda de Grave printed in appendices to his two editions. This conclusion appears as an appendix to the present translation.

Of the remaining manuscripts, *EF* and *HI* form separate but related groups, and *G* appears closer in its readings to *EF* than to the others. But the filiation is complex. After careful examination of all variants, Salverda de Grave has been unable to provide a genealogy which will indicate adequately the relations among the extant manuscripts.

Salverda de Grave's first edition of the romance, a critical text, was published in 1891 as Volume IV of the Bibliotheca

Normannica. It is based on *Manuscript A,* corrected by readings from the other manuscripts, and with the orthography normalized. His second edition, published in 1925–29 as two volumes of the Classiques Français du Moyen Age, is an edition of *A,* in the original orthography and generally consonant with the principles of editing laid down by Bédier. Variants from other manuscripts have been included in the critical apparatus, but the text has been corrected from them only when the reading of *A* was unintelligible. The line numbering remains the same as that of the earlier edition.

In the critical edition, Salverda de Grave rejects the readings of Heinrich von Veldeke's adaptation (c. 1170–c. 1185) as an aid in establishing the French text, despite the fact that the German work is far earlier than our earliest manuscript of *Eneas.* He finds Heinrich's narrative too free in both expansions and abridgements of the original to be useful, and believes that Heinrich's manuscripts show some evidence of revision by scribes who were familiar with the French text. More recently, Cola Minis has defended the value of Heinrich's readings as an aid in establishing the French text.[8] Minis' conclusions are significant: that Heinrich's *Eneide* helps in numerous instances to establish the *Eneas* author's original text; that in the case of *Eneas* the older practice of constructing a critical text is more useful than the newer practice of editing the text of a single manuscript; that Salverda de Grave's critical edition of 1891 provides a more satisfactory text than his later edition of *Manuscript A;* and that at least the first half of *D,* in conjunction with the group *EFGHI,* reflects a more primitive state of the text than *A.* The arguments do not appear conclusive, but it must be conceded that

---

[8] C. Minis, "Textkritische Studien über den Roman d'Eneas," *Neophilologus,* XXXIII (1949), 65–85. The author presents the argument more at length in *Textkritische Studien über den Roman d'Eneas und die Eneide von Henric van Veldeke,* Studia Litteraria Rheno-Traiectina V (Groningen, 1959).

the problems of text and manuscript tradition have not yet been entirely solved. Meanwhile, we can agree with Salverda de Grave's comment on his second edition, that though it is certainly not the original text, it is "at least an historical reality."

III

Although its author does not mention the name of Vergil, *Eneas* is a French adaptation of the *Aeneid* to the tastes and attitudes of a twelfth-century courtly audience. With the important exception of the Eneas–Lavine love story, the medieval versifier follows the general outline of the *Aeneid* with relative fidelity. There is little exact translation from the Latin source, but sufficient similarity in many lines to suggest that the adapter was working with a manuscript of Vergil before him. Yet, in matters of detail and narrative turn, and especially in *sen,* or theme, or attitude, the work is thoroughly independent. The French versifier's method was (if we can judge from results) to study a Vergilian episode, to shape and reformulate it in terms of his own imagination and the taste of his society, to decorate it and elaborate it with the flotsam of his exceptionally wide reading in classical and contemporary literature, and to set it forth in accordance with rules learned from his formal schooling in rhetorical poetics.

Part of *Eneas'* singular interest is that it permits us to view in detail the transformation of a major classical literary work into the spirit and idiom of another civilization, a transformation through which we can study the *differentiae* that distinguish the new worldview. "Neither the *Roman de Troie* nor the *Roman de Thèbes*," observes Salverda de Grave, "permits us, to the same degree as *Eneas,* to grasp the difference between the inspiration of a classical poet and that of a medieval poet."[9]

[9] *Eneas, texte critique,* p. xxxvi.

The *Eneas* poet's originality lay not in the ingredients of his romance, which he found already at hand in one form or another, but in his own mixing of them, in the freedom with which he culled from and combined the materials of his learning and experience. He was steeped in Ovid, familiar with the *Roman de Thèbes,* probably familiar with Wace's *Brut, Piramus et Tisbé,* and other contemporary verse, and in command of a wide variety of medieval Latin books of travel and marvels, bestiaries, chronicles, and encyclopaedias.[10]

But his great contribution to the new genre, apparent in both his love episodes, is his naturalization of Ovid's love books to the increasingly self-conscious sentimental requirements of his medieval audience. Ovid's preoccupation with the passion and sentiment of love suited the versifier's taste. The ardors and laments of his lovers are in the spirit of, and inspired by, the outpourings of the feminine heart in the *Heroides,* though they are also packed with imagery and narrative detail drawn from all the other major works of Ovid. Auerbach has remarked that the *Eneas* author, with most of his generation, misunderstood the stylistic level of Ovid's books of love, written for a Roman society of elegant courtesans, and that he therefore attempted to transfer the Ovidian themes and images to a social class and a narrative level to which they were unsuited.[11] Yet the echoes of the *Eneas* love passages in later romances show that this mismatching was unquestionably the most important reason for the work's great popularity among contemporary authors and audiences.

The success of *Eneas* was immediate. Echoes of its imagery and narrative turns, its love monologues and stichomythic dialogues, its introspective psychology and physiology of in-

[10] For scholarship on the sources of *Eneas,* see notes 4 and 5 above, but esp. Faral, *Recherches.*

[11] E. Auerbach, *Literatursprache und Publikum in der lateinischen Spätantike und im Mittelalter* (Bern, 1958), pp. 161–62.

cipient passion, its descriptions of natural and artificial marvels, began to appear in the works of contemporaries. From
Vergil's shadowy symbol of cultural union, Lavinia was transformed into one of the great lovers of the Middle Ages. Dressler has found strong echoes of *Eneas* in the early works of
Chrétien, in those of Gautier d'Arras (especially *Eracle),* in
Partenopeus de Blois, Floire et Blancheflor, the *Roman de
Galerent,* the *Roman de Blancandin,* and *Amadas et Ydoine,*
among others.[12] Later scholars have added to this list the *Lais*
of Marie de France and the *Roman de Troie,* to name but
two.[13] Courtly narrative during the remainder of the twelfth
century was dominated by the influence of *Eneas,* directly or
indirectly. Nor was its immediate influence confined to
France or French-speaking England. Within fifteen years of
its appearance, the Flemish Heinrich von Veldeke began an
expanded adaptation (1170) which was completed, after a
long interruption, about 1185.[14] Through this interesting
translation (discussed briefly later in the introduction) *Eneas*
helped to found the German court epic.

But more significant than the direct influences, borrowings,
and echoes recorded in Dressler's cautious study is the fact
that *Eneas* established for the following century a pattern
after which writers of romance could treat the theme of romantic love. Lavine's pains and sorrows over Eneas, like the
later Petrarch's long-deceased woes over Laura, were oft re-
suffered.

[12] Cf. Dressler, *Einfluss,* pp. 117–51.

[13] Cf. esp. Faral, *Recherches,* pp. 171–87; Hoepffner, "Marie de France et l'Eneas"
(see note 6); Salverda de Grave, "Un imitateur du Roman d'Eneas au XIIIe siècle
en France," *Studi medievali,* n.s., V (1932), 300–316; F. Warren, *"Eneas* and Thomas'
Tristan," *MLN,* XXVII (1912), 107–10.

[14] Heinrich von Veldeke, *Eneide,* ed. G. Schieb and T. Frings (3 vols., Berlin,
1964–70).

IV

It will be profitable here to examine more closely the *Eneas* poet's treatment of his major source, and perhaps to draw some conclusions about his method of composition, his interests and attitudes, and those of his audience. I will not attempt a detailed comparison of the romance with Vergil's *Aeneid;* that has been supplied in meticulous tabular form by the editor of *Eneas* in his first edition,[15] and I have called attention to the more significant changes in the footnotes to this translation. I will concern myself rather with the several types of suppression, change, or addition made by the medieval poet, and with the conclusions that can be drawn from these variations.[16]

The most obvious omissions and suppressions suggest that the romancer, like so many later French writers, speaks as an apostle of *clarté*. He is a rationalist, writing for a civilized, sophisticated, and enlightened Christian audience, and he is clearly embarrassed by Vergil's gods, perhaps disturbed that an ancient poet so noble, and a story-teller so polished, should be encumbered by an anthropomorphic polytheistic superstition. Whatever his feelings, he omits as much Olympian material as he can. He appears to understand nothing at all of the tradition of epic machinery, or of Vergil's superb use of Olympian episodes for heroic breadth and sublimity, for uni-

[15] Salverda de Grave, *Eneas, texte critique*, pp. xxxvii-lxii.

[16] Numerous commentators have analyzed the narrative effects of the *Eneas* poet's divergences from Vergil, especially in the Carthage episode and in the treatment of Vergil's epic machinery. We may mention J. Crosland, "Eneas and the Aeneid," *MLR*, XXIX (1934), 282–90 (highly disdainful of *Eneas);* two essays by A. Pauphilet, "Eneas et Enée," *Romania,* LV (1929), 195–213, and "L'Antiquité et *Énéas,*" in *Le Legs du moyen âge* (Melun, 1950), pp. 91-106; A Varvaro, "I Nuovi valori del *Roman d'Eneas," Filologia e letteratura,* XIII (1967), 113–41; R. Petullà, "Il *Roman d'Eneas* e l'*Eneide," Filologia medioevale e umanistica,* CII (1968), 409–31; and R. Jones, *The Theme of Love in the Romans d'Antiquité* (MHRA Dissertation Ser., 5, London, 1972; esp. pp. 30–42); but scattered observations on the subject can be found in almost all discussions of *Eneas.* I have profited from many of these, especially from the remarks of Pauphilet.

versality, as metaphor, and as lofty decoration. Or, if he is aware of these things, he cares for them not at all. Vergil's poetic and philosophical sophistication is so far above his own that he fails to recognize it. Rationalism here, as in many later authors, is accompanied by a somewhat blight-ed imagination.

These suppressions show no sign of what the Renais-sance would call "monkish narrowness"; rather, they are made in the spirit of enlightenment. Though the *Eneas* poet willingly moralizes about many things throughout his narrative, he has no quarrel with "payens corsed olde rites." Only once, in passing (vv. 9443-48), does he com-ment briefly (and humorously) on the inefficacy of the pagan gods, and only once (1006–7) does he absent-mind-edly endow a pagan rite with Christian trappings. While keeping within the pagan frame of his *matière* with surpris-ing consistency and deference, he prefers to ignore its su-pernatural elements.

The *Eneas* poet's rationalism, then, causes him to discard almost all divine interference and apparitions, all encoun-ters of gods with gods or with men, and similar superna-tural occurrences unnecessary to the narrative frame. Thus, from Book i of the *Aeneid,* Venus' interview with Jupiter and Jupiter's consequent prophecy of the future of Rome disappear, as does Aeneas' interview with Venus on the Libyan coast, Venus' concealment of Aeneas on the road to Carthage, and her substitution of Cupid for Ascan-ius. The adapter removes from Aeneas' account of the fall of Troy the episode of Laocoön and his sons, Aeneas' dream of Hector, the divine omens which appear over Julus' head, and the appearance of Creusa's ghost. The angry encounter of Juno and Venus (Book iv) does not appear in the ro-mance, nor does the lovely passage in which Iris releases the soul of the suffering Dido. The elaborate episode in

Book vii, where Allecto stirs up the war fury of the Latins, is omitted from the romance, along with Juno's opening of the temple of Janus in Laurentum. Many more instances are indicated in the notes.

The omitted divine or supernatural elements are replaced in various ways. Where possible, the whole episode is ignored, as in the detail of Creusa's ghost. Sometimes the *Eneas* author alters the outcome of an episode to conform with the demands of realism or natural cause and effect. In Book ix of the *Aeneid,* for example, Aeneas' ships are supernaturally transformed into sea nymphs when Turnus attempts to burn them. In *Eneas,* the ships are simply allowed to burn. In place of Allecto's frenzy at the opening of Book vii, the French poet expands the episode of the killing of Silvia's pet deer into a long and vivid feudal incident which arouses passions and precipitates hostilities.

But there are numerous supernatural elements in Vergil's narrative fundamental to the frame of the story, with which the *Eneas* author could not dispense. Eneas was, after all, the son of Venus and under her special guidance and protection. To do away with her would be undesirable. The adapter accepts such necessities, but nevertheless attenuates the incidents, suppressing as much detail as he can. He especially avoids depicting the pagan divinities in action. Though Venus communicates with Eneas more than once, we never see her doing so (e.g., vv. 32–41, 4563–64). Though Juno is hostile to the hero, we do not see her visiting Aeolus to raise a storm. We are simply told that she did so (183–89). Though the gods must command Eneas to leave Carthage, the French author removes Vergil's picture of Mercury bringing the message, and tells us merely that "a messenger came from the gods" (1616). Though Venus must aid Eneas in finding the golden bough, the romancer spares his audience Vergil's picture of the goddess' twin doves directing the hero's feet. He tells us only that Venus aided him "by a marvellous revelation and a very great divine sign" (2339-40).

In one instance, the *Eneas* poet manages some light humor out of these supernatural necessities. When Eneas, in the agonies accompanying the onset of love for Lavine, is uttering his Ovidian complaints against the cruelty of the god of love, part of his sorrow springs from the fact that *Amor,* who is dealing with him thus harshly—more insolently, Eneas laments, than if he were a vile chambermaid—is his own brother (8940–45)!

Occasionally the romancer explains supernatural elements by ascribing them to sorcery, a concept relatively acceptable to his audience, for whom science and sorcery walked hand in hand. The Cumaean Sybil, for example, with her dark, wrinkled skin, her beetling brows, her deep-set eyes, her knowledge of divination, astrology, necromancy, medicine, and the liberal arts (2201–9, 2267–94), is the *Eneas* poet's picture of the complete sorceress. She compounds a magic salve which protects Eneas from the stench at the entrance of hell (2393–96) and she quiets Cerberus, not by throwing him drugged cakes, as in the *Aeneid,* but by uttering a magic spell: "un charme et un anchantemant" (2598–2604).

There are two instances in *Eneas,* however, in which the poet not merely tolerates mythological material, but actually introduces or expands it. These are the episode of the Judgment of Paris (99–182) and the expansion of the Venus–Vulcan episode by the addition of Ovid's tale of Venus and Mars (4297–4393). But the gods of these episodes are thoroughly euhemerized; the poet is dealing not at all with divinities, but with proud maidens, and a domestic triangle. The episodes probably caught the author's fancy because they were full of the stuff of the human comedy, spiced in both cases with a touch of arch sensationalism. Both episodes convey sardonic implications about women which would assure the author of amused smiles from both sexes in a fashionable audience.

The *Eneas* author's rationalism likewise shows itself in the air of circumstantiality which he attempts to give to his narrative. His romance is full of specific numbers; exactly how many horses Latinus sent to Eneas, exactly how many men died at the bridgehead of Montauban, exactly how far Eneas' house in Troy was from the Greek plundering, exactly how long Turnus drifted in the Trojan ship before he came to shore, exactly how long the delay between Eneas' final victory and his marriage to Lavine. There is much realistic detail: how Sinon was able to make his escape (according to his fabrication) from the Greeks, how the fortifications of Montauban were constructed, how Turnus was seated at his meal when he learned that Lavine was to be given to Eneas, how the Carthaginians judged Eneas' gifts to Dido, how Eneas returned to his companions after leaving hell, how Camille waited for Turnus at the gate of Laurente, leaning on her spear, how the Trojans erred in revealing by their cheers that Eneas had returned with allies from Palentee. Vergil's epic embellishment is often replaced by homely *realia,* and sometimes by brief, bald, and dry recapitulations of fact. The work has been changed, as Salverda de Grave noted, from epic to simple narrative, and the French author views the world with the eye of a medieval realist.[17]

Nor is the romancer interested in Vergil's grand imperial theme: the divine mission of Roman rule ("regere imperio populus. . . pacisque imponere morem, parcere subiectis et

[17] *Eneas,* Cfmâ, I xxx. For a useful listing of realistic details see xxv-xxvi. The author's tendency to multiply facts and fall into prosaic realism had support in the rhetorical theory of the day. See the interesting comments and speculations of H. C. R. Laurie, "A New Look at the Marvellous in *Eneas* and Its Influence," *Romania,* XCI (1970), 48–53.

debellare superbos," *Aeneid* vi. 851–53), the praise of Roman glories to come, the concern with Roman and Italian antiquities and topography, the flattery of the Augustan family. Hence, for example, King Evander takes Eneas on no tour of the future site of Rome. Turnus' muster of the Italian tribes is much curtailed, Vergil's moving praise of the young Marcellus is omitted, and innumerable names of Trojan and Roman persons and places disappear from the narrative. The *Eneas* author likewise lacks interest in the *minutiae* of the Troy legend, which Vergil and Augustan Rome had valued as historical antiquities. In ignoring the imperial theme, the *Eneas* author reacted like most medieval writers, with the striking exception of Dante. Perhaps there lurks behind his reading of the *Aeneid* the common medieval image, *vita est peregrinatio,* probably Pauline in origin (Heb. xi. 13), which became so popular in the thirteenth and fourteenth centuries. The end of Eneas' pilgrimage, like those of later romance heroes such as Erec and Yvain, is not "Jerusalem celestial," but its secularized substitute—in the case of Eneas, the rule of Italy. The eschatological pilgrimage whose end is religious fulfillment becomes by analogy the secular pilgrimage whose end is worldly, chivalric fulfillment.

Gone also from *Eneas,* regrettably, is much of Vergil's bittersweet, melancholy magic, and especially the profound Vergilian sensitivity to the eternal tragedy of life: the stately and haunting sadness, the brooding lines and half-lines, the *lachrimae rerum.* Characteristic, tender Vergilian tableaux or episodes like that of the mothers of Pallanteum, first in terror at the rumor of war, then trembling on the city walls as they watch their sons march off to battle (viii, 556–57, 592–93); the anguished mourning of the brides, the mothers, the sisters, and the orphans of the Latin dead in Laurentum (xi, 211–17); the image of Latinus in wretched and lonely old age after the suicide of Amata (xii, 609–11); the pathetic death of young

Lausus, with Aeneas' moving regrets at the killing (x, 811–32); the painful parting of Evander and Pallas, aged father and untried son, as the young man leaves for the war (viii, 558–84); these and other similar passages, which have moved generations of modern readers of Vergil, the *Eneas* poet passes over, perhaps as incongruous with his chivalric theme. When he replaces them at all, it is with highly contrived, heroic-sentimental declamations in the manner prescribed by the handbooks.

These changes reveal a fundamental alteration in the *sen* or theme of the narrative. For Vergil the grand theme of the *Aeneid* was, as we have suggested, the glory of Rome: its noble past, its natural beauties, the greatness of its people, its love of peace supported by strength in arms, its divine mission as mistress of the world. These were to be exhibited through the legendary person of *pius Aeneas,* suffering the trials which led to the founding of Rome. Hence, lovers of Homer have long complained that Vergil's epic hero is irretrievably pallid in comparison with those of Homer, that Aeneas lacks the freedom, spontaneity, and personal magnitude of an Achilles, a Hector, an Agamemnon, an Ajax. Throughout Vergil's epic, but especially after Book vi, they insist, Aeneas is theme-ridden, overburdened by his household gods, by his submissiveness to duty, until the *Aeneid* becomes a sort of secular saint's life in lofty, sensitive hexameters, with Aeneas exemplary, rather than heroic, more symbol than character.

Eneas is not encumbered with this thematic burden, and its hero is much more nearly a free agent. The romance is fundamentally a narrative of a knight's fulfillment of himself, the realization of his potentialities, the accomplishment of his secular pilgrimage, his achievement of *joi* through love and war—a pattern later to be made familiar in a far more complex and sensitive manner by Chrétien de Troyes. The French poet reads his source with this theme primarily in mind. Surely the long Eneas–Lavine episode contributes to it, and was perhaps invented by the romancer partly for this purpose.

With a simpler *sen,* and with no regard for epic machinery, the *Eneas* poet could simplify his narrative and make it more episodic, perhaps with public reading in mind. He dispenses with Vergil's epic invocation and statement of theme as well as his opening *in mediis rebus* and resorts to the simple, direct opening which from the time of Geoffrey of Monmouth often characterized medieval tales born of the Troy legend:

> After the Trojan war, Aeneas, fleeing from the desolation of the city, came with Ascanius by ship unto Italy.
> (Geoffrey of Monmouth, *History of the Kings of Britain,* c. 1137)[18]

> When the Greeks had conquered Troy and devastated the whole country for vengeance against Paris, who had ravished Helen from Greece. . . .
> (Wace, *Brut,* vv. 10–13, c. 1155)[19]

> After the siege and the assault had ceased at Troy, the town destroyed and burnt to embers and ashes. . . .
> (*Sir Gawain and the Green Knight,* vv. 1–2, c. 1370)

But the epic formalities are the least of the *Eneas* poet's omissions for simplicity. Dissatisfied with the complexity of Aeneas' early adventures, he omits most of the detail from the hero's account of the destruction of Troy and dispenses with all the travels described in Book iii of the *Aeneid.* Almost all of the contents of *Aeneid* Book v—the funeral games for Anchises, the revolt of the Trojan women, and the death of

[18] Vol. I, p. 1. Tr. S. Evans and C. Dunn, Dutton Everyman Paperback (New York, 1958), p. 5. In the *Historia* this is preceded by a dedicatory letter and a paragraph describing the isle of Britain.

[19] E. Hoepffner suggests plausibly that the *Eneas* poet imitated his opening lines from these early lines of Wace. See "L' 'Eneas' et Wace," *Archiv. romanicum,* XV (1931), 249–50. On the medieval poet's hesitancy to throw the reader *in medias res* see A. Pauphilet, *Le Legs du moyen âge,* p. 95.

Palinurus—are gone from the romance. All that remains from that book is the founding of a city for the weak and unadventurous followers of Aeneas. The French author preserves far more of the incident of Vergil's last six books, though even here epic embellishment and thematic material (like the description of the engravings on Aeneas' shield and his tour of the future site of Rome) are suppressed. The *Eneas* author and his audience were presumably more interested in war, battles, and prowess than in travel adventure.

V

The medieval poet's additions to his source include most of those characteristics which made *Eneas* popular in its time, and an examination of them will help us define its genre. Many are in the form of set descriptions—descriptions of fine clothes, arms and armor, cities, buildings, fortifications, natural marvels, and in one striking case a woman—which replace Vergil's epic embellishment and alter both the tone and the movement of the narrative.

The *Eneas* poet frequently seems like a narrator in a hurry, overanxious to get on with his story, so that at times the narrative thins out to a dry chronicle of facts. This tendency works at cross-purposes with the romancer's delight in descriptions, tableaux and marvels. Thus, at the opening of the narrative, he moves quickly away from flaming Troy, offering little of Vergil's detail of the city's bloody destruction, only to bring his story to a complete halt while he recounts the long and rather remote tale of the Judgment of Paris (99–182). Likewise, he hastens sketchily over Vergil's muster-roll of the Italian tribes, but stops his narrative to expand the *Aeneid's* fifteen lines on Camilla into a set piece of school-text rhetorical description, 148 lines long (3959–4106). The reader will find numerous instances of this sort, in which the poet suppresses, attenuates, hastens his narrative with one hand, while adding, amplifying, delaying his narrative with the other.

The French author is also very fond of declamatory, sentiment-laden speeches, and many of his contributions are of this sort. Most of them are expansions or embroiderings of material already in the *Aeneid*. The brief outburst of Vergil's fleeing Nisus when he discovers that Euryalus is not with him, for example, is less than two lines in length: "Unhappy Euryalus, in what place have I lost you? How will I follow you?" *(Aeneid* ix. 390–91). The romancer develops this into a sentimental, self-accusing declamation of forty lines *(Eneas,* 5145–84). Aeneas' farewell to the corpse of Pallas occupies a scant three lines in the *Aeneid* (xi. 96–98), but in *Eneas* extends for sixty-two lines filled with voluble emotion. Dido's death speech (vv. 2039–67) and Eneas' speech on killing Turnus (9801–10) are similar, though briefer, elaborations of speeches found in the *Aeneid,* and there are numerous other expansions. A smaller number of speeches is invented without a hint from Vergil. The interchange between Tarcon and Camille (7073–7125) and Turnus' monologue over the dead Camille (7369–7426) are characteristic examples.

All these changes affect the movement of the narrative strikingly. While the genius of Vergil, working within his measured hexameters, could unify plot, character, and embellishment into a broad, stately, even-flowing narrative movement, his less-gifted adapter, working within rather urgent and precipitous octosyllabics, finds the combination too difficult to manage. His narrative tends to separate into its constituent parts, to move jerkily along by passages of hasty, almost factual, reportage, interspersed with complete halts, while he indulges himself in the details of a marvel, the description of a building, the delivery of a

speech, or the recounting of an amusing legend.[20] He is
thus digressive rather than synthetic, and in this he has the
support of literary theoreticians of his time.[21] The digressive
characteristic which tends to distress the modern reader was
undoubtedly attractive to his own audience, and was perhaps
in part dictated by the exigencies of public reading.

The *Eneas* poet's imagination seems not unlike that of the
innumerable manuscript illuminators whose work remains to
us, brilliant in contrasting colors, contemptuous of pastels or
chiaroscuro or perspective, offering stylized or formalized tableaux of the vivid moments of courtly life: tournaments,
feasts, solemn gatherings, the interviews of lovers. The romancer is often at his best in such briefly sketched tableaux.
Thus, he expands Vergil's ten-line description of Aeneas and
Dido ready for the hunt into a brilliant and effective picture
of the richly attired and godlike couple meeting at the foot of
Dido's grand staircase, surrounded realistically by scurrying
servants, arms-bearers, the barking hound pack and the
leashed tracking dogs (1445–1503). Or, in a briefer passage, he
gives us a fleeting glimpse of the fortress of Montauban, completed, stocked, and garrisoned, prepared for war, with a thousand richly embroidered pennons flying from its battlements
(4267–84). The poet cannot refrain from admiring the beauty
of this product of his imagination:

> Molt par senblot fiers li chastiaus
> et a mervoille par ert biaus. . . .

[20] An exception to the *Eneas* poet's love of description is his treatment of feasts.
Though there are feasts in *Eneas,* the poet declines to describe them, hastening over
them by the device of *occupatio*. His treatment of Evander's feast (4773–79) is
typical: "Eneas and his men washed, then dined very splendidly. I cannot give an
account of the dishes which came thick and fast, or of the good wines, plain and
spiced, but everyone had enough of them. Eneas rose from the dinner . . . ."

[21] For the importance of *descriptio* and *digressio* in medieval poetics, see E. Faral,
Les arts poétiques du XIIe et du XIIIe siècle (Paris, 1958), pp. 74–84, 118–51, and
passim.

Or there is the poet's delight in the sheer glamour of Eneas' colorful fortress of tents pitched outside Laurente (7293-7330): "ne fu pas forz, mes molt fu biaus."

The romancer's digressions on natural marvels, which he may have imitated from Wace's *Brut,* have received much comment.[22] The marvels are drawn from a variety of sources (indicated, where known, in the notes to this translation) and are displayed with evident satisfaction. We are thus introduced to the crocodiles and the dye-producing mollusks of Tyre, to the magnet, to the poisonous aconite, to asphalt, asbestos, the marvelous sea-born horses of Mesapus, the clairvoyant birds called *caladrii,* the healing herb, dittany (which appeared in the *Aeneid),* and other wonders.

These wonders, and the author's evident eagerness to teach his readers about them, may remind the modern reader of the fundamentally clerical—in modern terms, professorial—origins and orientations of early romance, for it is clearly out of the schools that the form arose. The three *romans antiques* which mark its beginnings are unmistakably bookish and pedagogical. They represent an important early stage in that long medieval process of the *vulgarisation* of clerical learning, which perhaps reached its climax in Jean de Meun's portion of the *Roman de la rose* (c. 1277), but which was still continuing in the fifteenth century (1475–90) when Caxton prepared his printed books for publication. One recalls the highly self-conscious didactic opening of the early *Roman de Thèbes,* so frequently imitated in later romance:

> He who is learned [*sage*] should not hide it, but should show forth his knowledge, so that when he is gone from this world he can be always remembered for it. If Master Homer and

[22] See Hoepffner, *Arch. romanicum,* XV (1931), 256–57. Hoepffner believes that the marvels of Wace are functional to his narrative. In *Eneas* they obviously are not. On the significance of the marvels see H. C. R. Laurie, "A New Look at the Marvellous in *Eneas* and Its Influence," 48–74.

Master Plato and Vergil and Cicero had concealed their learning, posterity would have never heard tell of them. Therefore
I will not be silent about my knowledge, or keep my learning
to myself, but wish rather to recount to you something worthy
of remembrance. (vv. 1–12)

These lines might well serve as prologue to the entire romance
genre.

Eneas and the other *romans antiques* became the means,
then, to convey to a new public the learning of the schools
about classical myth, legend, history, geography, and poetry,
and also to teach odd bits of information about natural history and science. They would do this by imitating the Roman
poets. Faral suggests the thinking of the time:

"We must cultivate the ancients; our poets should imitate
theirs": this is what was being repeated from the time of Ber-
nard of Chartres; and we can imagine what important conse-
quences this doctrine had for literature on the day when the
imitation, ceasing to be done in Latin, became available to the
public at large clothed in romance form, the day when, leaving
the school, some clerk put aside his Latin verse and decided to
make use of his erudition in the composition of a poem in
French. On that day the 'roman antique' was born.[23]

This imitation in the vulgar tongue has nothing in common
with the sort of neoclassicism which developed among Renais-
sance humanists. The early French adapters of the Matter of
Rome had no concern for the spirit and attitudes of classical
antiquity, for ancient literary and critical principles, or for the
sort of close imitation which produces a neoclassical literature. They were, in this sense, modernists. The imitation of
the ancients meant the depiction in a form agreeable and
intelligible to contemporaries of the actions, manners, and
achievements of strange peoples, thus providing models and
standards for one's own time. The past was called to the

[23] Faral, *Recherches,* p. 399.

service of the present. The Matter of Rome lived not as history in its own right, or as formal literary model or pattern, but as Humanities, *sub specie aeternitatis.*

All this is to say—and we are perhaps belaboring the obvious—that the twelfth-century romancers lacked the historical sense or historical orientation which dominates every educated man's world view today. The medieval romancer made no attempt to absorb and recreate the spirit of a historical past. Judgments of truth or falsehood were ethical, rather than historical, and perspective was pursued no more in time than in space. The historical past emerged, like the stylized background of the illuminators, as a depthless—or timeless—plane against which contemporary men moved, thought, and felt.[24]

In the eyes of their authors, then, the *divertissement* provided by the early romances probably found its justification in didactic function. Hence, the *Eneas* poet will entertain and instruct his audience with the marvels of natural history, as well as those of arts and crafts. The city of Carthage, with its magnetized fortifications, its rich marble, its five hundred towers and seven gates, its wealthy markets, and its acoustically perfect capitol, is an excellent example of the poet's didactic craft. He has discovered such features scattered throughout his readings and assembled them into a single fictional display for the education of his audience.

But the *Eneas* poet's architectural triumphs are his tombs, especially that of Camille. The romancer developed it as he did Carthage, gathering together into a single monument a number of wonders culled from his reading, unifying them by the free use of his imagination. The product strikes modern readers as an ultimate in garish bad taste and architectural

[24] On the view of history reflected in *Eneas, Thèbes,* and *Troie* see the useful observations of G. Raynaud de Lage, "Les Romans antiques et la représentation de la réalité," *Moyen âge,* LXVII (1961), 247–91.

instability. That it has nothing to do with the architectural practice of the twelfth century, or any other period, is obvious and gratifying. But it is rich, colorful, bizarre, and exotic—a marvel—and this satisfied the poet.

The *Eneas* author delighted not merely in tombs, but in all funerary pomp: long laments (in carefully contrived rhetoric) over the body of the deceased, processions carrying the corpse on a rich and ornate bier, the embalming of the corpse, the construction of a tomb with one or more marvels like an eternal flame, the composition of an epitaph,[25] the final sealing of the tomb. Some of these details appear in the narrative of Dido's death, but the author gives full rein to his interests in treating the deaths of Pallas and Camille. The two events—the deaths, the laments, processions, embalmings, burials, descriptions of the tombs, and epitaphs—occupy over 800 lines of the romance.

Having argued that the *Eneas* poet's justification for these details is at least partly didactic, we must observe that his manner is hardly that of the professor or philosopher, that he seems to concern himself more with surprise and mystification than with causes or essences. He writes rather as if he were conducting a side show, leading his readers down the narrative corridor until he stops them to gaze at an exhibit: Camille and her wonderful horse, the monstrous serpent called *crocodile,* the Judgment of Paris, the grotesque creature called Cerberus, or whatever it may be. His transitions from narrative and digression are abrupt and undisguised. "I wish to recount very briefly the occasion of this judgment" (99–100), begins the digression on the Judgment of Paris; and the natural marvels are

[25] Faral *(Recherches,* p. 100) has shown that epitaphs were a popular genre in the Latin literature of the twelfth century, though the *Eneas* poet might easily have drawn the idea from Ovid himself. See Salverda de Grave, *Eneas,* Cfmâ, II, 133.

introduced with equal abruptness, usually by a phrase calling attention to the unusual nature of the phenomenon to be described.

If we would not today consider this fascination with oddities as learning, yet it bears testimony to the consuming curiosity of the author and his audience, a curiosity certainly nourished by the classical studies of the schools. But the *Eneas* poet also makes another group of additions to his source, whose function is quite the opposite of his excursions into the exotic. These elements are the details and incidents of feudal interest which serve to naturalize the action of the romance to twelfth-century France. Most of them develop from the poet's reimagining the Vergilian narrative in terms of his own society. Hence, the conversion of the *Aeneid's* warfare to the clashes of armed knights, its armor to that of the twelfth-century West, its fortifications to medieval castles and walled towns. The *Eneas* author seems pleased with his knowledge of arms and armor, of the technical details of fortification, of the conduct of modern warfare, and he dwells on them frequently. He modernizes Turnus' firebrands to "Greek fire," a term familiar enough in France after the Second Crusade. The accumulation of this sort of contemporary detail is instrumental in converting the fable from a classical to a medieval narrative.

Vergil's Aeneas calls a number of councils of his followers, but councils of barons, in which the leader confers with his people "toz comunaument," play a far larger part in *Eneas*. The give and take of parliamentary argument is vivid, and the confidence which the leaders place in the decisions of their councils is emphatic (e.g., 66–71, 6537–6828; cf. esp. 6617–26). Such councils were an established part of the older *chanson de geste,* as readers of *Roland* will recall, but were probably also a common aspect of medieval government even as late as the twelfth century.

The romancer's development of feudal material goes well beyond external detail. His expansion of the episode of Silvia's tame deer turns the entire passage into a feudal military incident, with the aggrieved parties fighting for what they conceive to be their feudal rights. Likewise, the entire strife between Eneas and Turnus becomes in the romance a feudal conflict over inheritance, in which both parties present the reader, at various times, with the arguments for their respective claims. Turnus' right resides in a prior agreement with the ruling monarch, attested and consented to by the barons of the realm—on any human level an irrefragable case. But Eneas' right is based on divine decree, attested by divine omens, and further clarified by prophecy, solemnly confirmed by Jupiter himself—though the truth of this claim is denied by Amata and Turnus. The inevitable result is a feudal war of succession, whose outcome is at length established by single combat between the two lords. The feudal picture is complete.

Paradoxically, then, *Eneas* is in part a product of two conflicting types of addition to the source story: on the one hand, those elements which naturalize the narrative to the Middle Ages, which are comfortable and easily recognizable to the romancer's audience; on the other hand, those elements which carry the audience off into the world of the exotic and strange, which stir their imaginations with the wonders of ancient times.[26] These contrasting elements complement, rather than oppose, one another; but the feudal details are much more thoroughly a part of the spirit of the story than the *exotica,* which are imbedded in the fabric of the piece like curious and brightly colored gems, presented for the few moments of wonder and delight which they might bring. The truly mysterious—the atmosphere of Broceliande, utterly dif-

---

[26] On the manner in which the *Eneas* author was able to integrate the familiar and the marvelous in a single instance, see A.-M. Macabies, "Que représente le Carthage d'*Eneas?*" *Revue des langues romanes,* LXXVII (1967), 145–51.

ferent in quality from these *merveilles* of the *romans antiques,* and soon to enter the fabric of romance through Celtic
legend—is not yet a part of the genre.

In a narrative so thoroughly feudalized as *Eneas,* it is re-
markable that almost no specifically Christian imagery, piety,
or theology is to be found.[27] There is an occasional exclamato-
ry reference to a god who might equally well be Christian or
Vergilian; there is the isolated image of Calchas equipped as
a Christian priest with cross and stole; but there is little else
of the sort. The only considerable passage which might be said
to reflect Christian preoccupations occurs during Eneas' visit
to hell, when the Sibyl discusses the peculiar nature of the
tortures of the damned: these souls, explains the priestess,
suffer the tortures, but continue to suffer the fear of torture,
which among the living disappears when the pain itself has
arrived (2763–82). To this she adds some comment on the
nature of eternity, a rather brief piece of amateur speculative
theology.[28]

VI

Romantic love in *Eneas,* especially as it appears in the long
yearnings of Eneas and Lavine for each other, is the French
poet's greatest, and most crucial, contribution to the genre.
Love, as Wilmotte remarked, "is the essential element of our
romances and the sole justification for their popularity,"[29] but
before *Eneas,* there is no expanded treatment of it in the long
vernacular narrative. There are rudimentary beginnings in
Thèbes, in the amorous interests between Atys and Ismene,
and Parthenopeus and Antigone. But these are little devel-

[27] M. Wilmotte, in *Origines du roman en France: l évolution du sentiment romanesque jusqu'en 1240* (Brussels, 1941), pp. 206–8, has commented succinctly on the
paganism of the early *romans antiques,* as well as those of Chrétien.
[28] This is not to deny Pauphilet's assertion ("Eneas et Enée," 211) that the *Eneas*
author changes Dido's dying sentiments from those of vengeance to those of Christian reconciliation, thus adding to both her nobility and her pathos.
[29] Wilmotte, *Origines,* p. 212.

oped, the men concerned are killed, and the total effect is slight. In the *Brut,* too, Wace reflects his awareness of an interest among his audience in love literature. Certain of his minor expansions of Geoffrey of Monmouth's text clearly glance in this direction.

Yet it remained for the author of *Eneas* to develop the hints of these earlier narrative writers, to work out ideas already common among the Provençal lyricists and known in the shorter northern narrative of *Piramus et Tisbé,* to bring sentimental love, with the help of Ovid's language, imagery, and love psychology, to a position of central importance in vernacular narrative. The *Eneas* poet's treatment of his love episodes is neither polished nor profound, though it has verve. His love psychology is clumsy and rudimentary compared with that of Chrétien. Nevertheless, the appearance of the romance wrought a revolution, and all the later French romancers of the twelfth century, including Chrétien, became its debtors. As Wilmotte remarked long ago, "The date of 1160, assigned to *Eneas,* is perhaps the most memorable, in that respect, in all French romance; with it came the dawn of a new art."[30]

Whether there is any historical or literary reality corresponding to the popular term *courtly love* seems highly debatable. If, following some scholars, we define courtly love as the sort of rigorous formalization of erotic passion which apparently originated in the Langue d'Oc, which was developed into a sort of mystique by some of the Provençal troubadours, was reflected brilliantly by Chrétien in *Lancelot,* depicted (and perhaps satirized) by Andreas Capellanus,[31] and, in re-

[30] Wilmotte, *L'Evolution du roman français aux environs de 1150* (Paris, 1903), p. 55. The judgment has been repeated by numerous scholars since Wilmotte gave this lecture.

[31] Scholars are no longer accepting Andreas, or the general concept of "courtly love," with solemnity. See esp. D. W. Robertson, "The Subject of the *De Amore* of Andreas Capellanus," *MP,* L (1953), 145–61, and *A Preface to Chaucer* (Princeton,

cent years, identified tersely by C. S. Lewis as having "the four marks of Humility, Courtesy, Adultery and the Religion of Love;"[32] if this is "courtly love," surely the romantic passion in *Eneas* has nothing to do with it. Scholars and critics, like others, are often at the mercy of the phrase makers, and Gaston Paris unwittingly did literary history a notable disservice when he coined, many years ago, the phrase "amour courtois." Since its invention it has been applied by the careless, the hasty, and the handbooks to almost every shade and variety of love between the sexes which made its appearance in medieval literature. The term as defined above in fact describes only a very narrow range of medieval literary production; but love in the courtly literature of twelfth-century France has as much variety as that in most other literatures.

The author of *Eneas* presents his audience with two love affairs, neither of them "courtly" except insofar as the lovers are members of a courtly class, and possess in an idealized way the virtues thought proper to that class: in the woman, beauty, great sensitivity or sensibility, loyalty or fidelity, a dignity of person befitting her age and rank, a strong sense of personal honor—*pudeur;* in the man, honor, nobility of appearance, courage, seasoning in battle, generosity, discretion in speech and conduct; in both, *mesure*—moderation, a respect for the ordering of things human and divine. In *Eneas,* as in later romances, there is a constant tension between this last virtue and the volatile hearts of the lovers; for lovers, as

1962), pp. 391–448; W. T. H. Jackson, "The *De amore* of Andreas Capellanus and the Practice of Love at Court," *Romanic Review,* XLIX (1958), 243–51; E. T. Donaldson, "The Myth of Courtly Love," *Ventures,* V (1965), 16–23. The "courtly love" which H. C. R. Laurie, "Eneas and the Doctrine of Courtly Love," *MLR,* LXIV (1969), 283–94, finds in *Eneas* is a sexual love deepened by a Christian Platonic understanding of the universe, and leading naturally to marriage. P. Grillo, "The Courtly Background in the *Roman d'Eneas,*" *Neuphilologische Mitteilungen,* LXIX (1968), 688–702, likewise sees in the love of Lavine and Eneas an "amour courtois conjugal" (p. 700) similar to that found in the romances of Chrétien.

[32] *The Allegory of Love* (Oxford, 1936), p. 12.

medieval authors knew from Ovid, are not given to *mesure*. This tension is usually the subject of the interior dialogues that occupy so much of the poet's attention: the lover's sense of *mesure* against the tugging of his passions, judgment against emotion, modesty against desire, head against heart.

Dido's tragedy—surely not a "courtly love" episode—is one of *amor desmesuré,* of a mad passion thrust upon her, like that of Tristan and Iseult, by supernatural powers: "Dido embraced him [the enchanted Ascanius] and was inflamed. The lady drank mortal poison; to her great sorrow she did not notice it. With the kiss she caught such a madness of love that her body was on fire."[33] The *Eneas* author makes no effort here to alter the *sen* of the Vergilian episode. Though he lacks Vergil's genius and sympathy, he reproduces in his own manner the mature, noble, and dignified queen wracked by a destructive infatuation. It is a "wrong" love, and the French poet, like Vergil, goes to considerable length to describe its destructive effects on her judgment and her realm (cf. esp. 139–1432, 1567–1614), though he offers no reason for its wrongness other than the Vergilian divine mission of the hero. In the end, Dido herself views it as a quasi-adulterous passion, through which she has betrayed her vow to her dead husband—a betrayal from which she continues to suffer in hell. The author's final comment on her, in her epitaph, summarizes the theme of *desmesurance:* "ele ama trop folemant,/savoir ne li valut noiant" (2143–44).

In the Eneas–Lavine episode, which is equally remote from "courtly love," the French author is completely free from the constraints of the Vergilian theme and fable. He can develop

[33] 810–14. The metaphor of the enchanted kisses as a poison potion suggests the Tristan legend. Since this legend was almost certainly known in some form in France by 1155, it is possible that the *Eneas* author was familiar with it. Some recent scholars, however (e.g., R. Jones, *The Theme of Love,* p. 33), have seen in the Dido of *Eneas* a strong attraction to Eneas even before the Ascanius episode, and hence find her "far more responsible for her actions than in the *Aeneid.*"

the love as he wishes, and the more than 1600 lines which he devotes to his episode becomes, in consequence, a landmark in the history of erotic narrative. It should be observed first that the love begins with the woman: she is the first smitten, she makes the overtures. This beginning the *Eneas* poet undoubtedly learned in part from Ovid, whose works are far more concerned with feminine than with masculine love psychology,[34] but it reminds the reader of the transitional nature of Lavine as heroine. In her emotional simplicity, the nearly instantaneous character of her enamourment, and her willingness to act on it, she is quite like the numberless maidens of older medieval narrative who, inflamed by the sight of the hero, are willing enough to spend the night with him, in a passing and unsentimental amour.

But we are never given an opportunity to look into the minds and emotions of these earlier maidens; and therein lies the difference, the new approach which the *Eneas* author brings, out of Ovid, to his subject. One side of Lavine is exactly like that maiden of the *chansons,* but on the other side is *mesure, pudeur,* in conflict with her precipitate passion (cf. esp. 8712–15). Thus, the inner conflict develops, in lengthy dialogues of the lover with herself, dialogues also replete with her doubts, fears, fantasies, erotic anticipations, and amorous agonies. This opening to the reader's view of the consciousness of its characters is perhaps the most significant achievement of the new romance, an achievement which placed narrative poetry on the long road whose ultimate end is the modern novel.

The psychology of the *Eneas* author and of his heroine is obviously cruder than that of later romancers like Chrétien

[34] See Auerbach, *Literatursprache und Publikum,* pp. 157–62. Readers interested in the *Eneas* poet's Ovidian sources and in the Ovidian inspiration for the medieval language of love will find rewarding the chapter entitled "Ovide et quelques autres sources du roman d'*Eneas,*" in Faral, *Recherches,* pp. 74–157.

and Thomas of Britain. We have suggested that Lavine has affinities with the transient maidens of earlier narrative, and Wilmotte remarked with some justice that she "is only a younger sister of Belissent and those other indistinct heroines of our songs, fragile and amiably sensual."[35] The *Eneas* author is a pioneer, and his efforts show the faults of pioneer work. Lavine is introduced to the reader far too abruptly, without preparation—perhaps because she was late inspiration of the author. In the opening scene with her mother she is too persistently obtuse. Her later sufferings, monologues, and self-probings are often awkward, forced, and mannered, as the author strains to invest them with all the Ovidian reminiscences he can muster. He is too obtrusive in the use of physical symptoms, too repetitious (to even the most sympathetic modern taste), and above all too long. Nevertheless he has created a character with a real and sensitive self-consciousness.

Much of Lavine's simplicity is in fact the eternal, sensual innocence of the romance *ingénue*. She is introduced as hardly more than a child: her opening scene, one of maternal indoctrination, is the author's device to make this obvious to the audience. The comments of the mother are sufficient to mark the childlike responses of the daughter. Love, then, is for Lavine, as for many characters (usually male) in later romance, an initiation, or at least a symbol of initiation, and her rapid mastery of love's joys and distresses introduces her to the significance of life, and her function within it.

But here the *Eneas* poet is inconsistent. His *ingénue,* who at the beginning of the episode is wholly unaware of the meaning of love, a day later understands fully its sexual fulfillment, and in two days has become somewhat of an expert in its perversions. Her ruminations about the possible homosexuality of Eneas are highly informed and stated in the blunt-

[35] *Origines,* p. 205.

est of language,with an imagination which has far too much immediacy for her age, experience, and breeding. Professor Adler's suggestion that Lavine is an example of the medieval *topos, puella senex,* seems justified.[36] From the modern reader's point of view, the romancer, in his eagerness to discourse on all aspects of his subject, has overreached his characterization.

The short poem (921 lines) of *Piramus et Tisbé,* a free adaptation of the tragic tale from Ovid's *Metamorphoses,* is full of the sentiments, imagery, and language which the *Eneas* author worked into the Eneas–Lavine episode.[37] If Faral's suggestion is correct, that *Piramus et Tisbé* probably antedates *Eneas* and influenced its author,[38] it is possible that its extremely young lovers provided the model for Lavine's youth and naïveté. But whatever the inspiration, Lavine's love is a youthful, spontaneous, and uncomplicated emotion based on physical attraction, sudden, warm, unconditional, sensual, and unconcerned with formality or ceremony. Except for its language it is quite like the dawn of young love at any time, or in any literature. And except for their common Ovidian language, it has nothing to do with that elaborate, formal minuet of the emotions, that quasi-mystical *cultus* of the lady, with its various grades and degrees, its concern for secrecy, and its demand for a complicated *service d'amour,* which troubadour ingenuity had fashioned, and which has been called "courtly love."

As Lavine gazes down on Eneas from her tower chamber, young love comes suddenly to birth, and in the passages which follow the reader is thoroughly indoctrinated in the pangs, the problems, the wild imaginations, and the hopes

[36] A. Adler, "Eneas and Lavine: *Puer et Puella Senes.*"

[37] *Piramus et Tisbé,* ed. C. de Boer (Cfmâ, Paris, 1921). See esp. vv. 23-46, 202-61, 366-73, 543-61. Most recently discussed by R. Jones, *The Theme of Love,* pp. 3-10.

[38] *Recherches,* pp. 16 –21.

which mark its beginnings. The *Eneas* author is concerned only with these beginnings. In treating Dido he follows the lead of his source from beginning to end, but when he freely develops his own love episode, although he spins it out to great length, he loses interest before love is consummated. The lovers marry and achieve *joi,* but this is a postscript of little concern to the poet. He drops his scrutiny of the lovers' emotions before they have an interview or exchange a single word. There are no lovers' quarrels to surmount, no *service d'amour* to pursue, no trysts to arrange or aubades to sing. The pains and pleasures of this love, its doubts and difficulties, are those of the overture, before courtship, and the *Eneas* poet chooses to chronicle only the dawn of tender emotions.

We have stressed the author's didactic attitude in *Eneas;* certainly his didacticism extends to the doctrines of love. Long passages in the introspective monologues and dialogues of the lovers are obviously designed as pleasantly entertaining disquisitions on the nature of love and the principles of conduct for lovers. Many of the verses (often Ovidian in inspiration) have a proverbial or aphoristic character. We learn that "it takes two to make a pair, and each should be submissive to the other"; that over love "there is no lord anywhere"; that love cannot be divided; that "he who loves truly cannot deceive"; that the lady who succumbs too easily to love may be suspected of *légèreté* by her beloved; that there is no defense against love, nor is it possible to turn back, once the lover has succumbed; and a multitude of similar doctrines, some frivolous, some earnest.

The queen's lectures on the nature of love, spiced by the light, commonplace oxymorons about the delicious malady, are likewise vehicles for doctrine. One suspects that the poet hoped his best lines would be memorized and quoted by fashionable ladies in his audience. But he must also have hoped that his love episode would convey some sound advice on conduct, manners, and attitude for those absorbed in the new cult of sentiment. The episode represents, among other things, the first clumsy and tottering steps of an infant *préciosité*.

This dual position of the childlike Lavine as a new and confused initiate into love's service, and at the same time a teacher of love's doctrine to the romancer's audience, perhaps explains the *Eneas* poet's use of the *puella senex topos* in his treatment of her.[39] It is almost necessary to her dual function. The most brilliant example of such a *topos* in medieval literature, used for a similar, though loftier, purpose, is the Beatrice of Dante's *Paradiso*.

The message of Amata and Lavine on love is of course Ovid's message; but Ovid with a difference. The old, cursory gloss which describes medieval literature of love as "Ovid misunderstood" undoubtedly misses its mark;[40] as if one were to call the philosophy of St. Thomas Aquinas "Aristotle misunderstood." In both cases the language and concepts of an ancient author are adopted and consciously refashioned to meet the demands of another day. It would appear not that the study of Ovid called into being the cult of sentiment in the courts of twelfth-century France and England, but that when the cult of sentiment arose—for whatever reasons or by whatever accidents—the incident, imagery, and language of Ovid were at hand, through the learning of the schools, to give it utterance. The literary clerks of the schools did not thrust love literature and Ovidian sentiments on the audiences of the day. Rather, they supplied them when they were demanded.

The Ovidian tones which were rejected, as they are rejected by every age of sentiment, are the tones of cold sensuality, cruel epicureanism, light cynicism, and sharp irony which especially characterize the *Ars amatoria* and the *Remedia*

[39] See note 36 above.
[40] See Lewis, *The Allegory of Love,* pp. 5–11.

amoris. Though twelfth-century romances drew on these books freely for language and imagery, they adhered to the gentler, more gracious, and more sentimental tones of the *Heroides* and some of the tales (like that of Pyramus and Thisbe) in the *Metamorphoses*. Certainly these medieval writers were not humanists with a sense of obligation toward Ovid himself. They dealt with the Ovidian inheritance as they wished, and while the romancers were plundering it for the language of love, the satirists and moralists were finding it a source of sardonic ethical commentary. "Ovid has the makings of a moralist," notes E. K. Rand, "as the Middle Ages were well aware. He does not cry sermons from the housetops, but his works are stored with acute observations on men and morals which, if the context be forgotten, might be fitted into a letter of St. Paul's or a satire of Juvenal's."[41] The uses of the classical past were thus manifold, and Ovid, whatever way he was interpreted, wrote for our doctrine.

There is a singular failure in the *Eneas* author's treatment of love psychology, obvious to even the hasty reader. Since the romancer elaborated most of his doctrine from his knowledge of Ovid, sentimentally interpreted and adapted to the *ingénue,* and since Ovid was largely concerned with feminine love psychology, his treatment of the dawn of love suited the young Lavine rather admirably. Her private doubts and fears and jealousies, her innocent sensuality, her sleepless agonies, her tender outpourings of the heart, and her passionate vows of eternal fidelity to an absent and unwitting beloved—all these may seem wildly exaggerated and humorous (as they were surely intended to be), but in essentials they do not strike a psychologically false note. The reader will recognize in the symptoms the tender and attractive extremism of the adolescent.

But when the romancer must examine the dawn of love in

[41] *Ovid and his Influence* (New York, 1928), p. 111.

the heart of Eneas—that middle-aged widower, veteran of the greatest of all wars and of the love of Dido, father of a grown son, experienced leader of men—he handles his subject in almost exactly the same way as it was treated in Lavine. There are the same swoonings and sleeplessness and changes of color, the same agonies of desire, the same misgivings, the same complaints to the god of love over his cruelty. This does not fit at all: the piping song of the skylark in the heart of a lion.[42] Though we cannot tell how he was received by contemporary audiences, most modern readers will find this Eneas, groaning, self-pitying, and bed-ridden in the throes of his love agony, something of a grotesque.

There is a further oddity in the *Eneas* author's two love episodes. Although the writer is wholly familiar with the formal *descriptio* taught in the schools, and though he demonstrates his descriptive versatility (he describes storms, cities, horses, armor, and buildings in great variety), he fails to produce any description of either Dido or Lavine. We are given some cursory indications of Dido's beauty, especially as she and Eneas prepare for their hunt. But of Lavine, we see nothing at all, and her physical appearance remains as shadowy as it had been in the *Aeneid.* Since medieval *Artes poeticae,* like that of Matthew of Vendôme, taught that a full description of a beloved's beauty was necessary in order to motivate the lover, this is a singular omission.[43] Perhaps it is because love in both cases begins with the woman. The romancer describes the awe which Eneas creates as he rides into Carthage, and later shows Lavine at the window of the tower of Laurente, admiring

[42] It is this incongruity which causes Adler ("Eneas and Lavine," 74-78) to conclude that Eneas is an example of the *puer senex,* who, by finding the true meaning of love through his relationship with Lavine, undergoes a spring rejuvenation.

[43] See Faral, *Recherches,* pp. 101–5, and Matthew of Vendôme, in Faral, *Arts poétiques,* pp. 118–19.

the hero's noble bearing. But Eneas falls in love without the author's providing him with physical motivation.

The romancer reserves his single extended effort at personal description for Camille, whose physical charms he describes along with her moral and spiritual graces, her military accomplishments, her clothing, her horse and its rich trappings. Faral notes that such laudatory descriptions were recommended by the theorists to move the reader's sympathy,[44] and its function in the romance is obviously to increase the pathos of her death.

VII

It is virtually certain that the *Eneas* poet and his audience considered the essential basis of his story as historical fact. A glance at the manuscripts which contain *Eneas* in company with other works—all except two of the nine extant manuscripts—is revealing. Two contain *Eneas* in company only with *Thèbes;* in two it precedes *Brut;* in one it follows *Troie;* in two it follows *Troie* and precedes *Brut.* In one of these manuscripts some scribe has tied *Eneas* and *Brut* into a single narrative, altering the closing lines of the former to lead directly into verse 67 of the latter.[45]

The contents of these manuscripts suggest that they were designed as narratives of the establishment and growth of civilization in Western Europe. *Thèbes* and *Troie* provided the two great histories of ancient Greece; *Eneas* described the founding of Rome consequent upon the fall of Troy; and *Brut* described the establishment of Roman civilization in the Western Isles. *Thèbes* had already made its appearance when

[44] *Recherches,* pp. 101-2. The description echoes the briefer one of Antigone in *Thèbes* (Cfmâ, vv. 4045-84). G. Angeli, *L'Eneas e i primi romanzi volgari* (Milan, 1971), pp. 137-38, suggests that the *Eneas* author wrote the description in deliberate rivalry with the *Thèbes* author, a fellow clerk in the employ of the court of Henry II. Clearly the *Eneas* author shows little interest elsewhere in set descriptions of individuals.

[45] *Eneas,* Cfmâ, I, iv-v.

Brut appeared, but this arrangement of narratives by later copyists suggests that the appearance of Wace's chronicle may indeed have inspired the *Eneas* author to contribute another part of the story in vernacular verse. It is especially noteworthy that these copyists, ignoring our modern distinction between chronicle and romance, joined Wace's *Brut,* which was written as a historical chronicle, with the *romans antiques.* Each narrative told its part of the secular history of the West, and latter-day critical distinctions did not concern the scribes. The clear affinities among these works argue strongly in favor of Giovanna Angeli's recent suggestion[46] that their authors were all members of a Norman literary *atelier* subsidized by Henry II to help further Plantagenet interests.

In our preoccupation with detecting, describing, and evaluating the *differentiae* of romance in the early *romans antiques,* we have been prone to forget that these romances almost certainly fell upon the ears of their first audiences as essentially true histories, constituent parts of the world's great chronicle, accounts of the glories of the past, which had given way to the glories of the present. "Our books have taught us," wrote Chrétien in a famous and strikingly sanguine passage at the opening of *Cligès* (c. 1167), "that Greece had the first honor in chivalry and learning. Then chivalry and the highest learning passed to Rome, as it has now come to France. God grant that it be kept here, and that the place be so pleasing to it that it never depart from France."[47]

Certainly some of "our books" are the *romans antiques,*

---

[46] *L'Eneas e i primi romanzi volgari,* esp. pp. vii-ix.

[47] Vv. 30–38. Even this concept of *translatio studii,* a parallel to the medieval idea of *translatio imperii,* had already begun to develop into a rhetorical *topos,* though Chrétien appears to have been the first to give it full formulation. See E. Gilson, *Les Idées et les lettres* (Paris, 1932), pp. 182–86, and E. Curtius, *European Literature and the Latin Middle Ages,* tr. W. Trask (New York, 1953), pp. 28–29. See also the remarks of M. Wilmotte, *Origines,* pp. 201–10.

fortifying the learning and chivalry of France with that of the past, providing models, materials, patterns of conduct, and marvels for sheer wonderment. We have discussed both the didactic impetus and the nonhistorical orientation of these twelfth-century poets. In their works the past exists for the present, and the fictionalizing of what was accepted as history—the addition of love affairs, marvels, descriptive *tours de force*—added both to their palatability and to their didactic comprehensiveness without disturbing their audience's view of the material as history.[48] Surely the *Eneas* author's belief that he was gilding French learning with ancient truths had its effect on his treatment of the inherited fable.

The humor of *Eneas* deserves comment, which indeed applies to much twelfth-century romance. The modern reader often ignores the humor of these narratives, especially when he reads them in prose translations. But the Eneas–Lavine episode is saturated with it, and the lovers, especially Lavine, are treated with the benign and tolerant amusement with which the world has always viewed young lovers. They are ridiculous to the world at large and perhaps to each other, while at the same time intensely and solemnly absorbed in one another. Especially amusing is their ingenuity in creating air-castles, building causes and conflicts, mental chasms and mountains, aphorisms and casuistry, out of nothing at all, and utterly without the knowledge of their partners. The running

[48] It is precisely this fictionalizing which produced the seed of essential Romance in the *romans antiques*. The world their authors created was fundamentally, as G. Raynaud de Lage eloquently remarked, "un monde à leur façon, qui ne correspond effectivement ni à la 'vraie' Antiquité, ni au train quotidien de l'existence au XIIe siècle; c'est un monde qui n'est ni antique, ni moderne, plus brillant d'habitude, plus riche, plus beau que le vrai, un monde où l'on trouve ce qu'on a voulu y mettre: une société, des héros, que l'on rêve sans doute á partir de ce que l'on connaît d'expérience, mais qui n'existent nulle part en fait, un monde de l'aventure, une Antiquité aussi romanesque en un sens que le pays de l'Astrée ou que la patrie des bergers de don Quichotte." See G. Raynaud de Lage, "Les Romans antiques et la représentation de la réalité," *Moyen âge*, LXVII (1961), 289–90.

contrast between cold fact and the monstrous fictions of their fervid imaginations is a stable basis for humor. The touch is consistently light, and the lovers' cries of death and despair are never intended to be taken seriously.

The knowing, winking *gab* of Eneas' barons as they watch the lovers gaze at one another, she from the tower, he from the plain before Laurente (9230–55), establishes the tone very well. In the same whimsical tone the author describes Lavine's kisses from the tower, wasted on the air: "She kissed her finger, then extended it to him, and Eneas understood well that she had sent him a kiss, but he did not feel it, nor did he know of what savor the kiss was: he would have been very glad to know. She sent him two hundred of them that day, there where she stood in the tower, but he never knew how they tasted, for they did not reach him" (8877–86).

Undoubtedly the *Eneas* author learned much of his humor from Ovid, though he lacks Ovid's subtler, and often harsher, irony. But he established the light tone of the love passages in the romancers who succeeded him and, indeed, for centuries afterward. For English-speaking readers this tone is perhaps best preserved in Chaucer's late *Knight's Tale,* in the speech of Theseus when he finds his former prisoners, Palamon and Arcite, fighting "up to the ancle" in their own blood, over a lady who is unaware of their existence, and in a country in which their discovery meant their death:

> Now looketh, is nat that an heigh folye?
> Who may been a fool, but if he love?
> Bihoold, for Goddes sake that sit above,
> Se how they blede! Be they noght wel arrayed?
> Thus hath hir lord, the god of love, ypayed
> Hir wages and hir fees for hir servyse!
> And yet they wenen for to ben ful wyse
> That serven love. . . .

But Theseus, though the professed enemy of the two young lovers, finds sympathy for them in the memories of his own youth:

> But all moot ben assayed, hoot and coold;
> A man moot ben a fool, or yong or oold,—
> I woot it by myself ful yore agon,
> For in my tyme a servant was I oon.

This was the tone of the romancers from the beginning. The passage may serve to remind us that love in medieval romance was rarely treated in the tense manner which we often assume.[49]

There is humor elsewhere in *Eneas,* thought it is usually more sardonic or ironic, verging on the play of wit. The author finds a grim humor, for example, in the inability of the Latin seer, Rannes, to foresee his own death (5053–74). He is provoked to a smile at the sight of King Latinus rescuing his helpless gods from the unforeseen melee outside Laurente (9439–48). He and his audience certainly found humor, however maladroit it may seem to the modern reader, in the coarse taunts which Tarcon addresses to Camille (7061–7106). He amuses us with the rich interchange of sarcasms between Drances and Turnus (6633–6804, 6864–6904). He decorates the Vergilian narrative of Venus wheedling from Vulcan the armor for Eneas with touches of domestic comedy (4297–4393). And he elsewhere touches his narrative with quiet humor.

Eneas is not structurally impressive; certainly its author lacks the fine sense of structure and proportion which Chrétien displays in his best works. Nevertheless, he makes use of a certain amount of conscious patterning, usually by balancing episodes added to, or found in, his source. Thus, the

---

[49] *The Works of Geoffrey Chaucer,* ed. F. Robinson, 2nd ed. (Cambridge, Mass., 1957), Fragment I, 1785–1825, pp. 34–35.

addition of the Judgment of Paris is balanced by the later addition of the adultery of Venus. The deaths of the friends, Nisus and Euryalus, are balanced by the deaths of father and son, Mesencius and Lausus. In the more important balanced episodes there is an order of ascending length and complexity. The episode of Dido's "wrong" love, which he found in his source, is the prelude to the longer, more elaborate "right" love episode of Lavine, which he invented. The relatively modest tomb of Dido is followed by the more sumptuous tomb of Pallas, which in turn yields to the enormously elaborate tomb of Camille.

But Dido's tomb is better taken as a prelude to the major pattern. The deaths of Pallas and Camille occupy an important section of the central part of the story and are exact parallels, providing a dual core around which the author can order the warfare before the beginning of the Eneas–Lavine episode. The author describes the death of each in battle, but forestalls mourning for them by other actions. These are followed by truces for the burial of the dead. During the truces, elaborate and expensive biers are prepared for the deceased, over whom the bereaved utter long funeral laments. The corpses are then carried on long journeys to their homes. The romance describes the mourning for them when they are received in their own cities, the preparation and embalming of the bodies, the construction of magnificent tombs with epitaphs, and the final sealing of the tomb. Whatever we may think of these extended episodes themselves, the *Eneas* author makes excellent use of them as static points around which his central battles revolve, as the earlier and later episodes tend to revolve around Eneas' two loves of Dido and Lavine. The romance is not entirely without a structural rationale.[50]

---

[50] R. Cormier, in his study, *One Mind One Heart* (Romance Monographs, 3, Uni-

Nevertheless, the reader's total impression of *Eneas* is not that of a carefully ordered work of art. He finishes the narrative with the impression of a bewildering and disorderly riot of incident, color, texture, grotesquerie, noise, and emotion, each item sharply delineated, each demanding its own share of attention, careless of subordination, and often only casually related with its context. He will perhaps be reminded of the similar colorful profusion to be found in parts of ecclesiastical architecture or manuscript illumination. There are no muted tones in *Eneas,* no neutral shades, no meticulous *encadrement* or scaled perspective. The reader drifts on a rich stream of flamboyant detail and incident from beginning to end.

The *Eneas* author and his successors often interrupt their narratives to praise *mesure* (e.g., *Eneas,* vv. 677–84), but as narrative artists they are not practitioners of that great classical virtue. On the contrary, the watchword of these early romancers is extravagance; extravagance in entertainment and *largesse,* in dress, armor, and equipage, in cities, castles, and temples, in sentiment and emotion, pains and pleasures, oddity and grotesquerie, feasting and fasting, warfare and bloodshed. *Mesure* might be an excellent rule of life, but "sweet Competence," as it was once celebrated by an American poet,[51] is hardly good entertainment for a baronial audience eager to be surprised, delighted, and distracted.

The *sen* of *Eneas* is considerably less clear and self-conscious than that of later and more distinguished romances. It

---

versity, Miss., 1973) finds, thematically speaking, a distinct tripartite structure in the work. Part I (vv. I–2144), including the escape from Troy, the Dido episode, and the departure from Carthage, is thematically concerned with "Despair and Temptation." Part II (vv. 2145–7724), including the underworld *catabasis,* the confrontation with Turnus, and the deaths and burials of Pallas and Camille, is thematically concerned with "Hope and Struggle." Part III (vv. 7725–10156) including the Lavine episode, the final battle with Turnus, and the conclusion, is thematically concerned with "Fulfillment." See the summary presentation in R. Cormier, "The Structure of the *Roman d'Eneas," Classical Folia,* XXVI (1972), 111–13.

[51] Timothy Dwight, *Greenfield Hill* (New York, 1794), Part II, vv. 1–164.

is obviously controlled in part by the author's acceptance of the historical truth of his fable: *Eneas* first of all celebrates the glamour of the spread of civilization and chivalry from Troy to the West, *translatio studii et imperii.* But it is also the narrative of a knightly hero's fulfillment of his nature by overcoming nearly insuperable—often supernatural—obstacles, and conquering a kingdom, a wife, and a lover. It is a chivalric success story which begins with disaster and ends, as do most later romances, as well as the great romantic comedies of Shakespeare, with a *solemnitas,* the formal ceremony which marks the knight's achievement of *joi* and his assumption of a new position in society. Through its hero's conduct and achievements it celebrates the knightly virtues which he embodies; not the *pietas,* spiritual fortitude, love of peace and moderation which characterize Vergil's hero, but the handsome manner, noble bearing, lofty skill at arms, *largesse,* and sentimental sensibility which suit the emerging personality of the twelfth-century knight in literature.

Finally, *Eneas* is a celebration of the infinite variety of art and nature, "Goddes foyson," by a clerk who has learned the wonders of the world, past and present, from his studies, and is eager to delight his audiences with them. He would teach his readers not only a pattern of the nobility of the life of arms through the exploits of his hero, but also the glamour, strangeness, and color of the world through his embellishments of the fable.

One should add that *Eneas,* as an early representative of the romantic revolution of the twelfth century, documents a most significant social phenomenon: a new self-consciousness and sense of civilization among at least one portion of the knightly class in Western Europe, a new recognition of social responsibility, even a subtle flowering of individualism. It is this dawning self-consciousness, this gradually growing recognition of the individual psyche, so difficult to define, that the

Eneas poet and his successors recognized, encouraged, and elaborated in their works. The feeling is best epitomized, perhaps, in Chrétien's image of the motionless and solitary Perceval gazing at the three drops of blood in the snow, oblivious to the outside world, submerged in the contemplation of the noble beauty of his absent Blancheflor.[52] The romances thus record a notable change in the spirit and temper of a part of the dominant social class. And with *Eneas* the romance genre had achieved definition.

VIII

The twelfth-century adaptation of *Eneas* into German by the Flemish Heinrich von Veldeke (c. 1170–c. 1185) deserves special comment. It is a work of curious interest, significant as an instrument of the narrative's diffusion in German-speaking areas, important as a model for Heinrich's courtly successors, and absorbing (with *Eneas)* for a comparative study in individual and national temperaments. Undoubtedly, Gottfried von Strassburg was thinking especially of this work when he composed his famous tribute to its author: "Heinrich von Veldeke had every poetic gift. How well he sang of love. . . . I hear the best (those who were masters in his day and since) voice their opinion and accord him the glory of having grafted the first slip on the tree of German poetry."[53] Though Gottfried's praise may seem excessive to modern judgments, most scholars will agree with him that the appearance of *Die Eneide* marked the beginning of the German court epic.

Heinrich's work is a free adaptation of "the French book," as he explains, "which was translated out of the Latin."[54]

[52] *Perceval,* vv. 4162–4602. See R. Bezzola, *Le sens de l'aventure et de l'amour* (Paris, 1947), pp. 19–32.

[53] *Tristan und Isolde,* vv. 4726–39; tr. A. T. Hatto (Penguin Classics, 1960).

[54] *Eneide,* ed. Schieb and Frings, vv. 13507–8. Line references in the text are to this edition. The most exhaustive treatment of the relations of *Die Eneide, Eneas,* and

Though he knows the *Aeneid* and mentions Vergil a number of times by name, he remains relatively faithful to his French source in the main line of the narrative. In matters of detail he exercises great liberty, abridging in a few places, expanding in many more, so that he enlarges the 10,156 lines of *Eneas* to 13,528 lines, rhyming in couplets. A considerable amount of this expansion is the result of Heinrich's style and syntax. Though *Eneas* can hardly be considered terse, *Die Eneide* is even less so. Heinrich's verse is looser, more casual, conversational, and circumstantial, less rhetorically controlled, more given to padding and filler rhymes than that of *Eneas*. The Flemish adapter often takes two or even three lines to say what *Eneas* says in one. The French author, with a well-developed tradition of verse narrative behind him, is simply a better craftsman in his versifying and, hence, less wasteful of words.

Heinrich's fidelity to his source is greatest in the early part of his work. He becomes increasingly independent as the work progresses, and at its close his modifications are extensive. The author of *Eneas* required only 341 lines to bring his narrative to a close after the death of Turnus (the *Aeneid* ends abruptly at that point), but Heinrich takes 922 lines. An enumeration of Heinrich's major alterations and additions to this limited section will suggest the translator's tastes and attitudes.

Many of these changes are a part of his consistent effort to increase the elegance, the courtly decorum, and the magnificence of his French source, and to shift the main characteris-

Vergil's *Aeneid* is M.-L. Dittrich, *Die 'Eneide' Heinrichs von Veldeke. I. Quellenkritischer Vergleich mit dem Roman d'Eneas und Virgils Aeneis* (Wiesbaden, 1966). The most useful concise summary of the differences between the two medieval works remains that of G. Ehrismann, in *Geschichte der deutschen Literatur bis zum Ausgang des Mittelalters,* II ii, (2), 87–92. See also G. Schieb, *Heinrich von Veldeke* (Stuttgart, 1965), pp. 39–56.

tics of his hero from those of the conquering warrior to those of the noble, correct, and open-handed courtier, worthy to found a race of kings. At the death of Turnus, Heinrich allows an encomium of the dead Latin's courage and nobility to pass through the minds of his forlorn followers (vv. 12607–34). He increases the delay in the wedding of Eneas and Lavine from eight to fourteen days (12648–49), perhaps to allow himself narrative room for his other additions. He takes pains to depict the hero displaying *largesse,* first to his own followers (12689–704), later in his gifts to the ladies of Laurente (12983–13006), and he describes some of the wedding preparations, including the sending of invitations by Eneas and Latinus to their followers (12758–80). But to provide space for all this, and perhaps also to change the nature of Eneas' character, he collapses the hero's long love agonies and laments, which had occupied 172 lines of *Eneas,* to a mere thirty-eight lines (12705–44). They occur only at night, when Eneas lies down to sleep. In the day he is busied with preparations and courtly activities. The effect of this change is to dissipate most of the impression of mooning adolescence which the lovelorn Eneas so frequently leaves with the modern reader of *Eneas.*

Heinrich, like the French reworker of *Manuscript D,*[55] is dissatisfied with the abrupt manner in which the *Eneas* author brings the love story to its marriage consummation, with no chance for the doubting lovers to exchange messages, meet, or resolve misunderstandings. But while the French reworker provides only for an exchange of gifts and messages through a trusted messenger, Heinrich allows his hero to call on Lavine at Laurente, with all the magnificence of a state visit. For this Eneas dresses his finest "like a lord. . . rich in possessions

[55] For the alternate ending to *Eneas* in *Manuscript D* see the appendix to this translation. Certain striking similarities between the ending of *Manuscript D* and that of Heinrich's translation suggest relations between the two which have not yet been clarified.

and joyful of spirit," (12800–802), so that he looks more imposing than any emperor, Christian or heathen. Escorted by 500 selected knights he rides into the city, to the sound of pipes, trumpets, strings, and song. At the palace he is received by Latinus, who conducts him to Lavine. The two sit alone and talk, exchanging vows of love, and Eneas gives the maiden a golden ring, which she kisses thirty times. Before the author returns Eneas to his camp, he offers a generously long description of the festive atmosphere at the palace. The entire episode of the visit occupies 200 lines (12781–12982).

But besides establishing the courtly magnificence of his hero and arranging a satisfying meeting between the two lovers, Heinrich also ties up some of the loose threads in his source's narrative. Vergil had shown briefly the embittered old Queen Amata hanging herself as Aeneas and his army approached Laurentum, in the mistaken belief that Turnus had already been killed in battle. The *Eneas* author ignores the episode, and has forgotten Amata entirely in his haste to reach a conclusion. But Heinrich introduces, after Eneas' visit to Laurente, a long scene in which the Queen, shrewishly angry at her daughter's joy and bitter over the death of Turnus, accuses Lavine of causing the deaths of Turnus and many other brave men. She regrets her daughter's birth, and regrets that she herself ever knew King Latinus. Lavine defends herself with spirit, and the scene concludes with Amata falling back on her sick-bed. The decorous Heinrich eschews Vergil's account of her suicide by hanging and merely remarks in a few lines that after some days of illness, death overcame the old queen's heart (13012–92).

Not until he has disposed of Amata is Heinrich ready for the wedding, which he then describes in detail and at great length, comparing it with the contemporary lordly festivities of Kaiser Friedrich at Mainz (A.D. 1184). All of this occupies about 200 lines of verse (13093–13286), and is followed by a

100-line genealogy of the Roman rulers, descendants of Eneas, which ends only with the birth of God's son in Bethlehem, and which is characteristic of the translator's historical interests (13321–13420). Finally, Heinrich concludes with another 100 lines discussing himself and his work.

A comparison of this summary with the text of *Eneas* will suggest how freely Heinrich dealt with his source at the end of the narrative; but the passage is not representative, for most of Heinrich's expansions are considerably less consequential. They come about in part, as we have said, from the looseness of his rhetoric, but also in part from his historical interests, his love of ceremony and *Festlichkeit,* his concern for the love theme, and his absorption in the motives of his characters. For example, he expands greatly the Dido episode, making much of Dido's magnanimity; he expands likewise the initial love conversation between Amata and Lavine, and also Lavine's falling in love, altering freely many small details within these episodes. Lavine, even more stubbornly innocent and literal in Heinrich's work than in the French romance, demands how she can live if she gives her heart to another (9791–93). When later she sees Eneas from her window, Heinrich makes use of Love's arrow, here shot rather inappropriately by Venus herself (10036–39). And the translator dislikes Lavine's stammering out the name of Eneas in syllables to her mother; in his version, she spells it out, letter by letter, on a tablet with a golden stylus (10619–31). He dislikes also the physical feebleness which in *Eneas* overcomes the hero as a result of his lovesickness, and which delays Eneas' appearance before Laurente on the day following the enamourment. Instead, he attributes the delay merely to the hero's oversleeping after a restless night (11475–87)!

But Heinrich's changes are not all expansions. He is even less interested in Vergilian mythology than the *Eneas* author, and often further abridges the mythological references. He reduces the *Eneas* author's ninety-line excursus on the Judgment of Paris to a brief thirteen-line allusion (vv. 156–68). And however much he enjoys descriptions of dress, manners, and festivities, he seems not to have been aroused by the French author's descriptions of architectural marvels. He sharply curtails his source's description of Camille's tomb, and although his description of Pallas' tomb is virtually the same length, the looseness of his composition gives it considerably less substance. Significantly, however, he interrupts this description for an account, drawn from a tradition recorded by William of Malmesbury, of the finding of Pallas' tomb by the Emperor Frederick.[56] Such historical vignettes seem to have interested Heinrich considerably more than architectural refinements.

Other characteristic alterations may be summarized briefly. Heinrich's concern for the external decorum of courtly life—the rules of *gentillesse* according to the book—has frequently been noted. This concern causes numerous small changes which tend to idealize the characters and to make their conduct more correct or more gracious. Thus, Heinrich suppresses the grosser parts of the conversation between Lavine and Amata about Trojan sodomy; he softens the language of the quarrels between Turnus and Drances; he elaborates at some length on Dido's nobility of soul so that she will not appear merely a loose woman; he curtails Tarcon's insulting address to Camille, not perhaps so much to soften the insults to the woman as to suppress the references to Trojan cowardice; and he repeatedly stresses Eneas' courtly (as distinguished from heroic) qualities of graciousness, generosity, and *Festlichkeit*. He likewise tends to insulate his nobles from the contact with the lower estates which occasionally takes place in *Eneas*. The archer who shoots the arrow for Lavine

---

[56] For William of Malmesbury's account of this tradition, see note 113 to the text of this translation.

for example, is a young nobleman, a relative of the king, and the native Latins who fall afoul of Ascanius when he kills the deer are elevated from peasants to castellans.

These, then, are the most significant types of change which Heinrich introduces into his narrative of the fortunes of Eneas. If the Flemish versifier is more devoted to elegance, courtliness, festivity, and decorum, he is also more diffuse, often more wooden, and more rigidly bound by his respect for the externals of *courtoisie*. His characters, though considerably less fresh in conception, lead a somewhat more complicated and self-conscious inner life, and German literary historians are probably not wrong when they see in *Die Eneide* the rudimentary beginnings of spiritual qualities which later distinguish the great court epics of Gottfried and Wolfram from their French predecessors.

IX

Countless translators of ancient verse into modern prose have voiced their sense of frustration at the effort, and it is needless to add my own protests. To convert verse into prose is dangerous enough, but the attempt to express in a modern language the heart concepts of an alien culture, long dead, foredooms the translator to some sort of failure. His best defense is that in most cases his effort is better than nothing at all.

The translation which follows has been made from J.-J. Salverda de Grave's edition of *Manuscript A*, Paris, 1925–29. The edition is excellent and poses few problems for the reader. The language of the *Eneas* author is simple and direct, in the rather barren literary vocabulary of the mid-twelfth century, its syntax fundamentally paratactic, though subordination is more frequent than might be expected. His language is far less complex, *nuancé* and elegant than that of Chrétien. Though its morphology shows some signs of disintegration, the verse nevertheless suggests a pronunciation somewhat antique, formal, and bookish, befitting the bookish character of the author and his *matière*.[57]

I have made the translation as literal as possible commensurate with coherence and intelligibility. Though I have sometimes followed the author into syntactical turns or word order not common in modern English, I have avoided any attempt to give an antique flavor to the language. It has been necessary to introduce some order into the chaotic verb tenses which characterize the composition of the period, though occasionally I have permitted the tenses of the translation to shift with the original in the hope of suggesting some of its flavor. I have often followed the lead of the author into the narrative present, which he especially favors. Many of the poet's rhetorical–poetic devices are unfortunately obscured in translation, but an attempt to reproduce them would have been unbearably mannered, if intelligible. I have preferred to retain the French forms of major proper nouns instead of their Vergilian originals, if only to remind modern readers that they are encountering not the translation of an epic, but an entirely new form.

The notes have been made copious in the hope that they will provide a running commentary to assist students unfamiliar with the characteristics of early romance in understanding the nascent genre. Narrative turns which seem typical of the author or the form have received comment, as well as some of the stylistic devices discernible in translation. I have indicated sources where they are known, and have referred the reader freely to the more important scholarship on the romance, but have not discussed *Eneas'* influence in the notes.

Readers unaccustomed to the sound of Old French metrical texts are cautioned that the rhyme and meter of the original

[57] See S. de Grave, *Eneas,* Cfmâ, I, xix.

contribute most significantly to its total effect. They should also be reminded that much of the syntactical inversion and tense-shifting of the original text result from the exigencies of rhyme and meter, as well as from rhetorical mannerism.

The bibliography does not claim to be complete, though it lists the most significant twentieth-century scholarship devoted primarily to *Eneas,* at least through the end of 1971. I have tried to be more thorough in listing the scholarship of the past twenty-five years than in dealing with earlier studies.

ENEAS

[1-24] When Menelaus had besieged Troy, he never departed until he had captured it, laid waste the land and all the
kingdom, in vengeance for his wife. He took the city through
treachery, overthrew everything, towers and fortress,
burned the countryside, destroyed the walls: no one within
them was safe. He overthrew the city completely, gave it over
to fire and flame. The Greeks seized the citizens; no one
escaped their hands or avoided a shameful death. They spared
neither prince nor count: noble birth did not avail, nor courage, nor prowess; and there was no place left for defense. The
city was turned wholly to ashes. King Priam was killed there
with his wife, with his children: never before had there been
so great a slaughter. Menelaus has taken his vengeance. He
has had the walls completely leveled for the wrong done to his
wife.

[25–47] On one side of the city, Eneas held a domain, a very
large part of the town. When he heard that uproar, he looked
toward the fortress and saw the great destruction; it is no
wonder if he was afraid. Venus, the goddess of love, who was
his mother, informed him that the Trojans were undone: the
gods had taken their vengeance on them. She commanded
him to depart without delay, before the Greeks should seize
him. The gods commanded him thus: that he should go in
quest of the country from which Dardanus, who founded the
walls of Troy, came to this land. Eneas was not safe. It was

two long leagues and more from the place where his house stood to where the Greeks were lighting their fires. He knew well that they would be approaching him; he could not defend himself against them.

[48–60] There was sufficient time for him to take all his possessions. He had all his followers assembled and his treasures carried off; he took many possessions and great wealth and riches, and went out through a postern gate. He led away fully three thousand warriors. He carried with him his father, Anchises, who was a very old man, and he led his son by the hand: now they are given over to great hardship. A large number of his followers went out after him. They gathered there where he was fleeing.[1]

[61–82] When they had escaped from the city, under a tree far outside, he gathered his followers about him. He asked them all in council if·they wished to hold with him and to suffer both good and evil with him, or if they wished to return inside to avenge the death of their kinsmen: he is ready to do their pleasure, to return or to flee. They all said that to return or to offer battle was of no use, for their forces were not at all large; the Greeks would kill them all. They wished rather to

---

[1] The *Eneas* author has rejected both Vergil's epic invocation and statement of theme, and his Homeric plunge *in medias res*. This causes some inconsistency when Eneas later describes his adventures to Dido. For example, following Vergil, Eneas tells Dido of his fierce armed resistance to the Greeks at the sack of Troy, and of his loss of Creusa (vv. 1177–96), but in the opening episode of *Eneas* he does not give battle, and Creusa is not mentioned. In both sections of the romance the Vergilian narrative of the sack of Troy is condensed to a sketchy summary, showing little of Vergil's interest in the legend for its own sake. The romancer's love of directness is reflected by the absence of the rhetorical opening—the exordium headed by a proverb or general maxim—so common among early romances (e.g., *Thèbes, Troie, Erec et Enide, Perceval*). Angeli (*L'"Eneas" e i primi romanzi volgari*, p. 106) suggests plausibly that the omission results from the conception of *Eneas* as an "intermediate" work, designed to yoke a Troy romance to Wace's *Brut*.

E. Hoepffner ("L'Eneas et Wace," *Archivum romanicum,* XV, [1931], 249–51) sees in the opening lines of *Eneas* (vv. 1–4, 19–24, 55–57) the influence of the opening lines of Wace's *Brut*, though E. Frederick ("The Date of the *Eneas,*" *PMLA,* L, [1935], 184–96) denies the priority of *Brut*.

flee with him than to return within and die; they made him
their lord and master. Then they looked toward the left; a star
which had risen showed them the road, which ran from in
front of them toward the shore. In that direction the wretched
band went in flight.

[83–98] Eneas searched the shores, and found there twenty
ships which the Greeks had abandoned, well fitted out and
supplied. He went aboard them with all his followers, and
found in the ships fresh water, wine, and wheat in great plenty.[2] From the beach they embarked and set sail on the high
seas, for there was no time to delay. But Juno, who was
goddess of the sky, was a very cruel enemy to them. She held
everyone from the city of Troy in great hatred, because of the
judgment which Paris had made: on his account she hated the
whole country.

[99–130] I wish to recount very briefly the cause of this
judgment.[3] One day, Juno and Pallas and Venus, the goddess
of love, were in conversation. Suddenly Discord came upon
them; she threw a golden apple among the three of them,
then she departed. It was inscribed in Greek that she was
making a gift of the apple to the most beautiful of the three.
There was great strife among them over it: each of them
wished to have it, but they wanted someone else to decide to
whom the apple belonged. They could find no man who could
speak more justly about it than Paris, who was in the woods.

[2] Hoepffner (*Arch. romanicum,* XV, 251–52) sees in this convenient discovery of
the Greek ships and the immediate departure of Eneas the influence of Wace's *Brut.*
In *Aeneid* (ii. 804, iii. 6–7) Aeneas and his men built the ships while taking refuge
in the Phrygian mountains.

[3] The romancer's interpolation of the Judgment of Paris episode, curiously de-
tached from its context in the wedding of Thetis and Peleus, supplants a mere
passing allusion by Vergil, confined to two lines (*Aeneid* i. 26–27). Though it has
attracted considerable attention, its source—if there is a single source—remains
doubtful. Faral (*Recherches sur les sources latines des romans courtois,* p. 75) has
suggested that the author used a commentary on the *Aeneid,* perhaps that of Dona-
tus. See also Salverda de Grave in *Eneas, Cfmâ,* II, 130. The episode is the first
appearance of the judgment of Paris in French vernacular literature.

They showed him the words on the apple, to be given to the most beautiful of the three. Since he knew the laws well, they came to him to judge the question. Paris recognized them well. He gazed at each of them and considered them at length; he reflected to himself that he should not pass judgment hastily, without great consideration, and he asked them to return to him on the third day, by which time he would have considered the matter better; then he would judge their beauty.

[131–144] When he put them to a delay Paris was playing a clever trick. He thought to himself that meanwhile they might come to him with offers, and he could turn them to his profit. The goddesses returned to their homes. He had thought correctly; first Juno came back to him, and promised him that she would give him more than his father owned, that she would make him an exceedingly rich man, if only he would present the apple to her and declare as the truth that she had the greatest beauty.

[145–168] She departed. Immediately afterward, Pallas, who is goddess of battle, came to him and begged him not to fail her, but to hold with her in the judgment, and she would give him courage and such excellence in warfare that he would never in his life find anyone better than or equal to himself; never would any man be able to defeat him. Pallas departed. Venus returned, she who holds sway over the army of love and is its mistress and goddess. She made him this promise: if he would hold with her in the judgment, she would soon give him the most beautiful woman in the world. She departed. After the offers which they made him, he considered in many ways with which of these three he should hold, for he coveted wealth greatly and desired prowess much; but far more was he pleased by the woman whom Venus had promised him.

[169–182] The goddesses did not delay, but returned on the appointed day and asked for the judgment. However much

Paris may have hesitated over it, he gave the golden apple to
Venus and judged that she exceeded the two others in beauty.
Then he was well rewarded by her, for she gave Lady Helen
to him: she found no woman more beautiful. Pallas and Juno
were enraged and held the people of Troy in hatred: for the
act of Paris alone they henceforth hated the whole nation.

[183–209] Juno saw Eneas on the sea. She took great pains
to trouble him; a full seven years she tormented him, and
waylaid him through many seas; she held all his race in great
hatred. One day she raised up a great tempest against him,
stirring up the sea most violently.[4] The ships began to scud
before the wind. It thundered and rained, the wind blew and
the lightning flashed: very foul weather began to arise. Thunderbolts fell thickly,[5] the sea tossed violently, it became so
dark that the men saw nothing and could not hold their
course. They saw neither light nor sun. They could devise no
plan among them: they saw no port in any direction, and the
sky and sea promised them death. They see neither moon nor
stars; their ropes snap, their sails fall, their masts and helms
break; they move with great confusion and labor. Neither
captain nor helmsman is certain of the right course; they do
not know in what direction they are turning, or whether they
are going forward or backward: they have put their lives in
jeopardy.

[4] Juno's raising of the storm is in keeping with the romancer's consistently rationalistic or "naturalistic" treatment of Vergil's pagan divinities. Juno—whose hostility
the romancer finds necessary to his narrative—occupies two lines in raising the
storm. But Vergil had devoted over fifty lines to a decorative recounting of Juno's
brooding rage, her visit to Aeolus, the office of Aeolus as keeper of the winds, his
conversation with Juno, and his release of the storm winds. Vergil likewise devoted
much space (i. 124–56) to Neptune's intervention to calm the waves, which the
romancer quiets in a line, from natural causes. The *Eneas* author had no feeling for
epic machinery, and presumably saw in the gods merely a regrettable superstition,
unworthy of an enlightened modern audience. The decorative, or metaphorical, or
symbolic uses of mythology are lost on him.

[5] Cf. *Thèbes*, v. 638. All references to *Thèbes* are to the edition by G. Raynaud de
Lage (2 vols., Cfmâ, Paris, 1966–68).

[210–230] Sir Eneas cried out loudly.[6] "By the gods," he said, "those men were born lucky who were cut down and killed at the city of Troy! Why did I flee from it like a wretch? I would rather that Achilles had killed me, or the son of Tydeus, there where so many nobles were killed, than that I should die here with such shame! Why did the Greeks not kill me? The gods have held me in great hatred: I cannot remain on land and I fare worse on this sea; they have harrassed me very long, and take no pity on me. They have promised me I know not what land, and I know not where I can seek it. I have found many isles in the sea, and have not heard tell of that land, but I go on searching in very great distress, as fortune leads me."

[231–241] Eneas lamented much, and declared himself most wretched and miserable for escaping from his land, since he suffered such warfare on the sea. Rather he wished he had been killed at Troy with his kinsmen, with his friends, there where Hector and Priam were killed, and counts and dukes. His companions were in great fear; they wished for nothing except death. It seemed to them that death delayed very long.

[242–262] In front of the king was a barque. Its helm was shattered and its mast and sail plunged into the sea. It spun about thrice in a very short time. A wave dashed over it, striking it so hard on one of its sides that it smashed and splintered the timbers. The bolts and the seams burst, and the water poured in through the cracks and filled it suddenly. In a moment it had sunk. These men have finished their suffering: they will never more fear any tempest; no land will ever be conquered by them, nor castles burned, nor towers besieged. The wind attacks the other ships; masts, sails, and yard-arms are torn to

[6] For Eneas' first speech, the romancer remains relatively faithful to Vergil (*Aeneid* i. 94–101).

pieces and scattered over the sea, and Eneas wonders greatly. He thinks he will never come to port: both sky and sea promise him death.

[263–279] The fugitives from Troy suffered so for three days that they felt no joy. When the fourth day dawned the winds died down and ceased completely.[7] The sun rose, it rained no more, the sea lay completely at peace, the tempest was calmed. Then Eneas raised his eyes, looked straight ahead, and saw the country of Libya. He urged all his companions on, and they pulled strongly in that direction, rowing and sailing until they arrived at the port of Libya. They disembarked from their ships as quickly as they could. Of their twenty ships they had only seven left; these they tied up on the shore.

[280–304] They found the countryside very wild. They saw neither hut nor house nor town nor city, but only woods; nevertheless it pleased them greatly. Eneas went into the forest, taking a single youth with him. Both were carrying their bows, and they hunted harts and hinds; his men carried back many of them. They lit fires on the beach and prepared the food which they had taken joyfully in the woods. Often they looked toward the sea, hoping to sight the ships which the wind had separated from them. They were worried about these, but were most distressed over those whom they saw drowned, whom they did not expect to recover: In the others they had very great confidence, but for the dead they had no hope at all. They kept watch on the cliffs and looked long at the sea; when they did not see the ships they feared greatly that the deep sea had swallowed them up.

[7] Hoepffner (*Arch. romanicum*, XV, 261–62) notes many similarities between this description of the tempest and similar descriptions in both the *Brut* (vv. 2530–39) and *La Vie de la Vierge* of Wace, and has suggested that the *Eneas* poet may have been familiar with both works. He believes that Wace's tempest descriptions established the standard elements of such descriptions for virtually all twelfth-century writers of romance.

[305–356] Then Eneas assembled those who arrived with him. No more than a third of his company were there. He began to comfort them for the evils they had undergone at sea. "Sires," he said, "noble knights, be not at all dismayed if you have suffered terror on this sea, and evil and sorrow. In the future this will give you pleasure when you recall it; you will find it good to recount the ills which you have had upon the sea. A man who travels to another land to conquer a kingdom cannot achieve a great lordship if he cannot bear both good and evil. He who always has his will and has never experienced evil will never know, it seems to me, what good is; but if he suffers a little unpleasantness so that he does not get everything he pleases, I think that he will afterwards value greatly the good, when he has it. We have now suffered much pain, on many seas, for more than seven years, and we have labored much, and fasted much and kept vigil; if we ever gain any rest, a little good will please us greatly. Though we suffer torment and evil and pain, as fortune leads us, the gods will conduct us to the place which they have promised us in fief, in Greater Lombardy; thence came our ancestors. We are a large company, and yet we have very little food; we must seek provisions, but I see here a very strange land. I do not know if there is any grain or castle or town or city here; I have seen nothing wilder. If we find no provisions here, we have no reason to stay, but rather we should again put to sea and seek another country. Besides food, there had better be found fresh water, hay, and oats for the horses, who are hardly alive."[8]

[357–377] Then Eneas chose ten brave and hardy knights to go and search the countryside, who could report to him in what country they had arrived, and whether there was any man in it, or a grain of wheat. The messengers departed thence and went to search the country. They wandered

---

[8] This speech, which occupies forty-five lines of *Eneas*, is a characteristic expansion of Aeneas' terse words of comfort to his men in *Aeneid* (i. 198–207).

through valleys and over mountains, through thickets and through fields; they wandered far, but saw no one who could give them information, nothing that lived, not even a wild beast. They wandered through the thickets until they entered a pathway. From this ran a broad highway. The messengers held to the road, which was wide, until they saw the city of Carthage, whose fortress Dido held.[9]

[378–406] Lady Dido ruled the country better than any count or marquis would have ruled it. No domain or realm was ever thereafter better governed by a woman. She had not been born in this land, but was from the country of Tyre; Sicheus was her husband's name. One of her brothers had had him killed and had driven his sister into exile, because he wished to take possession of the realm. She fled by sea, together with a large company of followers, carrying away very great treasures of silks and cloth, silver and gold. She arrived in this land and went to the prince of the country. With great cleverness she went to ask him if he would sell her as much of his land as the hide of a bull would enclose, and she gave him gold and silver for it. The prince, not suspecting a trick, granted it to her. Dido cut the hide into very thin thongs; with these she took so much land that she founded there a city. Then she conquered so much by her wealth, by her cleverness, and by her prowess, that she possessed the whole country, and the barons submitted to her.

[407–440] Her city was named Carthage, and was situated on the coast of Libya. The sea beat against it on one side: it would never be attacked from there. On the other side were pools, and great, broad marshes, and large moats with barbi-

---

[9] The landing of Eneas on the Libyan coast illustrates the author's rationalistic handling of his source. He suppresses Aeneas' interview with his goddess-mother, the divinely conjured cloud which makes the hero invisible to the Carthaginians, and the miraculous element in the survival of the lost ships. Instead of substituting Cupid for Ascanius, the French writer's Venus merely confers on Ascanius the power to cause love.

cans made in the Libyan fashion, and trenches and palisades, fences, barriers, drawbridges.[10] Before one could reach Carthage there were many difficult spots and many hard defiles. High up on a corner of land by the shore was a great natural rock; there the walls were laid. The stones were of marble—gray, white, indigo, and red—all set in regular order with great skill and care, all of marble and adamant. The walls were made with columns, with pillars and with niches, carved with beasts and birds and flowers. The outside of the walls was covered with marble of a hundred colors, without red and without blue. Around the walls were placed with very great skill three rows of magnets, made of a stone which is very hard. The magnet is of such nature that no armed man approaches it whom the stone does not draw to itself. Thus, if men came near it wearing hauberks they would be immediately drawn to the walls.[11]

[441–470] The walls, which feared no assault, were thick and high. They had five hundred towers around them, besides the principal fortress. Inside, facing the city, the walls were arcaded with arches and canopies of great stones, all marble.

[10] The description of Carthage, like much else in the Dido episode, is thoroughly independent of Vergil. As Vergil had reconstructed primitive Carthage in the image of Augustan Rome, so the *Eneas* author reconstructs it as a coastal fortress in the image of medieval Europe—with the addition of a few "marvels" to give it what medieval audiences accepted (in view of the Alexander legend) as the flavor of antiquity. The medieval writer knows none of Dido's associations with Roman history or Augustan politics, and is unaware of the symbolic nature of the Dido–Aeneas romance. He sees it only as a moving, melancholy, and pathetic episode of love gone wrong, and his additions and changes consistently develop this view. On the episode as a whole, see Pauphilet, "Eneas et Enée," *Romania*, LV (1929), 195–213. For a list of the *Eneas* poet's specific additions to, or amplifications of, the episode, see Faral, *Recherches*, p. 119.

Hoepffner (*Arch. romanicum*, XV, 263–64) believes the plan of the description of Carthage to be patterned after the description of Carlion in Wace, *Brut*, vv. 10466 ff.

[11] Faral (*Recherches*, p. 89) calls attention to the *Commonitorium Paladii*, which describes the magnets set on certain islands in the Red Sea, in order to draw ships to them. S. de Grave (*Eneas*, Cfmâ, II, 130) mentions the magnetized mountains in the *Voyage of Sinbad*.

The road ran beneath. There was always a large market there, where men sold silk, furs, quilts of satin, coverlets, purple cloth, gowns, colored clothes, precious stones, spices, and plate. Rich and beautiful merchandise could always be found there. One could imagine no luxury in the world which was not there in plenty. In the city there were broad streets and numerous rich palaces, wealthy burghers, halls and towers, galleries and parlors. There were beautiful buildings in large numbers within the city. It had seven principal gates.[12] A count lived over each one, and for this reason held his fief and his land: if war broke out at Carthage, each count had to serve in it and to provide seven hundred knights.

[471–496] In the sea by Carthage, near the shore, they catch a sort of fish, not large but small; they cut these fish at their tails so that red drops fall from them; from this they extract the precious Tyrian purple.[13] There are few fish of this kind; people call them *conchylia*. From the blood of these small fish, which are very plentiful there, comes the royal purple color. Likewise they make black dyes in Carthage from the blood of a great water serpent, which is called the *crocodile*, of which there are many on an island. These serpents are enormously large, and of a very unusual nature; when one of them has devoured his prey, then he falls asleep with gaping jaws.[14] He has no bowels whatever. The birds enter inside his body and during his sleep feed on what he has previously eaten. He does not purge himself otherwise, for he has no fundament.

[12] The following lines (vv. 465–70) on the seven gates of Carthage are imitated from *Thèbes* (vv. 5399–5410).

[13] This *merveille* could have been derived directly or indirectly from Isidore of Seville, *Etymologiae* xii. 6. 50. Faral (*Recherches*, pp. 162–63) argues plausibly that the *Eneas* author found it in the *Letter of Prester John*.

[14] The tradition of the birds which scavenge in the entrails of the crocodile can be found in Pliny, and after him in many medieval works, but the birds are described as causing the death of the reptiles by puncturing their intestines. See Faral, *Recherches*, p. 92. S. de Grave (*Eneas*, Cfmâ, II, 131) mentions the birds in Apuleius which aid the crocodiles by removing leeches from their mouths. But no exact parallel to the version of the romance is known.

[497–527] On one side of the city Dido established her stronghold. It had strong towers and a good fortress, which feared nothing smaller than a thunderbolt. No man could harm it by any assault, by spear or by arrow, nor could any engine harm it, unless it came out of the sky. The palace was beneath the tower. None so handsome was ever seen or built by king or emperor. A hogshead of precious stones were set in the wall, and seven thousand enamel plaques were placed there on the pillars, on the battlements, on the gateways, on the arches, on the joists, the windows, the glazing, and the window-frames. Dido had built a temple nearby, rich beyond measure, where Juno was worshipped. It would be tiresome to describe all the details of its construction. The goddess Juno wished that Carthage would become head of the world, and that all the kingdoms in it would be completely subject to her, but she could never bring this about. It was destined to be quite otherwise, for the gods had decided that the head must be at Rome.

[528–548] The Capitol was situated on the right, outside the castle, to one side. There by common consent the senators would gather to do justice, to uphold the right, to curb the wrong: this was the place where court was held. It was made with wonderful ingenuity, very beautiful and spacious within, with two hundred vaults and arches. However softly anyone might speak, he would be heard immediately throughout all the Capitol around him.[15] The twenty-four senators were chosen there. Later, at an age long distant from that one, Rome had the power which Dido wished to bring to Carthage. Her city was not yet entirely completed; Dido was still having work done on the walls around it, to strengthen them.

[549–598] The messengers hastened until they entered Carthage. They inquired and asked who governed the city, and were told that a woman was mistress of the whole realm. They inquired where she was, and followed exactly the directions. They found the queen in the hall of the castle beneath the tower, with a very great assembly. The messengers came before her. Ilioneus, who was very wise and brave, spoke first. He greeted her and then said to her, "Lady, hear us a little. You have surely heard a long time ago that the Greeks warred against the Trojans. They burned the city and destroyed it, overthrowing everything, large and small. Not one of those whom they could seize was able to save himself from death; they completely ravaged the city. There was in Troy a rich baron of celestial lineage; the gods protected him well from the great slaughter which the Greeks did that night; they put him outside the city. He had gathered a large following around him. By the gods' command he is going to seek Italy, a distant land. We have searched for it by sea for seven years, but cannot yet find it. The other day we had a great storm, which sank one of our ships. We saw its men drown, and we were separated from a large number of our other ships, nor do we know yet whether they are sunk or not.[16] The smaller group has landed very near here in your country. Eneas has remained there, waiting for his other ships; he has sent us here to you so that he may be safe in your country and may not have to fear your people, as long as there is storm and wind, and until he has somewhat repaired his ships, which the storm has damaged."

[599–640] Dido answered the messenger. "I know well," she said, "the great loss and destruction of the Trojans; I heard much of it long ago. You who were preserved from it have since suffered much for it. Never since then have you been

[16] In the *Aeneid* (i. 520–58) Ilioneus delivers this speech to Dido as a representative of the separated ships, and is observed by Aeneas and Achates, who are hidden from sight by a cloud evoked by Venus.

without sorrow, and you are in great need of a rest. If you wish
to sojourn here, to repair and mend your ships, have no
fear, I assure you, of any men in this country. Be reassured, fear not. If Eneas wishes to come here, I will be at
his service in my city. My possessions will be at his dispos-
al. I myself was even more wretched when I came to this
country, for I was not born here; through my own experience I know, I have learned it well, that I should indeed
have pity on a man, if I see him disconsolate. If Eneas
wishes to sojourn and remain here in passing, he will never
have to spend a penny for anything he may need; I will
have him provided for completely out of my goods, and I
will give him much at his departure. I will do more for him
than I have told you; if in the end he should wish to
remain here and give up the folly which he is seeking, he
would have a part of my land for himself and for his
company; my people and his would be one. If he wishes
to live in community with me, I will not hold my Tyrians
more dear than I will hold his Trojans. Return to him
quickly at the shore, and tell him that he should come to
Carthage to lodge with me: he is thoroughly weary of
seafaring."

[641–662] The messengers took leave and returned very
joyfully to their lord. Eneas saw them from a great distance, went out to meet them, and said to them, "What
have you found?"

"Our good fortune."

"And what?"

"Carthage."

"Did you speak to the king?"

"No."

"Why?"

"There is no lord there."

"What then?"

"Dido is the ruler."

"Did you speak with her?"

"Yes."

"Does she threaten us?"

"By my faith, no."

"Then what did she say?"

"She promises us good: 'Be secure, fear nothing.' Thus speaks the Tyrian lady. If you wish to remain and rest in this Libyan land, to restore your ships and repair them, you need fear nothing, for she reassures you thoroughly. Through us she asks that you sojourn with her in her tower. Her aid will not be lacking to you as long as you please to accept it."

[663–692] While the messengers were searching the countryside, the ships which they thought lost had come to port. Each of them anchored; all were there except one, which they had lost by the storm, for which they had no more hope on earth. Eneas rejoiced greatly over the news which he heard, and over his ships, all of which were safe except one. Fortune was very favorable to him: fortune, which before had afflicted him, was now encouraging him. Therefore no man should despair if he has to endure evil, and in turn he should not rejoice too much if he has all his desire; he should be neither too much dismayed by great evil nor too much delighted by great good, but accept both the one and the other in all moderation. Neither a good nor an evil lasts forever. Fortune changes in a very short time, and he who weeps in the evening laughs the next morning: in the evening Fortune is ugly, in the morning beautiful, as she turns her wheel. The man whom she sets on high one day, on the next she turns down below: the higher she has placed him, the greater the fall he takes downward.[17]

[17] On the medieval commonplace of Fortune and her wheel see Faral, *Recherches*, p. 100, n. 3; and esp. H. R. Patch, *The Goddess Fortuna in Medieval Literature* (Cambridge, Mass., 1927). Hoepffner (*Arch. romanicum*, XV, 268) notes that Wace,

[693–719] Eneas advised his barons of the lady's answer and her offer, and of what she had told him: that he should go to her in the city. They advised him in council that he should go there quickly, and thus he did; he did not delay. He dressed himself in very fine clothes and mounted a palfrey. He had one hundred forty men mount with him, and he rode straight for Carthage, as he was led by the messengers who had been there earlier. Before nones he came to the city. His men went in front of him, riding by twos. Burghers, ladies, and knights came into the streets and to the windows to look at them in wonder. There was no need at all to ask who was lord of the company; without any of them having heard tell, they recognized the king immediately.[18] One man would point him out to another with his finger. He was very handsome and gracious, a sturdy and large knight; he seemed to everyone the most handsome of them.

[720–763] He dismounted at the castle; Dido had come out to meet him, and he went forward and greeted her. She took him by the right hand, and they seated themselves in the opening of a window, far from the others. She inquired about his condition, and he gave her a long account of how he had

in the lamentations of Lear described in his *Brut*, vv. 1965–84, had already made extensive use of the personification of Fortune. On the proverb about tears and laughter see Dressler, *Der Einfluss des altfranzösichen Eneas-Romanes auf die altfranzösische Literatur*, p. 69.

[18] Though they seem formulaic, vv. 712–13 ("N'estovoit nul demander/qui de la compaignie est sire") are perhaps a conscious echo of *Roland* (vv. 118): "Gent ad le cors e le cuntenant fier:/ S'est kil demandet ne l'estoet enseigner." (S. de Grave, *Eneas*, Cfmâ, II, 131). The entry of a heroic stranger into a fortified town, followed by the curious and admiring gaze of the townspeople, becomes a commonplace of romances. Faral suggests that the insistence on Eneas' handsome appearance, a detail unmentioned by Vergil, reflects the medieval poet's use of school rhetoric. He cites Matthew of Vendôme, who noted that when the power of love is an author's subject, the love must be motivated by a full description of the beauty of the person who inspires it. See Faral, *Recherches*, p. 101. For the text of Matthew of Vendôme and other medieval handbooks of poetic see Faral, *Les arts poétiques du XIIè et XIIIè siècle* (Paris, 1958).

wandered and how he arrived. When he had told her all, Eneas called his chamberlain and sent him back to the ships for his son, who had remained there. He asked that he be brought very quickly, and commanded that three garments which he owned be brought also. He thought to himself that he would give them to the queen of Carthage, who had shown him very fine hospitality. There was a marvelous brooch—none more precious—and a cloak which was very valuable. Its fur was cut in squares, from an animal of a hundred colors; the whole mantle was hemmed with other furs richer and finer, in front and on the bottom border. The lining was very costly, and the outside was worth much more: it was all embroidered outside with gold. The fasteners and the buckles and the buttons and the tassels alone were worth more than three castles. There was also a gown which would become a queen, of purple starred with gold.[19] King Priam had placed these adornments with his treasures when he was about to be crowned; his wife Hecuba wore them on the coronation day. The chamberlain returned, having accomplished everything very quickly, as his lord had told him.

[764–780] Eneas' mother knew and saw that her son was in Carthage. She feared greatly in her heart that they would threaten him with evil, that he was among a very savage people. She held the power of love. When she saw that Eneas had sent for his son, she took Ascanius sweetly in her arms and kissed him very closely. With this kiss she gave him great power to cause love. Whoever kissed him after her would be inflamed with the fire of love. Venus told those who were conducting him that no man or woman should kiss him except the queen and Eneas. They departed immediately.

[781–800] Ascanius with his followers came to Carthage, to

[19] The description of the cloak (v.v. 741–52) is elaborated from Vergil's terse "pallam signis auroque rigentem" (i. 648), and signalizes well the romancer's taste for the flamboyant and exotic in costume—a taste shared by his successors.

his father, who had him present to Dido the gifts which he
had caused him to bring. She received them most gratefully,
and accepted the rich present. She prized it not so much for
its own value as for him who gave it to her. The lady and all
the Tyrians looked at the Trojan's gifts; they esteemed them
most highly, and made much conversation about them, and
great ado. They could not decide among themselves which
one should be most valued. When they looked at the coat they
praised it exceedingly; but, looking in turn at the dress, they
considered the mantle as nothing; and when the brooch came
afterward, they did not value all the other things at an egg.[20]

[801–822] The queen sent the gifts to her chamber; then she
called the child, who had come to his father. She embraced
him, held him gently, and kissed him very closely. In this she
acted most unwisely: whoever touched him around his face
or his mouth was acting much the fool, for Venus had placed
her fire there. Dido embraced him and was inflamed. The lady
drank mortal poison; to her great sorrow she did not notice
it. With the kiss she caught such a madness of love that her
body was on fire. Eneas in turn kissed him, and then Dido
kissed him again quickly. Love hastened from the one to the
other; each in turn drank deeply of it: whoever kissed him
more drank more of it. It was Dido who was the more mad-
dened; she took then a mortal intoxication: now love has her
in great distress.

[823–838] The queen gave herself over to kissing Ascanius
until it was fully night, and time for supper; with that the
washing of hands was sounded, and then they sat down to eat.
It would be tiresome to enumerate and recount all the foods
which came, thick and fast, and to name the plain and spiced

[20] The depiction of crowds of onlookers evaluating or admiring rich gifts, or spec-
ulating on the worth of knightly jousters, became a common *topos* in medieval
narrative. See, e.g., Chaucer, *Canterbury Tales*, V, 189–262 (SqT). The *Eneas* author
repeats it (vv. 909–32, 4556–58).

wines, but everyone there had enough of them.[21] Everyone
was very well served, and when the dinner was finished the
servants removed the tablecloths. In the palace the brightness was very great; so many candles were burning there that
the light would have been no brighter by day.

[839–858] Dido remained at the head table, where only the
noblest of her barons were seated. The rest of her household
had departed. She begged her guest to tell her of the destruction of Troy, and to recount its betrayal. Everyone became
quiet throughout the palace, and listened in deep silence.
Eneas hesitated a little, then addressed her. "Lady," he said,
"you remind me of my very great sorrow and my sadness; I
could not begin to tell it. To this hour I feel great pain when
I recall that deep sorrow. I would not tell it of my own will,
but since you wish that I tell it to you, now you will hear a
very large part of it. I will tell you the truth about it, for I was
there, and I saw and know it.

[859–878] "Troy was indeed a wealthy city, built with great
magnificence. It was very long and broad, a whole day's journey across. When Menelaus besieged us for the crime which
Paris committed, he found us very strong and brave. We had
many good knights. In those days we would hold frequent
tourneys, where Menelaus lost many of his men, and then
there was a truce of three months or more between us—such
a time it was—when we enjoyed a long rest. I do not know
why I should describe to you the battles and tourneys which
we had there so often. You have heard all of that, but you
have never heard all of how we were destroyed. Know that we
were betrayed.

[879–905] "When Menelaus had sat ten years at his siege,
which was very great, and saw that he would never take us

<hr />

[21] The curtailed *occupatio*, or refusal to tell, is a frequent rhetorical "color" in
Eneas. See, e.g., vv. 518–19, 872–75, 1172, 3955–56, 4002–4, 4007, 4775–78, 5641–45,
9433–36.

by force or constraint, he was very close to returning home, when Sir Ulysses promised him that he would try if he might succeed in something by treachery. If he could not capture us that way, then it would be useless to remain. He had a large horse built out of wood, on fifty pairs of wheels, so that it could be drawn. He had it well hollowed out inside, and there, within, he had large platforms built; he had five of these structures built inside; none was so small that a hundred knights could not stand there. The horse was completely filled with hardy and brave knights, well armed with all kinds of weapons. The others, who departed, took their pavilions and tents and put to sea in ships. They all rowed to an island near the coast; there they waited.

[906–944] "In the morning the army departed, and great joy was felt through the whole city of Troy. They ran to open the gates, and the knights and the burghers began to go forth. King Priam went out, and we along with him; we all were issuing forth joyfully and going through all the places where the Greek tents had been. One would point out to another with his finger: 'there stood the king's pavilion; there was the lodging of Achilles; here Ajax stayed, there Ulysses, and there the tourneys were held.'[22] Everyone gazed and looked; there were barriers, palisades, and great moats between them and the city. The king gazed at the horse, not knowing whether the Greeks had raised it there so near the city for good or for evil. The crowd talked much about it, and gazed all around it; they spoke their guesses about it, but they did not know the truth. It would have gone much differently if they had known with certainty what the horse had in its body: of all those within not one would have gotten out without being cut to pieces and killed; not a single man of them would have

[22] Faral (*Recherches*, pp. 112–13) sees in the conjunction of these great names the influence of Ovid's treatment (*Metamorphoses*. xiii) of the quarrel of Ajax and Ulysses over the arms of Achilles.

come out alive, but all of them would have died. If they had
been known to be within, they would have been burned inside
the horse, and Troy would yet have had no harm, nor would
we have been thus destroyed. Through this treachery we all
perished.

[945–960] "There where we were by the horse, before the
eastern gate, gazing all around—there the shepherds led a
man whom they had found in the trench, bound and completely naked. The Greeks had left him there. By this man we
were deceived. The king spoke to him first, asking him in turn
what his name was, who he was, and who had thus mistreated
him. We were all gaping at him and attentive to his words. We
urged him strongly to speak, and he gave the appearance of
weeping.

[961–1002] "He had little care for his life when he placed
himself in such hazard and in danger of death, in order to
deceive and betray us. He undertook an act of great boldness.
Sighing he spoke to the king. 'Sire,' he said, 'I am from Greece,
but it troubles me greatly that you do not take vengeance on
me, for I have no hope of life. I know that I am close to my
end. Ulysses, who has held me in great hatred and mistreated
me much, would desire this greatly; he has abused me most
wrongfully. Because of one of my uncles, whom he killed, I
quarreled with him, and told him that if I got back to my own
country, I would indeed not rest until I had taken vengeance.
He was a powerful man, and had me seized. Out of caution
he would never release me, but held me long in captivity and
very great misery, until the other day, when it happened that
Menelaus held a council. He complained that it grieved him
not to return to Greece: he had made too long a stay, but he
could not get the right wind. If a good wind which could bring
them to Greece did not blow when he wished to enter the
ships, there was no help; already he has tried it ten times, but
always the winds cheated him. He asked advice concerning

what he could do about the winds, which were so contrary to him, and they all advised the king that through the high priest of their religion he should make inquiry of all the gods how they might return to their land.

[1003–1029] "'Then Calchas—a prophet highly honored— was sought out and given the duty. He took his cross and his stole and made a great sacrifice to the gods; then he inquired well into the matter, and the gods showed him the truth of it, all in order.[23] When he came on the morning of the next day, everyone returned to the diviner and asked what they should do. He answered on behalf of the gods that their departure would be fruitless if Aeolus, the god of the winds, were not first appeased, and that a Greek should be sacrificed to him: if they wished to depart now, it was necessary for one of them to die. Everyone was frightened by this, for each man feared for himself, that he might be condemned to death. They were about to cast lots to determine on whom the chances would fall, who would release the others, when Ulysses had me brought forward: he said that I was condemned to die, that I had forfeited my life.

[1030–1064] "'There was no opposition at all; each one who feared for himself gladly settled on me. I was seized and stripped wholly naked, and my hands bound behind my back; I was basely tormented, just as you see me here now. All the priests of the faith made their signs over me, and they led me to the altar; on my head they placed salt, wine and oil, meal and ashes. I was about to extend my neck, and beside me stood the man who was about to behead me. My death was all readied. Thereupon a quarrel broke out between two barons far out in the army.[24] The king went there very quickly,

[23] This anachronistic picture of Calchas sacrificing with cross and stole is the lone occasion on which the French author permits formally Christian accouterments or images to enter his poem. Among medieval authors he is unusually careful in this respect, perhaps because he had the *Aeneid* before him as he worked.

[24] The detail of the quarrel in the army is a characteristic addition of the *Eneas*

and all the others together with him. They abandoned me: I was alone. I took to flight in the other direction, and went and hid in a distant wood. What they wished to do to me, I believe they have now done to another. They are at peace with the god of the winds; he has sent them a very favorable breeze, and they have departed to their country. I have remained behind like a wretch. I have lengthened my life a little, but my death remains very close to me. Among you I must die, and my death will seem late to me, for I desire it greatly. It pains me very much that I am not dead, if that is possible.'

[1065–1097] "When that traitor had told us this, he was quiet a little. We looked at the wretched man, and all of us felt great pity toward him. They untied him immediately, and the king ordered clothing to be given to him. He pardoned him both limb and life, and told him that he should not be at all dismayed, for through him he would come to no harm. Then he inquired about the horse, why it was made, and why it was of such large construction. The evil Sinon spoke to the king: 'Sire,' he said, 'I will tell you all the secrets of the Greeks, for I will never love any of them, nor will I ever return to them if I can live among you in peace. They knew well all the truth, that the gods had ordained that Troy would never perish as long as the Palladium was there. Pallas, who was goddess of battle, was sustaining you without fail, and her image was worshipped and much honored among you: through her you were all secure. One night, Ulysses climbed up through a breech in this wall; Tydeus was with him. They stole your Palladium from you, and were conveying it from here out to the army, when the image was broken.

[1098–1132] "'Hence Pallas was angry with them, and thereafter caused them much trouble for it. All the diviners

---

poet, always eager in a matter-of-fact way to explain causes or give details of operation. Vergil's Sinon (ii. 134) was satisfied to say that he broke his bonds and escaped.

and the magicians and the teachers of our religion told the king in council that he should quickly seek reconciliation with the goddess. Therefore, he had this horse built, and was going to arrange for Pallas to be sculptured and placed on top, fully armed with lance, sword, and shield.[25] But not long ago he lost the craftsman who was making it. Those who see the horse do not know why it was made to such measurements, so large, of such high stature; but I will tell you the reason why the evil Greeks did it. Gladly will I tell you their evil. They made the horse thus large so that you could not draw it inside, for it is such a sacred thing (this the hateful Greeks knew well) that evil would never come to the place where it was lodged. Here there is great hope of good: the Palladium which was stolen was not worth so much inside as the horse would be there; but it would be a detestable thing to the wretched Greeks, who know well that great honor and joy would come to you if the horse were inside: you would be preserved from all evils.'

[1133–1152] "We believed what he had said; there was no man great or small who did not advise drawing it inside.[26] A hundred feet of the wall were torn down: the gate and the entry were small, the horse immensely big, and it was necessary to make a large road. We tied ropes on it for drawing. Three thousand men were pulling from the front, and behind it were as many more, who pushed with their hands and with levers. They worked very willingly. The horse was brought within the city with the greatest rejoicing. Maidens were singing in front of it, and harps and fiddles were sounding; with such great joy and happiness we led our sorrow into Troy. It was left in front of the temple. Sinon was hidden beneath.

[1153–1176] "When we had all departed and were asleep,

[25] The proposed statue seems to be the French author's own *merveille*. S. de Grave (*Eneas*, Cfmâ, II, 132) believes that it may have resulted from a misinterpretation of *Aeneid* ii. 183–84: "hanc. . .moniti. . .effigiem statuere."

[26] Again characteristically, the *Eneas* poet suppresses the supernaturally contrived deaths of Laocöon and his sons (*Aeneid* ii. l 198–233).

toward midnight, Sinon, who knew the construction of the horse, opened the doors and the windows, and all those who were in the body came forth. They shouted the Greek battle-cry and set fire to the city. The others, who the day before had given the appearance of going away, came to port by night. When they saw the fire of the city, they all went in that direction, and entered it at the same time. They found no opposition, nor did they encounter a man great or small from whom they took any ransom except his head: never has man heard tell of such slaughter. I cannot describe a tenth of it. There King Priam was killed. The Greeks destroyed everything. They dragged Helen from the tower and returned her to her lord.

[1177–1196] "I saw the great destruction and gathered many of my followers. With a great force I went out; my wife Creusa followed after me to accompany me, but I was so occupied with fighting that I lost her in the crowd. From this I had great sorrow, for I never saw her again. I became all wearied with killing Greeks. Venus, my mother, came to tell me on behalf of the gods that I should depart and go to the land from which Dardanus, our ancestor, came. I saw that it could not be otherwise. My mother caused me to withdraw, and with twenty ships I put to sea. Since then I have never ceased to suffer evil, and I have had many a great misfortune. It has been almost a year since my father died at the port of Sichans."[27]

[27] Aeneas' long, detailed narrative of the horrors of the sack of Troy and of his own escape (*Aeneid* ii. 268–804) is here compressed into forty octosyllabic verses. Among the more significant suppressions are the scenes between Aeneas and his father, Anchises, his search for his lost wife, Creusa, and the appearance of Creusa's ghost. The French Eneas thinks of his father—who will be necessary for the Hades episode—only in the final lines of his recital: "Pres a d'un an qu'as Sichans porz/fu Anchises mes pere morz." The author thus dispenses with Anchises' death and burial, and indeed all of the wanderings described in Book iii of the *Aeneid*. The 347 lines (vv. 849–1196) of Eneas' recital replace all of Books ii and iii of the *Aeneid*, 1522 Latin hexameters.

[1197–1218] While Eneas was telling his tale the queen marveled at the evils, the sorrows, and the losses, and the pains which he had suffered. She looked at him sweetly, as love urged her. Love goads her, love spurs her; often she sighs and changes color. When it is time to sleep she has the beds prepared. She leads him to the chamber where the beds are readied with covers and good sheets. Eneas, who is very tired, goes to bed. The queen is present at his covering, and can leave only with great difficulty. Four counts lead her away, and she enters her chamber. A hundred noble damsels are there, daughters of counts and kings, none of whom is not a maiden. They serve the queen at her retiring.

[1219–1265] When the chamber is quiet, Lady Dido does not forget him for whom the god of love has now put her in great turmoil. She begins to think of him, to recall in her heart his face, his body, and his form, his words, his deeds, his speech, the battles of which he has told her. It is for naught that she lies down to sleep: she turns over, then turns back again often, she swoons and stretches, she pants, sighs, and yawns. She is greatly agitated and troubled, she trembles and shivers and shakes, her heart stops and fails her. The lady is in very bad straits; and when she happens to forget herself she thinks that she is lying together with him, held all naked in his arms, and she thinks that she is embracing him in her arms. She cannot cover or conceal her love. She embraces her blanket, but finds no comfort or love there. She kisses her pillow a thousand times for love of the knight, and imagines that he who is absent is present in her bed; he is not there at all, but elsewhere. She speaks to him as if she hears him. She gropes and searches for him in her bed, and when she does not find him she beats herself with her fists, weeps and makes great lament, dampens the sheet with her tears. The queen tosses much, first on her face and then on her back. She cannot escape: she suffers much and passes the night in great sickness and pain. She is tortured in many ways. She does not know who has trapped her: she has drunk deadly poison. She does not understand who the child was whom she has held and embraced, who has given her this madness.[28] She cannot escape being tortured throughout the whole night. She thinks that she will never see daylight.

[1266–1278] When she could see light, at the break of dawn, she arose. She called no chambermaid, nor any of her women-in-waiting. She was burning with mortal fever, and the madness of love afflicted her greatly.[29] She went quickly to her sister: "Anna, my sister, I am dying, I will not live."

"What is the matter?"

"My heart is failing me."

"Are you sick?"

"I am completely healthy."

"What is the matter then?"

"I am weak with love; I cannot hide it; I love."

"And whom?"

"I will tell you; in faith, him. . . ." And when she was about to name him, she swooned, and could not talk.[30]

[28] Here the *Eneas* poet forgets himself for a moment and slips back into the Vergilian substitution of the disguised Cupid for Ascanius.

[29] Though the romancer contracts and compresses Aeneas' narrative of his adventures, here he expands at length. Love symptoms, love psychology, love dialogue, and love introspection are his stock in trade. Verses 1197-1272 are expanded from a single phrase of Vergil (*Aeneid* iv. 5): "nec placidam membris dat cura quietem." The symptoms described are in complete conformity with the love rules and love psychology recorded some twenty or twenty-five years later by Andreas Capellanus in *De arte honesti amandi*, though the spirit is not that of the troubadours, or "courtly love." Though the sentiment's flavor and nuance are peculiarly those of the twelfth century, Faral (*Recherches*, pp. 135–50) has made it abundantly clear that the source, model, and inspiration for the poet's language and love imagery are to be found in Ovid. Some specific Ovidian parallels to the above lines may be mentioned: *Ars amatoria*. i. 733; *Amores* i. 2. 1; *Heroides* xv. 123 ff.; v. 152; xix. 170; xii. 38; xv. 3. 27. "Il n'est pas possible d'oublier," remarks Faral (*Recherches*, pp. 150–51), "qu'au XIIè siècle Ovid a été considéré comme un habile maître de rhétorique: on a étudié avec prédilection les subtilités de son art, et les productions d'école de la même époque portent la marque de l'imitation constante qu'on en faisait."

[30] These stichomythic love dialogues (and monologues) grow to great length in the

[1279–1322] When she revived from her swoon, she began to speak again: "I love him who has suffered such evils, the Trojan lord whom fortune has sent into exile and who came yesterday to this country. I think that he is of noble family and of heavenly lineage. In everything he shows clearly that he is noble, and his son is very courteous. Yesterday evening I could not get enough of holding and kissing him. Never since I departed from Tyre, when my lord Sicheus was dead, do I recall any love until it came yesterday. I saw no man of any age, however rich or brave or wise he may have been, to whom I would have shown the least semblance of this affection, save only this one, whom destiny has led to my country. This man has fired my heart, this man has given me a mortal madness, for this man I am most certainly dying.[31] If I had not promised my love to my husband for my whole life, I would make this man my lover. But since I have given my love to my husband, it will never be violated by this man. I would rather die than be faithless to him and give my affection to another. I will preserve it and keep faith with him. May the earth divide beneath me and swallow me up alive, or may fire from the heavens consume me completely, rather than that I give my love, which I promised to my lord, to another. I gave it to him and he had it, and has it. He will never be wronged by me. I have no need to love another so long as I live. I can have nothing to do

---

Eneas–Lavine affair, and form one of the author's most important contributions to the new genre.

[31] This sort of anaphora ("cist a espris le mien corage/ cist m'a doné ja mortel rage. . . .") is a favorite rhetorical figure of the author. It appears repeatedly (e.g., vv. 1238–39, 1332–33, 1340–42, 8203–7, 8655–59, 8930–35, 9061–67, 4273–74, 9046–69), usually with the substantive "amors" as the repeated element, but the repetitions in each case are usually moderate in number. See Biller, *Etude sur le style des premiers romans français en vers (1150–75)*, p. 175 and *passim*.

with this other man. I never saw him or knew him, except only through what I have heard spoken of him. I have heard him called Eneas. . . ."

[1323–1354] When she recalled him, when she named him, she grew pale and swooned, so that she was very close to death. Her sister Anna comforted her: "Lady, why are you dying wretchedly? This love which you have for your lord amounts to nothing. He is dead, many days since, and your youth is being consumed in sorrow. From him you will never again have any devotion, from him you will have no children, nor sweet love, nor fine looks, nor protection, nor help. You have here a very foolish love. Since he can surely never do anything for you, why do you wish to suffer sorrow for him? Never will you have any good from the dead: take your pleasure in the living. In the dead there is never any recovery; set your desires on the living. He is a fool who has such regard for the dead. I know it is true, and I have also heard it said: the dead should hold to the dead, the living to the living; that is consolation.[32] Who will preserve your city, your land, your domain? A land or realm cannot well be long maintained by a woman. She accomplishes little by her command if it has no other support. If she must wage war she can endure no great burdens whatsoever.

[1355–1382] "This is a very strange land. War presses on you from all sides. You have made all the barons of this country your enemies because you would not consider one man from this entire area worthy to be your lord. You have held them in contempt; therefore they hold you in hatred, and attack you from many sides. They will destroy you sooner or later. Since you love this man, make him your lord; he will maintain you in great honor, for he is of very great valor. God led him to this country for your good, I assure you. When you

[32] On this common proverb see Dressler, *Einfluss*, p. 69. S. de Grave (*Eneas,* Cfmâ, II, 132) cites an example from the *Romans de set sages*, vv. 267–68.

are overcome by love do you think that you can in any way conquer it? You can do nothing against Love. If you take this man as your lord your power will increase greatly from it, and Carthage will be celebrated for it. To hide your aims you can say that he should stay with us this winter and have his ships overhauled, for now is not the time to cross the sea. Thus you can easily detain him here; later you can do your pleasure."

[1383–1390] The lady was already on fire, and her sister made it greater; she was thoroughly inflamed by love, for this increased her desire: her sister has comforted her poorly, for if Dido had never had any desire for Eneas and had never loved him, this would have excited her love.

[1391–1432] The queen is going mad with love. She does not stop or cease. She takes the Trojan, of whose love she is not yet certain, by the hand, leads him through the city, and shows him its wealth and her castle and her palace. She cannot be at peace for an hour. She very often speaks to him of a thousand things which do not concern him, for she only asks in order to have a pretext to speak to him. She asks him something a thousand times, and never finishes or ceases. In the middle of her tale she stops, not knowing what she is saying or doing. She loses completely her judgment and eloquence, for love has turned her from wise to foolish. She used to govern her land very well and wage war well, but now she has completely neglected these things and forgotten them in her heedlessness. Love has made her forget to govern and protect her land. If enemies lay waste the countryside, she values peace no more than war, for nothing occupies her any more except the love which so assails her. Henceforth, all her followers have very poor support from her; they get neither strength nor help from her. They no longer mount the walls and towers, and no account is taken of the work on the city. Meanwhile they have interrupted the work on the walls, high in one place, low in another: she has lost all for Eneas. She has neglected her rule, and she has not a man who does not complain that the Tyrians are demeaned by her hospitality to the Trojan. She who should protect her domain has abandoned all for her love.

[1433–1444] The queen was in such torture and such pain for a week that she had no rest, night or day, nor ever closed her eyes in sleep. She was in sorrow and great sickness, and did not know how to speak to the knight. She will not be cured for a long time unless she has other thoughts: either she must die of it or confess her love to the knight.[33] For a long time she suffered this anguish which she did not dare to admit openly.

[1445–1478] One morning she felt a great urge to go hunting in the woods, that she might divert herself from her sorrow and forget her love; for love is a much more grievous thing when one is lazy and rests, and he who wishes to escape well from it should never rest; and if one wishes to get far away from it, he must have another interest, for when one is occupied elsewhere, one recalls one's love more slowly.[34] She summoned her huntsmen and had her hunting horses saddled, and they took their bows, horns, and hounds, dogs and trackers and leash-dogs. The city rang with their preparations, with the yelping of dogs, and the confusion. Servants came from all directions, carrying bows, quivers, and arrows. The household was in great excitement. The queen had dressed herself in an expensive purple material banded very beautifully with gold all over the body as far as the hips, and likewise all over the sleeves. She wore an expensive cloak, finely decorated with gold in drops, trimmed with a golden thread, and on her head she had a band embroidered with gold. She had

[33] The pretense of dying of love is Ovidian. See Faral, *Recherches*, p. 148.

[34] Another Ovidian idea, expanded in the *Remedia amoris*. See Faral, *Recherches*, pp. 119–20. The romancer omits the maneuvering on Olympus between Juno and Venus which in the *Aeneid* precedes the hunt and leads to the consummation of the love.

brought with her a golden quiver which was taken from her treasure. There were a hundred arrowheads of pure gold, and the arrows were of fruitwood.

[1479–1494] She takes a laburnum bow in her hand and then descends from the tower, leading three dukes from the hall. The great lords descend after her. Sir Eneas, her lover, awaits her at the foot of the stairs with all his followers. When he sees the Tyrian lady she seems to him like Diana herself, a most beautiful huntress, who in everything resembles indeed a goddess. When she sees him she changes color because of her love.[35] She descends the stairs, and her horse is made ready, all covered with gold and precious stones. Her lover assists her in mounting.

[1495–1520] The Trojan was very well prepared for going into the woods. Horn around his neck, bow in hand, he seemed not at all ignoble;[36] he would have seemed to you as if he were Phoebus. He mounted without further delay and by her reins led the lady, who was in great pain from her love: her escort pleased her greatly. They went into the forest, where they took many deer, and hunted until noon. Then, suddenly, a great storm arose, and a great tempest; it thundered and rained, and became very dark; none of them was safe there. They turned and fled in many directions. The boldest man there was cowardly, and the bravest trembled with fear.[37] No two of them remained together except the

[35] Another Ovidian touch (*Ars amat.* v. 731), which quickly became part of the stereotype. See Andreas Capellanus, *The Art of Courtly Love*, tr. Parry (New York, 1947), pp. 58, 185.

[36] Litotes, as here ("ne sanbloit pas de rien vilain"), is sparingly used by the *Eneas* author, whose genius was more at home in hyperbole than in understatement.

[37] "li plus hardiz i fu coarz,/ li plus vasaus de peor tranble." These lines display clearly the care with which the poet has applied the concepts of school rhetoric to the construction of his narrative. Each line contains a hyperbolic oxymoron, and the two are united by anaphora. The lines are followed closely (vv. 1516–18) by this carefully pleonastic passage: "cil dui ne departirent pas,/ ne guerpi li, ne ele lui./ Tant vont fuiant ansanble andui."

queen and Eneas; those two did not separate; he did not leave
her, nor she him. They went fleeing together until they came
to a grotto. There they both dismounted.

[1521–1538] Here are the two of them together. He does
with her what he wishes, nor does he use very much force at
all, nor does the queen resist: she consents to him with all her
will, for she has long desired him. Now love is made manifest.
Never since her lord's death had the lady done anything
shameful. They return to Carthage. She feels great joy, nor
does she hide it at all, but shows herself most happy and
joyous. She says that she will be his wife, and thus covers her
misdeed; she cares no longer what anyone says of it. Henceforth, in every way, she does with him all her desire.

[1539–1566] The rumor goes through the country that Eneas has dishonored her. Rumor is a wonderful thing: she never
stops nor rests, she has a thousand mouths with which she
speaks, a thousand eyes, a thousand wings with which she
flies, a thousand ears with which she listens for any wonder
that she might spread about. She never ceases to lie in wait;
if she knows ever so little of anything, of very little she makes
very much. She enlarges it more and more, while she goes
both high and low; she enlarges with equal speed the false
thing, as well as the true. She makes a very small thing into
many tales, and always enlarges it, wherever she goes. From
a little bit of truth she tells such lies that it seems like a dream,
and she exaggerates it so that there is not the least truth in
it. First she speaks softly and in stealthy secret, but then she
goes shouting her tale: the more she rises, the more loudly she
speaks. When she has discovered a little she talks about it all
openly.[38]

---

[38] This influential image of Rumor, or "Fame," is derived from Vergil, but her
mythological identification (the youngest of the Titans, daughter of Earth, born to
spite the gods) is suppressed. Numerous later romances took the image over from
Eneas. See Faral, *Recherches*, p. 311 and Dressler, *Einfluss*, p. 104.

[1567–1581] Throughout Libya this Rumor announces the lady's misdeed: she says that a man has come from Troy, that Dido has kept him with her in Carthage, and that she now keeps him there in shame. Both of them pass the winter season in lechery, and are not troubled about it. Because of it, the lady ignores her duties. She hardly thinks of anything else, and he has abandoned his voyage because of it. In this both of them are acting foolishly. The lady is very greatly defamed throughout all the country of Libya, and they dishonor her name.

[1582–1604] When the barons hear it told—the dukes, the princes, and the counts whom before she would not take as her lord—they consider themselves much shamed, since she disdained them all for a man of less worth, who is neither count nor king. They say among themselves, and they are right, that he who believes a woman is very foolish: she does not hold true to her word, and thinks wise what is foolish. She used to say that she had promised her love to her lord, who was dead, and that she would not take it back during her lifetime; now another man has done his will with her, now she has belied her promise and broken the agreement she had pledged with her lord. He is a fool who trusts in woman. She has very quickly forgotten the dead—however well she may have loved him. She now puts all her delight in the living, and the dead she leaves in neglect.

[1605–1614] Now Dido has what she wanted: with the Trojan she does her will and her desire all openly. Now he holds her without concealment, has forgotten his duties, and abandoned his voyage. He does not want ever to part from her, and she thinks that she will keep him long. He is wholly given over to ruin, and holds the country and the woman for his own.

[1615–1644] One day when he was in Carthage, a messenger came from the gods and commanded him on their behalf to give up this distraction and go to Lombardy, to have his fleet

made ready, to abandon the Tyrian woman and all of the
Libyan land: this is not his country nor his fief; the providence of the gods is otherwise.[39] Eneas was much dismayed by what the messenger announced to him. He knew
that he could no longer stay, that he must of necessity
depart. It grieved him deeply to depart and abandon the
lady. He was very pensive, stricken and fearful, greatly
pained in two ways: he could not in the least ignore the
word of the gods or their command, and he feared much
the parting from the lady, lest she kill herself. He feared
that it would be disastrous for her, and nevertheless he did
not know what to do about the command of the gods; he
was also much in doubt whether to announce it to the lady
or to leave secretly. He feared that if he told her she would
delay him and he would depart late.

[1645–1664] He had his ships made completely ready and
decided to leave stealthily. He instructed his men well that
they should know that with the first wind he would depart
from her with his fleet. His followers were much cheered,
for this stay had troubled them, and each of them desired
greatly to go. There was no one whom the stay pleased,
except him who was at his ease; it would have pleased him
much to remain, but he went by necessity, as the gods had
ordered him. He had his ships provisioned secretly with
whatever was necessary for them. He thought he would
deceive the lady, but the queen noticed it; for he who loves
always suspects, lives in doubt and fear, and will never be
secure, night or day.[40]

[1665–1674] Rumor hastened to reveal it to the lady. She

---

[39] The *Eneas* poet here finds divine intervention necessary to his plot, but subdues
it as much as possible. Vergil's Mercury becomes simply "uns message," and his
elaborate narrative is condensed to ten lines.

[40] This is Ovidian (*Heroides* i. 12; xviii. 109; *Ars Amat.* ii. 517 ff.) See Faral,
Recherches, p. 121. It later became a romance commonplace. See Andreas Capellanus
(tr. Parry), pp. 28, 185.

told her of the treachery which the knight had prepared, how he had stocked his ships, how he wished to leave in secret. When the queen knew it, she did not rest from the hour that she heard of the treachery until she had spoken to him.

[1675–1702] She sat down beside him and sighed, and addressed him tearfully: "Speak, vassal, where have I done wrong, that you should kill me?"

"Now what is this?"

"You are surely having your ships provisioned."

"I?"

"True, you wish to flee from me."

"Rather I will depart all openly."

"Why then have you deceived me? Would you abandon me thus?"

"I can no longer remain here."

"Why?" she asked.

"The gods do not wish it."

"Ah, alas, what a wretched fortune. Why then am I not dead? To my great misfortune have I given the friendly aid, the fair countenance, the good hospitality which I have rendered you in Carthage. I will not fail to tell you: you planned a great crime and extraordinary treachery when you determined to depart and separate from me like a thief. How could you have planned it without asking leave of me immediately, or without having pity on me, or without my knowing it immediately from you? The Trojans keep bad faith.[41] Are these the rewards and the thanks that I have deserved from you?

[1703–1758] "But since Dido—who must die for it—can no longer hold you, nor can friendship nor love nor good service

---

[41] Faral (*Recherches*, pp. 113–714) believes that the references in *Eneas* to Trojan bad faith (vv. 1790, 3289, 6321–22, 6332) have their inspiration in similar repeated references in Ovid, based on the perfidy of Paris (e.g., *Heroides* vii. 67–68; *Metam.* xi. 215).

nor pity, do you wish to act so madly as to put to sea in such a storm? It is winter, and the weather is very bad. It is not sensible to sail now. First let the winter pass, then the sea will be calmer. I would pray you by all the gods—who are too harsh to me—by love and by the union which is pledged between us, that you take pity on me. If I die from your wrongdoing and you give me no comfort for it, you will have committed a very great sin. These men around me, none of whom I want as my lord, hate me because of your love. There is not a baron in this country who is not my enemy because of you. They all wish to dispossess me. I must fear such enemies very greatly, and I will have no help either near or far, for you are failing me in my need. They will drive me from this land, nor will I have to war against them first. This I fear, as well I might; but love for you, which spurs me greatly, distresses me still more. If this desire which I now have does not change, I will never live. I fear this parting very much, nor do I think I will escape death from it, for I will have nothing to comfort me. If I had a child by you who resembled you ever so little, whom I could kiss and hold and embrace in your stead, and who would comfort me for you, it seems to me that I would fare better. But I think that I will have nothing to give me comfort or cheer. I am most sure I shall die when I see you part from me. Sire, why have you betrayed me?"

"I have not, truly, my love."

"Have I ever done you any wrong?"

"You have done me nothing but good."

"Did I destroy Troy?"

"No, it was the Greeks."

"On my behalf?"

"On behalf of the gods."

"Have I killed your father?"

"No, lady, I assure you."

"Sire, why then do you flee me?"

"It is not on my account."

"And on whose account then?"

[1759–1790] "It is because of the gods, who have ordered me, who have fated and determined that I should go to Lombardy, where I must restore Troy. Thus they have spoken and destined it; for if it had been my will, and there had been no command except mine alone, given by me, I think that I would not now be going from this country. If it were not the will of the gods that I should govern anyone who remained after the slaughter by the Greeks, and restore the walls of Troy, and if it were my own pleasure, I would not seek to leave you. I take my departure against my will: never believe that it is for my own sake. I know that you have served me most handsomely in your kindness; you saw me in distress, and had mercy and pity on me. If I cannot now reward you for it, I will never be able to forget it, and will remember it as long as I live. I will love you more than all others. If I go away from this country, it is not for myself, I assure you. Give up this lamenting, for you will achieve nothing at all, but only pain me and abuse yourself."

[1791–1813] She looked at him sideways, her face dark with anger. Often she changed color, as love tormented her. Love had completely inflamed her, and she spoke like one mad: "You never sprang from the gods, for you are very evil and cruel, nor were you born of man; rather you were born of stone, and nourished by tigers or some other wild beasts. You never came of man—this I believe—since you have no pity on me. You have a hard and closed heart, and there is nothing which will make you feel pity. Alas, what more shall I say? Since I cannot have him, I give him up. I am speaking to no avail, since he does not hear me nor answer me with a kind word. I am rapidly approaching the hour of my death. My tears can never sway him, nor my sighs, nor my words.

[1814–1856] "What more shall I say? I am completely mad: he did not heed my laments enough to shed a tear over them, nor did he turn his eyes toward me. It means little to him if I suffer. He did not give me one kind look. I mean almost nothing to him. Alas, why am I not dead, since he comforts me in nothing? We feel very differently: I am dying of love, he feels none of it; he is at peace, I am full of woe. Love is not loyal to me, since we do not feel alike. If he felt what I feel and loved me as I love him, the two of us would never part.[42] He goes along mouthing his imaginations and inventing his lies, and saying that the gods have commanded him, have provided and ordained how he ought to lead his life, and ordered that he depart for Lombardy. Indeed the gods pay much heed to this, and labor without measure, and make a great business of commanding him what he should do! By my faith, it makes no difference to them whether he stays or goes! Since he says that he matters so much to the gods that he does nothing without their command, why then have they so afflicted him, and harried him daily by sea and by land? Nor did their warfare against him ever cease until he came to this land; when he arrived in this country he was distraught. How foolishly I acted in receiving him! Now I repent it, as well I should; he has done all his desire with me, and will not remain here for any plea. Since I can no longer keep him, let him go; and I must die."

[1857–1874] She wept, lamented, and sighed. She still

[42] The idea of the inequity of Love is Ovidian (See Faral, *Recherches*, p. 148) and became a romance commonplace. See Andreas Capellanus (tr. Parry), pp. 32, 47, 50. On the phrase, "we do not feel alike," ("ne senton comunalment") see R. Cormier, "*Comunalment* and *Soltaine* in the *Eneas*," *Romance Notes*, XIV (1972), 1–6. Cormier discusses the feudal connotations of the term *comunalment* and argues cogently that the phrase in this context implies "we do not feel a community of souls."

wished to say much more, when she fell into a swoon that deprived her of her reason. Her maidens carried her to her stone-floored chamber. Sir Eneas wept sorely and comforted the queen, but nothing he said was of help, for he could delay no longer. It was necessary for him to do the will of the gods, no matter whom it might trouble. Thus the Trojans departed from Carthage, came to their ships on the coast, prepared their equipment, and found the wind very favorable. They weighed anchor, launched their ships, and some of them hoisted the sails.

[1875–1898] Dido went up to her apartments, up to the highest windows. I do not wonder that she grieved when she saw the fleet made ready. She lamented and sobbed and wept and shrieked when she saw that her love was going away. She no longer cared for her life, for love has no judgment or moderation. She wished to try again if pleas were of any avail, and called her sister to her. "Anna, I am dying of great sorrow. Sister, look there where the ships are going, with Eneas urging them on; he does not in the least wish to remain. Go and tell him that I summon him. I did not destroy his country or kill his father; I did him nothing but good. Ask him to grant me a favor. I do not ask that he give up completely going to Lombardy, but that he stay with me a little and comfort me—this I hope for."

[1899–1926] Her sister went there and tried often, but Eneas did not change his intention at all. He hastened to sea immediately. Dido swooned and changed color. Since she had determined to die, she said, "Anna, now I have thought of and devised a very good plan: near here is a sorceress. The most difficult thing is easy for her: she revives dead men,[43] and divines and predicts fates, and makes the sun hide at high noon and return all backward toward the east, and likewise

[43] This power is ascribed to Amphiarus in a virtually identical line in *Thèbes*, v. 2060.

with the moon. She makes it new or full three or four times a week, and she makes the birds speak, and water flow uphill.[44] She draws the infernal Furies out of hell to announce their auguries to her. She causes the oaks to descend from the mountains and serpents to be overcome and captured. She makes the earth groan under her feet, knows well how to enchant and prophesy, causes people to love or hate, and does her pleasure with all things.[45]

[1927–1954] "She has told me that she will make the knight return, or will cause me to forget, so that I will not care about loving him; and to this end she has ordered that I have a large pyre built, and that I put there my adornments—all those things which he gave me as gifts—the sword which he left me, and the bed in which he shamed me; that I have everything burned and destroyed. Then she will so work by her magic, by marvelous enchantment, that love for him will not grieve me at all. Have a pyre prepared for me quickly and secretly in a chamber, and put there the Trojan's clothing, which is inside, all his arms, and the bed where we had our delights; I want to keep nothing of his. Have the sorceress come, and prepare me a sacrifice, which must be made at this rite." Anna went to prepare the pyre, since the lady had ordered it. She did not understand or realize why she had commanded it.[46]

[1955–1970] Dido remains in her lodgings, from which she gazes after the knight, who has already put out to sea. Her love stings and torments her, and makes her swoon often, and

---

[44] Cf. *Thèbes,* v. 2297.

[45] On the Ovidian additions to Vergil's description of the sorceress see Faral, *Recherches,* pp. 121–23. S. de Grave (*Eneas,* Cfmâ, II, 132) assumes that her ability to make the birds speak and to draw the Furies out of hell are the *Eneas* poet's own invention. J. Crosland finds the most important source for the description in Lucan's *Pharsalia.* See "Lucan in the Middle Ages, with Special Reference to the Old French Epic," *MLR,* XXV (1930), 47–48.

[46] The *Eneas* poet omits the supernatural omens of approaching death found in *Aeneid* iv. 452–73; the liquid of Dido's libations turning to blood, the voice of her dead husband, the mournful song of the owl, and the horrifying dreams.

quiver, and tremble. She wrings her hands and tears her hair, and with her sleeve of white ermine she waves him to come back a hundred times, and a hundred more; but this does not affect him at all, for he cannot return or go against the command of the gods. She calls and makes signs to him. Love pains and tortures her, and will not leave her, I think, until she has come to her destruction.

[1971–2006] When she sees that her beloved is going away and that her love is bringing her to her death, she begins to sigh and lament to herself: "Alas, since he is going away from here what shall I do now but kill myself? When I see how he has wronged me, can I not then hate my life? I will never have comfort from him; he is already far out of port, and I believe that I will see him no more; never again will he come to this country. Since I will never again have any good from him, why did I ever see him or know him? Why did he come to this shore? Why did I receive him in Carthage? Why did he lie with me? Why did I break the vow which I pledged to my lord? Thus Love has destroyed me indeed. Now the promise is belied, nor will I ever have anything from this man. For a very short time I have broken the faith which I had kept so long, but now that short-lived mistake is as bad for me as a great one: my faith is just as belied as if he had had me all my life. Since Eneas will not have me for his wife, shall I then go begging those whom I do not want as husbands? Would I commit such a dishonor? When they were willing, I did not deign; shall I now beg them in turn? I will not do it, truly: I would rather die, since I cannot otherwise defend myself."

[2007–2037] She gave herself to lamenting while the Trojans sailed, until she could no longer distinguish any of the ships. Then she thought she would die of sorrow, and she beat her breast and tore her hair. Her people made great lament, but they could not comfort her, and none of them dared speak to her. She wandered about as if mad, until she entered the chamber where her sister had made a great pyre and done what she had commanded. Before this Dido had caused her to be called away, and the room completely emptied of people. She did not want her to be there to oppose and interfere with what she had in mind. She is all alone in the room. There is no one there to interfere at all with the madness which she wishes to commit as she draws the Trojan's sword: when he gave it to her he never thought that through it she would lose her life. She holds the naked sword; she has struck herself under the breast. With the blow she jumps onto the pyre which her sister had prepared for her, and lies face down in the bed on the Trojan's garments. She welters in blood, and utters laments.

[2038–2074] She speaks with great difficulty: "I have loved these garments much and have kept them as long as it pleased God; I can draw out my life no longer.[47] Upon these clothes I wish to give up my soul. It was my misfortune that I first saw these garments, for they were the beginning of death and destruction for me. To my misfortune I first saw him who gave them to me; like a fool I loved him so much; it has brought me to great harm. On these garments, and on the bed where I was shamed, I wish to end my life. Here I have thrown aside my honor and my power, and left Carthage without an heir; here I have lost my name and all my glory. But I will not die so utterly without remembrance that men will not forever speak of me, at least among the Trojans. I was very noble and wise before love brought me to such madness, and I would have been most happy, had not the Trojan who

[47] In his most striking modification of Vergil's treatment of the Dido episode, the *Eneas* poet suppresses Dido's long, bitter monologue calling for divine vengeance, and swearing eternal enmity between Carthage and the Trojan race (*Aeneid* iv. 590–629). Vergil's Roman historical–political theme, developed in that passage, does not concern the French poet. He replaces it with a dying speech (vv. 2038–67) of remorse and forgiveness, "par nom d'accordement, de pais," and thus, as Pauphilet notes (*Romania*, LV, 211) provides Dido with a Christian death.

betrayed me, he through whose love I am losing my life, come to this country. He has killed me most wrongly, but I here pardon him my death. In the name of peace and reconciliation I kiss his clothes upon his bed. I pardon you for it, lord Eneas."[48] She kissed the bed and all the clothes. She was already drained of blood, and had lost her speech. She groaned and sobbed as death tormented her, and sighed with very great difficulty. Now all breathing failed her.

[2075–2110] When her sister came and saw her, only then did she understand her deceit. She saw the sword upright in her body, and the stream of blood flowing forth. She would have stabbed herself in turn if her maidens had not held her. She wept and cried out and shrieked, and pulled and tore at her hair. "Alas," she said, "unfortunate woman, I myself have prepared the death with which she has killed herself. Sister, is this then the sacrifice which you asked me to prepare? Was it then for this purpose? Truly I have killed you, but I did it unknowingly. I did what you commanded me; now I see well that you tricked me, now I repent it, but too late. Is this then the plan, sister, which you had to invent and provide for and devise, so that love would be easy to you? And where now is the sorceress who knows so well how to enchant, who was going to make you forget? I have done you most evil service, for, by my doing, you are killed. The sorceress was to have cast a spell by which you were going to forget. But here is a very evil enchantment: this we see clearly. You have drunk a deadly philtre to forget the knight. At last you will no longer remember your love for the Trojan."

[2111–2124] Her sister suffers great sorrow, so that her heart almost fails her. Dido is stricken to her death. Death

[48] If the *Eneas* poet is no Vergil, he has nonetheless composed a moving and pathetic death speech for his Dido. The rhetoric of the passage is very careful, using anaphora (vv. 2043, 2046) and especially *interpretatio* (vv. 2039, 2042, 2049–50, 2057, 2059). Anna's speech upon discovering her sister dying (vv. 2083–2110) is equally contrived.

presses hard upon her and torments her, and from one side the flame approaches, and engulfs and burns her whole body. She can speak neither loud nor soft, except that she whispers the name of Eneas. The flame has come so near her that her soul is separated from her body. She cannot protect her white and beautiful and tender flesh from the fire. She flames and burns and turns black, and in a very little time she is consumed.

[2125–2144] Her maidens and her barons gave vent to their great sorrow around her. They lamented deeply her courage and her wisdom and her wealth. When the body had become ashes, her sister had the dust collected. They placed the Tyrian lady in a very small urn. From there they carried it to the temple and buried it with great honor. Then they built a very noble tomb, made of enamel and inlay: no man has ever seen one more rich. On it they inscribed an epitaph, whose letters say

> HERE LIES DIDO,
> WHO KILLED HERSELF FOR LOVE.
> THERE WOULD HAVE BEEN NO BETTER PAGAN
> IF SOLITARY LOVE HAD NOT SEIZED HER:
> BUT SHE LOVED TOO MADLY,
> AND HER WISDOM AVAILED HER NOTHING.[49]

[2145–2160] Eneas was on the high seas, without thought of returning. He saw land in no direction. He wished to go to Lombardy, but as they rowed and sailed rapidly, far distant from port, a storm arose from one side, which drove them

[49] This is the first (and by far the most modest) of the tombs, and the first of the epitaphs, in which the *Eneas* poet delights. Epitaphs were a popular genre in the Latin poetry of the Middle Ages, though, as S. de Grave suggests (*Eneas*, Cfmâ, II, 133), Ovid himself liked to compose them. Cf. Faral, *Recherches*, p. 100. The poet calls Dido's love "soltaine," which S. de Grave glosses as "soudain." For the translation used here, see R. Cormier, "*Comunalment* and *Soltaine* in the *Eneas*," *Romance Notes*, XIV (1972), 6–8.

toward the right. He turned toward the port of Sichans, where his father had died. Sir Acestes, who was of the Trojan race, received them there and served them very richly. Eneas gave a great feast and held games at his father's tomb, for it was then the anniversary of his death.[50]

[2161–2190] The next night when it was dark, when everything was secure, when man and beast were at rest, and fields, forests, and woods were quiet, Sir Eneas was lying in his bed and his father appeared to him. Three times he called him by his name, and then spoke to him: "My son Eneas, hear me, for the gods have sent me here to you. They command that you go to Lombardy, and they say also that you can leave here the followers who will not be of use to you: the old and the weak who want peace, and who can labor no more. You will take with you the young, who will not be at all troubled at undergoing long, hard labors and fighting battles; for you will suffer many hardships, pitched battles and sieges. But you will be well protected in all this, and will be dismayed by nothing. Indeed, you will win the whole war and will then hold the land in peace. You will take the king's daughter as your wife, and there will be no end to your reign. A royal line will be born of you, which will be celebrated throughout the world.

[2191–2220] "But first it is necessary that you descend into hell to speak with me in the fields of the good, where I stay. It is not the evil hell. I am in the Elysian Fields, where there is neither pain nor sorrow: the abode of good men is there, and there we are in great repose. Sibilla, a woman who knows augury, can lead you there. She is a diviner of Cumae and a very wise priestess, who knows all that is and all that will be.

[50] Almost all of *Aeneid* v—the funeral games, the revolt of the women, and the magic mystery of the death of Palinurus—is replaced by sixteen dryly factual lines (vv. 2145–60). Only the appearance of the spirit of Anchises to Aeneas—necessary to the narrative—is retained.

I do not know anyone who is her better at divination. She knows of the sun and the moon, and of each of the stars, of necromancy, of medicine, rhetoric and music, dialectic and grammar.[51] You must first make a sacrifice to the infernal king. Then she will lead you to me. I will show you your future battles and will name for you all the kings which will be born of your line: they will be lords of all the world. I can no longer stay here, for approaching day presses me to depart." When he had spoken thus he remained no longer, and vanished in a very short time.

[2221–2240] Eneas thinks and sighs over what he has heard. He fears the evils—as well he might—which he knows he must suffer before he will possess a single furrow of earth, but he fears more the journey to hell: of that he is in great terror. He arises at the break of day and assembles all his barons, those whom he knows to be most prudent. He explains to them what the gods have ordered them, and asks them all in council if he should leave his weak followers behind. They tell him that he should do it, since the gods wish it to be thus. He can well leave with Acestes those who cannot endure the hardships, and Acestes will give them some of his land, for they have no care to conquer any other.

[2241–2260] Eneas followed their advice; he left there his weak followers who were not fitted for war and who could not labor, and laid out a city for them. And Acestes gave them a very large tract of his land. The others readied their fleet. Those whom he led away were not many, but they were able to suffer evil and pain. He took his leave of the remainder, and wept and sighed with pity. With his followers he entered the ships, and they weighed anchor

[51] The French poet, who considers learning and magic appropriate companions, invests Vergil's Sibyl with the panoply of medieval learning. But see A. Adler, "Eneas and Lavine: *Puer et Puella Senes*," *Romanische Forschungen*, LXXI (1959), 76–77.

and set sail. They sailed swiftly on the high seas, intending to go directly to Cumae: there lived the prophetess, Sibilla, the wise priestess. They sailed day and night until they arrived at that port.

[2261–2288] Eneas went ashore from his ships, and then went in search of Sibilla. He took with him only Achates, and both of them traveled on foot. They walked until they came to the temple where the priestess was. She was sitting in front of the entrance, all old and disheveled, with a face all pale, and skin black and wrinkled. Her appearance filled him with fear, for she seemed a woman of evil nature. The barons came before her and Eneas addressed her. "Lady," he said, "the gods have sent me here to this country, to you. I am of their lineage, born in ravaged Troy, and by their command I must go to speak to my father in hell. I cannot go there without your help, but they grant me you as a guide. Orpheus went there formerly, and Hercules and Theseus: several mortals have returned above from that infernal kingdom. I beg you that you lead me, that for the sake of the gods you do not delay me."

[2289–2332] When Sibilla heard him say that he wished to go to hell, she raised her eyebrows high, opened her deepset eyes, and looked at him fiercely: fear seized him from her look.[52] She shook her hoary head and answered the Trojan. "Sire," she said, "you see here the broadest entrance of great hell. Entry into it is easy enough, but the return is very painful; there are those who enter both night and day, but there are few who return. It is hard to make the return unless led by a good guide. But since the gods have ordered me, and your father has demanded it of you, I will lead you in all

[52] The French poet omits Aeneas' long prayer to Apollo and the oracular answers which the hero received in the temple (*Aeneid* vi. 51–101). Also suppressed is the death of Misenus, son of Aeolus (*Aeneid* vi. 149–89, 212–35), with its supernatural elements.

safety to him and bring you back. But if you wish to cross the river of hell twice, to return from that shadowy land, you must first seek a bough of gold which grows only in these woods. You must make a present and gift of the branch to the queen of hell. To cut it you will try iron in vain, or any knife of steel, but it will permit itself to be broken off if Jupiter wills and grants that you undertake this journey."

"And if he does not will it?"

"You can know this, for the branch will then be very difficult for you to take. No man can tear it away, nor can iron or steel cut it. When the bough is broken from the tree, another immediately grows there. Without this branch it is not easy to return here above from hell, but if you can find the branch and can bring it to me, then I shall go together with you. You will suffer no delay through me."

[2333–2350] Eneas departed from there and entered the forest. Through the forest he went seeking the branch and calling on all the gods. The goddess of love, his mother, showed him the tree where the branch was, by a marvelous revelation and a very great divine sign.[53] When he saw it he was very happy. He tore it off easily, and immediately another came in its place, similar to the one which was broken off. Eneas was joyous and happy. He returned straightway to Sibilla and showed her the golden bough. She prepared a sacrifice, offered it to the god of hell, and prayed to him very humbly.

[2351–2373] In that place there was a deep cavern—none more grim in all the world. Its entrance was great and wide. It was surrounded by woods and by a black and filthy stream. The cavern was ugly and shadowy, very horrible and stinking: no one who smells this stench will live a single hour longer. When birds fly above it and smell the strong stench

[53] The guidance given to Aeneas by Venus' doves (*Aeneid* vi. 190–209) is attenuated to this vague statement.

they immediately fall down dead. The people of that country say that here is the entrance to the infernal regions. Entering never ceases, night or day, but there is no crowd of people returning. When the soul is severed from the body, immediately after it has departed, it must go there and pass through this cavern. Eneas and the priestess, the Cumaean diviner, came together to the cavern.

[2374–2400] She spoke a little to him. "Vassal," she said, "Listen to me! This is the entrance of hell. If you wish to return from down there you must be brave and knightly. All the dead descend down there. Pluto holds the empire by decree. He is king of it, and Proserpine is goddess and queen. The gods of the heavens have nothing to do with it, and their power does not extend there. Since we must descend into hell, here we can begin the journey; see to it that you be not dismayed by all the things you will see there. There is little light in hell; carry your sword all naked. Follow me as I shall lead you, and I shall show you the way ahead." She gave him an ointment which she had carried with her. When he had smelled its odor the strong stench did him no harm. He drew his sword without delay. She went ahead and he after her, both pursuing their way in the darkness. They could see hardly anything.

[2401–2434] As soon as they started they found themselves among a very ugly gathering. There were Death and Sorrow, Famine and Poverty and Fear and Disease, sad Old Age and Cowardice and Sloth and deadly Care and Crime, Lament, Weeping, and Treachery, Hardship, Pain, Deception, Discord and Enmity, deadly Battles, War, Wrong, and Sleep, which is cousin to Death.[54] A branching tree stood there, very old, ugly, and mossy, with leaves hanging from it which were dreams, phantoms, and lies; during the day they are down in

[54] The *Eneas* poet doubles the length of Vergil's list of dark personifications at the entrance to hell (*Aeneid* vi. 274–81).

hell, but in the night they rise up to the earth. The Trojan was greatly afraid, but they passed these and went on. Nearby they found horrible monsters, huge and ugly and very terrible. They saw them nearby, and Eneas made ready a blow with his sword, which he thought would kill any of them. But the priestess began to speak to him. "There is no use in this," she said. "You will never be able to touch any of them, for they are all lives without bodies. Your sword was not out because of them. You should know that it was not for such business that I asked you to draw it, but in order to see by its brightness, to go through this gloom."

[2435–2468] They went along the deep vale until they approached the infernal river. There the press was great, where new arrivals were assembling on the shore. The water was deep, unpleasant, and black. Caro was ruler of the passage and guarded the crossing. He was old, ugly, and shriveled, all hoary and wrinkled. His face was gaunt and decayed, his head gray and lumpy, with large, hairy ears and great, mossy eyebrows, eyes red as coals and a long beard and whiskers.[55] This creature was lord of the fleet: he had a rotten skiff, old and battered and broken, worn out and patched up. Those who had died flocked to this shore from all directions, for the souls of the dead never stop until they reach this port. He carries over this water those who have received burial and have their tax penny and funeral rites, but afterward, none of them ever returns. Of the great crowd on the bank Caro received

[55] The *Eneas* poet's slight expansion of Vergil's description of Charon (*Aeneid* vi. 300–303) produces a medieval grotesque somewhat akin to the wild man common in medieval narrative. Cf. F. Bernheimer, *Wild Men in the Middle Ages* (Cambridge, Mass., 1952), and L. Benson, *Art and Tradition in Sir Gawain and the Green Knight* (New Brunswick, N. J., 1965), pp. 72–90. H. C. R. Laurie, in a valuable analysis, has examined the kinship among Caro and the Sibyl of *Eneas*, the *vilein* of Chrétien's *Yvain* (vv. 276–357) and *Dangier* of the *Roman de la rose*. Cf. "A New Look at the Marvelous in *Eneas* and Its Influence," *Romania*, XCI (1970), 62–74.

some and left others. Those who had not been buried remained there, abandoned: he could not ferry over a soul whose body was yet to be buried.

[2469–2482] Eneas heard the great tumult, looked at them, listened to them, and marveled at the gathering. He addressed Sibilla. "Lady," he said, "teach me what this might be on the shore. Great numbers are coming from all directions, gathering here in crowds, and there I see a mariner whose sailing never ends, who never ceases his coming and going. A very great crowd is waiting to embark, but I see him drive some far back, while he carries others over quickly."

[2483–2504] The priestess said to the knight, "You see here the infernal river and the marsh whose oath the gods dare not foreswear or violate. The great company who assemble here are souls; none can pass over whose body is yet to be buried. These go wandering on this side of the river, and will not pass over before a hundred years are out. The souls who have had their funeral rites correctly and whose bodies have had burial, those he passes without hesitation. Then there is no talk of returning. When they have crossed beyond they are immersed in a marsh. After they have drunk a little of it they forget everything that they have done up above, and they have no memory of the past. The name of this forgetting is Lethe."

[2505–2534] They delayed no longer, but approached the bank, where Caro noticed them and recognized them among the souls, for he saw the glittering sword. He addressed them first. "Speak, now," he said, "who are you who thrust forward armed in this shadowy realm? Speak, why have you come? What do you seek here? This is hell, not a human habitation. Here dwell nothing but souls, here we receive nothing corporeal. No mortal man ever came here who did not wish to do us all kinds of evil. Sir Hercules came here once and seized and carried off our gatekeeper. He carried him forth bound, and only with great difficulty did that porter ever return to our realm. Next Sir Theseus came, together with Pirithuous. They wanted to dishonor the king of hell and to seize and carry off his wife. No mortal comes here whom we like: they never do us anything but harm. Stay there; you have come for naught, for never will you pass here or come to the other side through my help. I cannot trust any man who is alive."

[2535–2556] Eneas was dismayed when he heard this, but Sibilla answered him. "Hold," she said; "this is Eneas, who does not come here to harm you. He comes here not to do you wrong, nor to shame or hurt you, but because he wishes to speak with his father. You can pass him safely, for our gods have sent him here. He comes by their wills, I assure you. You cannot doubt this, for he can show you proof of it." Eneas drew out the bough which he had under his cloak. When Caro saw it he became calm, turned the skiff toward him, and drove far away the souls who were ready to enter. Into his boat he received Eneas and the lady who was leading him: the boat rode deeply from the great weight, and water ran in through the cracks.

[2557–2586] Caro steered and rowed until he set them on the other shore. They left the skiff and arrived at the gate where Cerberus was gatekeeper. His duty was to guard the gate. He was ugly beyond all measure, and of a very horrible shape. His legs and feet were all hairy, with hooked toes and talons like a griffon. He had a tail like a bulldog, a pointed and twisted back, and a fat, swollen belly. On his back was a hump, and his chest was sunken and withered. He had narrow shoulders, but great arms with hands like hooks, three large, serpentlike necks, hair of snakes, and three heads like those of dogs: there was no creature so ugly. His habit was to bark like a dog. From his mouth would fall a froth, from which grew a deadly and evil plant. No man drinks of that plant without being drawn to death: no man can taste it without death. I have heard it called *aconite*; it is the herb which stepmothers give their stepchildren to drink.[56]

[2587–2614] When Cerberus saw them coming, he began to yelp loudly, so that all hell resounded with it. He bristled with wrath. The snakes which were around his neck stirred, and did not cease striking and writhing and hissing. Eneas was in such great fear that he dared not move one step forward. I do not wonder that he feared this. But the priestess spoke a charm and an enchantment in a whisper between her teeth, very quietly, and as soon as the charm was ended, Cerberus was completely asleep: he lay there curled up in a circle, in his filth, next to the gate.[57] Both of them passed by him through the gate in safety. When they had passed beyond, they found first the companies of children, the infants and sucklings, those whom death took from their mothers. These howled and cried and sobbed loudly. The noise there was very great from the sorrow which the infants suffered.

[2615–2650] Nearby, Minos was casting his lots and inquiring into the lives of the dead. To each soul he would send a fate in accordance with what it deserved. He sent the good to sweet fields and the evil to suffer pains. Eneas went forward, and in a vale found those who had lost their lives for love, a great company of them. Among the others he recognized well her who had died for love of him: here was the lady of Car-

[56] From the meager detail provided by Vergil (*Aeneid* vi. 417–20—who assumed his readers' familiarity with Cerberus— the *Eneas* poet has developed an excellent medieval grotesque, whose like is to be seen commonly on the gothic cathedrals and in the illuminated manuscripts. R. Palgen, *Das mittelalterliche Gesicht der Göttlichen Komödie* (Heidelberg, 1935), pp. 58–64, draws some interesting parallels between Dante's treatment of the inhabitants of Vergil's Hades and their treatment in *Eneas*. Faral (*Recherches,* pp. 111–12) notes that the French writer derived his comments on aconite from the tale of Medea in Ovid (*Metam.* vii), which is likewise responsible for the unexpected reference to stepsons. But the passage may also echo *Metam.* i. 147.

[57] The magic spell replaces Vergil's drugged honey-cakes, in consonance with the medieval poet's conception of the Sibyl as a sorceress and magician. Faral (*Recherches,* pp. 114–15) believes that the idea came from Ovid's tale of Medea (*Metam.* vii).

thage. He was very sorrowful in his heart that she was dead, and hastened toward her to speak to her. "Lady," he said, "for love of me you have suffered mortal sorrow. I was the cause of your death, but I have no guilt or wrong in it. I parted from you without my liking and against my will, and I swear to you by all the gods of heaven, and by the infernal ones, that I did not abandon you through my wish. I parted from you with great difficulty, and the departure was painful to me, but I could not do otherwise: the gods of heaven had commanded and ordained it thus. By their command I have come here and descended into this realm. When I parted from you I did not think that it would be thus, or that you would find no comfort to please you more than death."

[2651–2662] When Dido heard him speak thus, she could not look at him at all, for she was very hostile to him. She fled into a wood where her lord Sicheus was, who had a better right to her love. Because she had belied the faith she had pledged to Sicheus, she did not dare turn toward him, nor even to look at him at all, nor approach near him. By her misdeed she was dishonored.[58]

[2663–2698] The Trojan went forward with little delay until he came to the field where those were who had died in battle, and who had practiced chivalry all their lives in the world above. In that field were Adrastus, Polynices and Tydeus, Hippomedon, Parthenopeus, Amphiarus, and Capaneus.[59] He saw many men from his own country who had been killed at Troy. They all gathered around him, coming from every direc-

[58] Dido's hostility in hell, though faithful to the Vergilian narrative, is inconsistent with the speech of forgiveness with which Dido died in the romance (2063–67). In the Vergilian episode in Hades, Dido is represented as reunited with Sychaeus in mutual love and sorrow (*Aeneid* vi. 472–74). In *Eneas* her fate is far worse: filled with bitterness toward Eneas, she fears her former husband because of her infidelity, and is forever bereft of comfort or companionship: "por son forfet se vergondot." Cf. Pauphilet, *Romania*, LV, 211–12.

[59] S. de Grave (*Eneas*, Cfmâ, II, 133) suggests that the *Eneas* author drew the names of these Greek heroes from *Thèbes*.

tion. Hector and Priam came, Paris, Deiphobus, and many others of his country. Eneas did not dare turn his face to them but hid himself as well as he could, and felt ashamed in their presence, because he had stolen away from them as a fugitive when they were killed.[60] Next came the knights of the Greek company: the brave Ajax was there, and Protesilaus together with him, Agamemnon and Achilles, Menelaus and the son of Tydeus. When the Greeks saw Eneas armed, they feared that the gods had sent him to avenge the Trojan defeat, and they began to flee. When they saw him come toward them they gave the appearance of crying out, but they could not utter a word.

[2699–2719] Now Eneas looked toward the left and saw a large city. This was the chief seat of hell. The walls were all of iron, and a burning stream, whose name was Flegeton, flowed around it. From within the city he heard weeping and laments and very loud outcries, and beatings and very great tortures, the sound of hell and of chains. There was much mortal sorrow there, and he feared greatly what he heard. He stopped to listen, and addressed the priestess. "Lady," he said, "what can this be? I hear very loud cries here on the left, and see there a very large city, with a burning stream flowing around it; from within I hear outcries and beatings and very great pains and torments."

[2720–2752] The priestess said to the knight, "Mortal man cannot tell you the great sorrow nor the pains nor the torments which are within. No man who lives can tell you what

[60] The French poet here alters the Vergilian narrative strikingly. He suppresses entirely the moving interview with Deiphobus (*Aeneid* vi. 494–547), which described the hapless fate of the last Trojan husband of Helen, and he describes Eneas as filled with shame by his betrayal of the Trojan dead. There is of course no suggestion of this antiheroic incident in the *Aeneid*. It appears to reflect the medieval tradition of a traitorous Aeneas, associated with Antenor's plots to betray Troy. This tradition originated in the *De Excidio Troiae* of Dares Phrygius, was obscurely reflected by Joseph of Exeter and Benoit's *Roman de Troie*, and appeared in many later treatments of the Troy legend.

suffering is there and what torture, but I know it well, for I have been there and seen the city. Tisiphone led me there and showed me all the punishments.[61] The lord of this fortress is named Rhadamanthus. There he carries out his tortures and his scourges and his torments. There the giants are tortured, who through pride and haughtiness wished to climb to the heavens by force and dispossess all the gods. There is one within who wished to lie with Diana and dishonor her.[62] He is named Tityus. He lies on his back, and on top, on his chest, is a vulture which night and day eats his breast and all his entrails. His torment never ceases, for when the vulture has eaten, the entrails quickly grow anew. Tantalus is in the midst of a stream. From above loaded branches hang down to him as far as his throat. He is mad with hunger and thirst, but cannot taste the water or touch one of the apples.

[2753–2782] "There are various torments in that place, so that the abode is most hateful. Everlasting pains are there, suffering, and great fear; these torments are eternal. There is a permanent fire which gives no light or brightness, but which consumes and burns the damned, blackens and torments them, and from which they have no hope of rest. They exist in suffering and sorrow, and fear plagues them greatly: they are in fear even while they are suffering pain. Mortals are not thus, for when anyone fears a great torment he loses his fear as soon as he feels the pain; but fear torments these people together with the pain. The pains are great and fearful, the fire burning and shadowy. The torments draw them to their deaths, yet last without end, for there death lives and the end is the beginning; there conclusion has growth, and destruc-

---

[61] Here the French author contradicts his source. Vergil's Sybil has not been to Tartarus, but was told about it by Hecate (*Aeneid* vi. 563–65).

[62] This non-Vergilian detail on the punishment of Tityos is discussed by F. Warren, "On the Latin Sources of 'Thebes' and 'Eneas,'" *PMLA*, XVI (1901), 375–87. Originally the myth concerned the attempted rape of Latona, but it was later transferred to Artemis. Cf. S. De Grave in *Eneas*, Cfmâ, II, 133.

tion restoration. The fear of torture is never gone. It plagues and torments them much, and they have eternal life. It drives them utterly to their deaths and yet lasts forever.[63]

[2783–2810] They turned toward the right and moved away from the city on the left. Eneas left his bough, placing it at the fork of the roads. Those who had come there formerly would leave their boughs in that place when they descended into hell; the queen caused them to be taken there. The Trojan continued until he came to the Elysian Fields, where the good men were, who felt no punishment. In this field there was light and great repose and great beauty, and a sun and a moon. The people were there in great peace. The fields were everywhere in bloom, and there was much joy and delight. They were playing at gymnastics, for there was always gladness and festivity there. These people were not corporeal but spiritual. Some were singing and dancing, enjoying themselves with great delight. None of the damned lived in these happy fields, but the good men who observed justice and honored the gods.

[2811–2830] When the Trojan arrived with the priestess at the sweet fields, he saw his ancestors, from whose line he was descended. The ancients who founded Troy were there in great happiness. He went on, and saw his father, who was on the bank of a river, where he was counting all his descendants who were to come. He took care to arrange them as they

---

[63] Vergil's account of the tortures of Tartarus is considerably modified. The torments of Ixion, Pirithous, Phlegyas, Theseus, and others are ignored. That of Tantalus is added, probably from Ovid (*Metam.* vi. 602–6); cf. Faral (*Recherches,* p. 115). The torments of the others are replaced by a description of the nature of hellish suffering, almost certainly inspired by Christian meditations on this subject. On the striking idea that the fear of these torments persists even while the torments are under way, S. de Grave (*Eneas,* Cfmâ, II, 133) remarks, "Il serait intéressant de savoir où, dans quel sermon ou dans quelle description de l'enfer, notre poète l'a trouvée, ou s'il l'a imaginée lui-même." The eternity of these torments is hardly compatible with the transmigration myth (vv. 2911–22), which he has inherited from his source.

would be born, seeing them all in succession as one would descend from another, the father before and the son after; thus Anchises arranged them as the lineage would descend. These souls had yet to take bodies and to be born into the upper world from this subterranean world.

[2831–2866] When he saw that his son had come among the infernal perils he wept and sighed with pity. He had leave from the gods of hell to speak with his son, to answer him and converse with him. He stretched out both his arms and spoke to him first: "Son Eneas, now I know and see, since you have come here to me, that obedience has conquered fear. I have awaited you now many days, for I knew indeed without a doubt, and had always held the hope that you would come here to speak with me. I did not stop counting the days until you came here. I cannot find fault with my thought, which had foreseen all: it has not deceived me. Son, you have suffered many fears, pains, hardships, and great sorrows. I feared greatly that hospitality which you received in Carthage, lest you should forget all your duty or do yourself great harm."

"Father," answered Eneas, "I could not fail to come and speak to you. I was often full of anguish over it. Your image, which would appear to me every night, compelled me. I have left all my followers and my fleet at the port of Sichans, and have come here to talk to you amidst shadowy hell."

[2867–2888] Eneas wept and sighed, and could speak no more at that time. He wished to throw his arms about his father's neck to embrace and clasp him; but the image fled like a dream or the wind, so that he did not seize it. Anchises went forward. When he neared a hill he called them to his side, and both approached, the priestess and the knight whom she was conducting there below. "Son Eneas, I wish to show you your lineage, and to name all those who are to be born of you: they will be emperors and kings."

"Sire," said Eneas, "I wish to know if it can be true that

those who are now here below will ever take on bodies up above and have corporeal form, will ever be sentient and mortal."

[2889–2922] He answered: "Son Eneas, never doubt this. I will tell you the truth about it, and will not hide it from you. Those who die up above all come here below to hell. Here it is rendered to each one according as he deserved while he lived. If he was a good man while he lived, he suffers no pains or sorrows but comes to the Elysian Fields. Those who lived evil lives, who always committed crimes, suffer evil and torments, fires and tortures. When, through pains and sorrows, they have made the atonement which their evil deserved, they come to the Elysian Fields. Then they stay here in great comfort and repose, and they have no sorrow. When they have lived here for a time and it comes into their will to return above, then they go to a river down here in hell. A god is there who immerses them in it, and when he removes them from the water they are able to say nothing in the world above of what they found here below. Then no one remembers anything of what happened to him here. The god puts them again outside, and they return above to take a human body once more.

[2923–2968] "You see here a great company of those who are about to take on mortal life, who will be your sons and descendants. Look at them, and I will enumerate all of them to you. I will show you how they will come and how they will be born, all in order. After that I will name them to you, and I will tell you the battles and the evils which you will have to suffer before you can come to your empire. That youth who holds the lance skillfully in his hand will be the first of those in the air above. Lavine, the daughter of King Latinus, will bear him to you. He will be born in a wood and will be named Silvius. He will be a king and the father of kings, and will be ruler of Alba. The fourth after him will be that man who will strongly resemble you in name and in great piety, in bravery, and beauty; his name is Silvius Eneas. He will be a very rich baron, and of him will be born both kings and dukes. See that one there: that is Romulus, who will be the seventh of your line. Through him you will be greatly celebrated. This man, your descendant, will found Rome and impose his name on it: that city will be the head of the world, and its rule will extend everywhere. Of the lineage of Romulus and your son Julus will be born the noble Julius Caesar, who will surpass all in prowess. His rule will be over the world, but then the senate will kill him. This is what is promised you by the gods, from the earliest time. Caesar Augustus will be next. In his time there will be a very stable peace and much comfort and great beauty, and the world will be under his rule."[64]

[2969–2996] Thus Anchises showed him all—fathers and sons and nephews—as they would issue from him and come one after another. He showed him all the barons and told him their names, and explained to him well the rule over the city of Alba, which he would establish first of all. Later, the city of Rome would be head of all the world; his heirs would always govern it. Anchises showed him all, and then afterwards told him the battles which he would wage and the hardships which he would endure. Eneas was greatly fired by what he learned there. He was most joyful about his line, which he saw would be so famous that the world would submit to it; it would rule without end. He felt such great joy of it in his heart that he forgot the sorrow of Troy. Nevertheless, he was sober about the battles he would fight, and the evils he would have to suffer before he came to hold the land.

[2997–3020] There are two great gates in hell, and there is no wood or iron in either: one gate is of ivory and the other

[64] The *Aeneid*'s enumeration of the hero's descendants (vi. 756–892) is much abbreviated, and the touching description of the young Marcellus, bearing Vergil's flattering tribute to the family of Augustus, is omitted.

nearby is of horn. Through these gates issue our dreams, and those which prove to be false come through the ivory gate, while the true come through the horn. Anchises led them out by the ivory gate, and with great difficulty turned away from them and departed. He left his son most unwillingly, but he could remain no longer, for he had no leave to talk further, and he departed by necessity, for he could already see the light of day. He vanished in a very short time. Eneas wept at the parting. They went directly to his followers, who were waiting for him at the shore. The priestess conducted him until she had reunited him with his men, then took leave of the knight and returned to her own country.

[3021–3032] Eneas left the shore and set sail on the high sea; they raised the yards and sails and ran by the stars, sailing night and day until they came to Lombardy. This was the land and the country which Jupiter had promised them. The ships arrived at the Tiber, put down their sails and yards, and dropped anchor, but they did not yet know what country they were in.[65]

[3033–3050] They went ashore from the ships, wishing to go in search of food, but they did not expect to find it nearby and did not dare to go far. They took their provisions from the ships—what was still left to them—and sat down in the meadow to eat, for they had great need of food. They took loaves and crusts, and made tables and bowls of them. On these tables they placed the food, and out of the necessities of hunger they ate all. Ascanius began to laugh and by way of a joke said to them, "Hunger has surely tormented us greatly, since we have eaten even our tables. There is neither scrap nor table left which we have not consumed in our hunger."

[65] Vergil's introduction of King Latinus, his enumeration of the divine portents against Lavinia's marriage to Turnus, and the prophecy of Faunus (*Aeneid* vii. 45–106) are here omitted from the narrative.

[3051–3068] When Eneas, his father, heard this, he rejoiced greatly over it in his heart, for he knew then that they were in the country which the gods had promised to them, and which would be their home. What his father had said to him—he had it well written in his heart—came to his memory, that when hunger would so harrass him that he would eat his tables, then indeed he would know without a doubt that his home would be there, and his hardships would have an end. Eneas rose to his feet, weeping with joy and delight, praising all the gods of heaven, and encouraging his followers. They did not understand it until he addressed them.

[3069–3086] "My lords," he said, "this is the country which we have so desired, this is the land of Lombardy, which the gods have promised us. Here our hardships are ended, here will be our domain. The gods have brought us to this port. I recall well the saying of my father, who used to prophesy to me that when hunger would so harrass us that we would eat our tables, then it would be useless to search for another abode, land or fief, for the gods would give us the land where we then were. I have no wish to seek it further, since we have here in our need eaten all our tables. Here I will stay."

[3087–3104] It is no wonder that the Trojans rejoiced when they heard this, for they had long desired the land which they had now entered. They felt great joy, and praised the gods which they had carried from Troy.[66] They set them up, and also invoked the gods of the country, praying very humbly that they might have a propitious future. They worshiped all the gods of heaven and honored them with

[66] Hoepffner (*Arch. romanicum*, XVI, 163) notes a close resemblance between these lines (vv. 3088–93) and Wace, *Brut*, vv. 1058–62. He considers it probable that the whole episode of the landing in Lombardy was modeled on the arrival of Wace's Brutus in Britain.

a sacrifice. They ran to the water of the Tiber to wash
themselves and then to drink. They washed their hands and
their faces, praising the gods of the country and enjoying
great delight. That night they lay down and took their rest.

[3105–3142] When Eneas reached the country which the
gods had promised him he was happy, for he had not had such
delight since the siege had come to Troy. He had his ships
beached on the Tiber, thinking that he would never have any
more to do with them, and that they would be of no further
use to him. He was thoroughly tired of sailing. Now he felt
certain that his hardships were to be finished. But now there
would begin the great war to conquer the realm and the country: much time would pass before his hardships would be over.
He asked and inquired thoroughly who was the lord of that
country. He heard from several that its lord was Latinus, an
aged king. The city in which he lived with his barons was
named Laurente, and was not far distant from that shore.
Eneas called his messengers—as many as thirty knights—
gave them their instructions, and sent them to King Latinus
to seek peace and concord and love, and to ask that he be safe
in the land. To strengthen and support his request, he sent
the king rich gifts: a crown and a cloak, a scepter, a ring which
Dido had given him out of love when she was his beloved, and
a cup of expensive enamel-work which King Menelaus had
given him on the shore beneath Troy, when he had come to
him as a messenger.[67]

[3143–3168] The messengers departed and went to the king
in the city, while Eneas went searching along the cliffs by the
sea. He saw a very large plateau on the top of a hill; in its
center a spring gushed forth, whose stream ran down to the

[67] The details of the hero's gifts are altered from their source. Vergil (*Aeneid* vii.
245–58) describes the cup as a libation chalice of Anchises, the sceptre and the crown
as Priam's, and the robes as the work of Trojan women. Dido's ring and the enamel-
work of the cup are the French poet's romantic additions. Faral (*Recherches*, p. 116)
believes that the detail of the cup derives from Ovid (*Metam.* xiii. 680).

sea. The place was naturally strong. There he led all his men, toward the sea and up the mountain, and there he laid out fortifications for them. They worked night and day at trenching and ditching, at parapets and palisades, and at building drawbridges. Before twenty days had passed they had made such an enclosure, and a fortress so strong and high, that they feared no assault: they would never be captured without a great battle. There they carried all their food and arms and equipment. They placed their ships in a cove beneath the camp on the beach, next to a creek, at the base of a cliff.

[3169–3199] The messengers traveled straight for the city of Laurente, so that they arrived there the next day. They entered the palace—which was large—came to the king, greeted him, and bowed deeply to him. Ilioneus, who was very wise and knightly, spoke for them all: "Hear us, my good lord king. You have surely heard how the Greeks took and defeated Troy, laid waste the whole city, overthrew the towers and walls, and killed the inhabitants both great and small. A few people escaped from it, led away by Eneas. By command of the gods we slipped away from among the Greeks. We have since suffered many woes on many seas for more than seven years; great storms and great winds have driven us on many coasts; we have sailed the world, and now we have arrived at the Tiber.[68] Our small band remains there, and would move most unwillingly. Eneas has stayed with them to protect them and their ships. He has sent us here to you, that you might admit him to your country and receive him in your land. There will never be war between us but rather we will remain always your friends.

[3200–3222] "Our ancestor, who founded Troy and its fortress, was born here; I know that Dardanus was his name. By command of the gods we have returned here where our race

---

[68] Hoepffner (*Arch. romanicum*, XV, 252) suggests that vv. 3187–92 are modeled on Wace, *Brut*, vv. 21–35.

had its beginning. In your land we wish to remain. You will never have cause to complain of us that we have betrayed you in anything; we are not the sort of people who would want to lay waste your land, or to plunder or rob you. Though you may have great trouble in your land, it will never happen through our action. Sir Eneas sends you here a large part of his treasure: a very costly cup of gold, a scepter and a ring, a crown, and a cloak. If you wish to keep him and us, we will serve you at your pleasure."

[3223–3254] Then he gave him the gifts. The king received them very graciously and answered the messengers: "For my part, your lord is welcome in this country, as he will see in a very short time. I will sustain him as best I can. I am a very old man, and have no heir by my wife except one maiden, whose name is Lavine. Without wishing it, indeed against my will, I have promised her to a prince of this country, a marquis whose name is Turnus. My wife wishes him to have my kingdom and Lavine, my daughter, as his wife; but it is fated and destined, and all the gods have decreed, that a foreign man shall have her, and from them a royal line will issue. From what I have heard you say, I think that this man is your lord. I believe that the gods wish him to have the woman and the country. Let him come to me and I will give them to him. The gods grant it, I know well. I will send him three hundred ten fine horses, rich and costly, and not without bridles and saddles. You can say to him on my behalf that I will give over my land to him and make him the gift of my daughter."[69]

[3255–3276] The messengers were joyful when they heard this. It is no wonder if they were encouraged. The king had the horses brought, with bridles, saddles, and chest-harnesses, and had them delivered to the messengers. They turned them over to their squires, took their leave without delay, and

[69] Hoepffner (*Arch. romanicum*, XV, 253) indicates close resemblances between many of the above lines (vv. 3230–38, 3252–54) and Wace, *Brut*, vv. 41–51.

quickly began their trip home. They traveled so that on the fourth day after they had left their lord they returned to him at his camp, which had been all newly made. They told him what they had learned from the king to whom they had gone, of the daughter whom he had bestowed on him, and the horses which he sent him. They showed him the horses one after another, and presented them to him on behalf of the king. Eneas was most joyful. The gods which he had carried from Troy were brought forward, and he worshiped them and honored them with a sacrifice.

[3277–3298] King Latinus thought that he would arrange a marriage for his daughter, and in his heart he greatly desired the marriage with the Trojan; but the queen disapproved of it, and was sorrowful and angry over it. She went to the king, sat next to him, and told him her wish and her desire.[70] "King," she said, "I wonder greatly where you have gotten this idea, that you wish to give our daughter to the Trojan. Do not think of it: the Trojans have no honor at all, nor do they hold to any law. You have surely heard how Paris went secretly to steal the wife of Menelaus, for which Menelaus has since done the Trojans so much harm. He kept her in adultery until all Troy, with its empire, was destroyed and ruined for it. I will never believe in their lineage.

[3299–3330] "This man is in great need of repose, for he has labored many a day rowing on the sea. If you wish to give him your daughter he will take her very gladly, but as soon as he has a fair wind, he will abandon her to you. It will make very little difference to him if he has dishonored her. Never expect anything else from him, for he has done such a thing before. It was to her misfortune that Dido, the lady of Carthage, ever

---

[70] At this point the *Eneas* poet deals most freely with his source. The long account of the angry exchange between Latinus and Amata, Amata's warning to Turnus, and Turnus' reply (vv. 3277–3490) are his own. In the *Aeneid* the warning to Turnus is given by the fury Allecto herself.

granted him hospitality. He did his will with her, and when she had given him rest for a time, then he departed with his ship, and she killed herself with great suffering. Lavine can be sure that she will not have better fortune with him. I believe that he will surely take her, but he will never keep faith with her. Give her to him indeed, since you wish to do it, and he will bring her a very handsome dowry: all the sea on which he has been sailing since he left his country. He has no other land or fief. When the Greeks passed through his land they neither took anything from him nor gave anything to him. You can give her to him—I know no more of it—but Turnus has been promised both the girl and the land. He will never give them up without a great war."

[3331–3350] The king heard that the queen was concerned for the maiden; he knew well that she did not wish Eneas to have her as his wife. He answered her very briefly and told her what he felt about it. "Madam," he said, "the marriage over which you are sorrowing in your mind cannot come about in any other manner, for the gods have willed it thus. Turnus cannot have her, but this man must have her, and I see no other indication or omen. I will not give her to the one when the gods have granted her to the other. They have led him here because they have destined him for it. He is descended of their lineage and will make our own line famous."

[3351–3384] The queen heard that Latinus would not do otherwise with his daughter, but wished to give her to the Trojan. When she saw that she could not sway him, she retired to her chamber, weeping, and in a very ugly mood. She shook and trembled with anger, and beat her palms together. Later, when she could speak, she began to lament. "Alas," she said, "unhappy woman, that my daughter will be given to a man from a foreign land which is wholly ruined by war, one who stole forth from his city out of cowardice when it was captured. The cowards slipped away with him, drew together in one place, and made this vassal their king. Is he then a king? I know not of what, except a few ships, I know not how many. But I will have news for him. I think that very soon I will stir up such a war against him that he will abandon the land to us or quickly lose his life in it. He shall have none of my daughter unless he pays very dearly for her. Neither daughter nor mother will ever fall under his protection. I will die of sorrow if he takes her. Lavine was born in an evil hour if she is ever married to this man. But I do not think that Turnus will fail me in this, or that he will refrain from battle against him."

[3385–3402] When the lady had wept for a time, and had given vent to her sorrow and her grievance, she called a squire whom she made her messenger. She charged him with her message and sent him straight to Turnus, to warn him secretly: he should be fully aware that Latinus was breaking his word to him and was taking back his daughter; that he should ask Latinus to keep his bargain with him without delay, and wage such a war against the Trojan that it would drive him out of the land. The messenger departed, went straight to Turnus, and found him at his castle near the city of Laurente.

[3403–3436] Turnus was rising from his meal when he saw the messenger come. He knew him well and called him. The squire greeted him, then drew the marquis to one side, and they seated themselves at the end of a table. He began to speak his message. "Hear me, fair sir," he said. "The queen has sent me here, and warns you that a man has newly come into this country, one of the vanquished Trojans. He arrived the other day in the Tiber, and sent his messengers to the king, to seek peace and safety. The king has given up his land to him, and sent him three hundred ten valuable horses, all saddled. Moreover, he has granted his daughter to him as a wife, with all his kingdom. Know this well without a doubt: he is not keeping your agreement, and you will not have his daughter at all, unless you have very good help. But the queen, who wants you to have the girl, advises that you gain all the land and dominion with the help of your friends. Take soldiers, gather an army without delay, and press the Trojan with war, until he abandons the land to you, or you have conquered or captured him, or he departs a fugitive by sea.

[3437–3456] "Come to the city of Laurente. Since the king has given it all to you, hold it and defend it, and do battle for it with your whole army. Eneas has no defense against you. Know that he will never be so bold as to do battle against you. You have received the grant from the king: come and take possession of it all. The king is old, and has abandoned everything. Though he may make a show of arrogance, he will not take up shield or lance. The queen and the barons indeed consent to your rule over everything he has given you. Come, make yourself lord of all. It will be accounted a very great catastrophe if a foreign man falls upon you and conquers your possessions. Then you will be thoroughly dishonored."

[3457–3490] Turnus answered the messenger: "I had indeed heard the other day that Eneas had arrived. But that Latinus is giving him his kingdom and his daughter Lavine as a wife was hidden from me. He granted them to me long ago, and I will never let them go without reason. If this man wishes to seize her from me, may I never have wife or land unless I defend myself against him. I marvel greatly at such a conquered and fugitive people, that they still go looking for battle. Since they were conquered once, it is only right that they remain at peace. The king is old and very worn. If he has brought them against me, he can hardly sustain them. He has no right to break his word to me; I have done him many great services, and they are returned to me with ill will. But whether he likes it or not, he will have to do me justice: he has long ago given me possession of them; now he can never take back either the land or the maiden. Go, then, and tell the queen that I will be at the city of Laurente before the third day ends. If Eneas wishes for a battle, he will not fail to get one from me. If I should lose a single foot of land through him, I would not well be able to conquer another."[71]

[3491—3524] The messenger departs and Turnus remains, complaining to his close friends about the king, who has not kept covenant with him, or faith, or oath. He will be most sorrowful if he does not avenge himself, but he does not know how to act in order to begin a war against the Trojan. He says that if Eneas wrongs him by remaining, if he does not depart, he will not fail to attack him and meet him in battle. He broods night and day on the war he desires; yet he cannot decide how he might be able to begin it, how he might find the right occasion for battle, for contention, for embroiling himself with the Trojans. But before a little time passes he will be able to go to war, to throw lances, and strike blows, and will be able to have his swordplay and receive many a blow. Only fifteen days went by after Eneas had come to the country—and the war was begun which Turnus so much desired. The occasion for the battle arose from a small enough beginning, and the war, which was so harsh, in which a thousand men were killed and as many wounded and captured, opened from a very small accident.

[3525–3564] Near the city of Laurente was a little fortified castle, the domain of Tirus, a very old man of high lineage. He had two sons, and a daughter named Silvia: there was none more beautiful in all the country. The maiden had raised a deer, which she fed from her own bowl, to which she gave drink from her goblet, and which slept in her chamber. It had sixteen points on its antlers. Every day it went out through the fields and woods together with the wild hinds, and like-

---

[71] From this point the narrative assumes the form of a feudal struggle between two medieval barons, Eneas and Turnus, each defending what he believes to be his feudal right. The atmosphere is remote from the Vergilian, and the contrast is instructive.

wise with the domestic animals, but at night it returned to its home. The damsel used to play with it, and it knew her so well that whenever she called it it would kneel down at her feet. She would stroke its feet with her hand while it ate bread at her lap and drank wine in very great draughts. The maiden would not have lost it for sixty pounds of fine gold. The deer was so well behaved that at night it served at dinner, and acted as a candelabrum before the father and the daughter.[72] Its head was marvelously beautiful when a large candle burned on each of the points of its antlers. Thus it served each night. The maiden had taught it very well, and when the lord drank, then

[72] A striking expansion of the brief passage in the *Aeneid* (vii. 479–539) which describes Ascanius' killing of Silvia's tame deer, thus precipitating hostilities. The medieval poet composes an episode of over 250 lines (vv. 3525–3782) opening with the charming, pastoral picture of Tirus, his daughter, and her deer, and closing with the realistically conceived feudal clash which provides Turnus with an excuse to begin his siege. Though the deer's original is in the *Aeneid*, the *Eneas* poet's description is derived from that of a tame tigress in *Thèbes* (vv. 4511–30), whose death precipitates the first battle between the Thebans and their besiegers: "In the city [Thèbes] was a tigress whose equal was not known beneath the heavens. Now you can hear a great marvel: it never touched a sheep, for it was thoroughly tame, wholly contrary to its nature. If you gave it either meat or bread, it would eat out of your hand. It would drink a large copper basin full of wine, and then it would be drunk all day, leaping and playing until you were thoroughly exhausted. On the front of its forehead it had a brightly glowing carbuncle: I do not think that such a noble head was to be seen on any other beast. And its whole coat shone more than a bear's. The king would not have lost it for 300 pounds in Mans silver." The charming, if grotesque, detail of the deer's service as a candelabrum seems to be the poet's own (cf. Faral, *Recherches*, pp. 96–97).

In the clash between the Trojan youths and the rather sympathetically conceived rural Latins there may be a reflection of the sort of indignities actually suffered by the peasantry at the hands of the turbulent medieval knighthood. To make room for this incident, the French poet omits the long supernatural episode (*Aeneid* vii. 286–474) in which the fury Allecto, at Juno's behest, rises from hell and sweeps through the Latin countryside, whipping the women—especially Amata—into a Maenadic fury and the men—especially Turnus—into a rage for war. Mythology as metaphor—in this case for the spread of war-fever—has no attractions for the *Eneas* poet.

In the earlier part of Ascanius' hunt (vv. 3585–3600) Hoepffner (*Arch. romanicum*, XV, 262–63) has found a number of parallels with the description of Brutus' hunt in Wace (*Brut*, vv. 136–46).

the deer stood all erect. Never was there such an obliging beast, and never was one so intelligent.

[3565–3589] The youth Ascanius went to his father Eneas and begged that he permit him to go hunting, or to shoot only one deer. Eneas gave him leave to go. Ascanius gathered enough of his peers so that there were a good twenty companions, then he mounted his hunting horse and the others mounted theirs. One of his servants carried his bow and the other his hunting dog. Each of his friends took his sword, for they did not know the country; they did not go along to hunt, but to guard the youth. They traveled and rode much, and went far from their camp until they entered the woods of Laurente. They were wandering along a path when they saw a herd of hinds grazing there among the thickets. Together with the herd was the deer that was so tame, which the maiden had raised.

[3590–3616] Ascanius selected that deer from among the herd. If he could find the right moment he would make an attempt to shoot it. He got down quickly to his feet, took his bow and arrows, and drew near a very large tree, whither a youth accompanied him. The herd passed close in front of him, and he kept aiming at the large deer, which was coming last, at the end of the herd. He shot, and struck it in the belly, so that the arrow pierced both its sides. The deer felt that it was wounded, and immediately left the herd, fleeing with very great leaps into an enclosure of the house where it was raised. Its flanks bled heavily. Ascanius placed his dog on the trail, mounted his horse and pursued it, extremely pleased that he had shot well. The deer felt the mortal wound, and fled to its house, approaching its mistress with difficulty. Then it came to her with its breath failing, fell to the ground right at her feet, and looked as if it were seeking mercy.

[3617–3644] The maiden saw it bleeding and ran quickly from her chamber, calling for help in a loud voice. Both her brothers heard her. They asked her what was the matter with her, and she told them what it was, that her father's deer was dead. As soon as they had forces they rushed forth and saw those who had shot the deer. They did not stop to speak with them, but began to deal blows immediately, wielding poles and clubs against the naked swords of the Trojans. The peasants of the district rushed to the conflict and attacked the Trojans. Tirus was there with his two sons, who wished to avenge the deer, but they paid for it dearly. They rushed forth like fools to receive great blows, and encountered the Trojans, who pierced their sides. Before the deer's carcass was taken, many a soul was drawn from its body, and there were many bloody and wounded from among those inside.

[3645–3668] Ascanius was holding his bow. He placed an arrow (he had no more) in the notch and shot at a man who was pursuing him. It reached the elder of the brothers and cost him a blood-letting. Its point penetrated his throat, completely disjointing the neck-bone and cutting the windpipe, so that the breath came out his neck. He fell dead next to his brother. Tirus, his father, was doleful over it. His men made efforts to avenge him, and began to press forward. Tirus made an assault against the Trojans, and Ascanius cried out to his men: "What are you doing, noble knights? The deer is waiting to be flayed! We can delay here so long that it will never be cooked for dinner. Let every man lay on with his sword, and we will make here a good, strong pepper-sauce! Draw near to the meat, for everyone needs that!"

[3669–3684] He encouraged them very well, and they laid on with their polished swords, cutting off hands and arms, making heads bloody and peasants cry out. They dispersed the peasantry, who were not trained for battle. Sir Galesus, a wealthy man, had come there only for his good name and to stop the conflict; but he received there such a blow that he fell dead immediately to the ground, with never a chance to ask for a doctor to heal his wound. There was no need to bandage him, or apply a salve or ointment. He did not languish at all long.

[3685–3692] As soon as the battle had begun, a squire had returned to the camp to announce it. He said that those in the camp should go to help them, for they were assailed in the woods, and were attacked with force. If they did not have quick help, the peasants would capture them all.

[3693–3726] When Eneas knew that his son was being attacked in the forest, he had confidence in nothing. He sent him quickly a hundred knights, very well armed, riding rapidly, as the squire led them. They found the others defending themselves with difficulty, for the clamor had become very widespread. Hence Tirus was so reinforced, and so full of hatred, and was making such an attack on the Trojans, that they were suffering much grief. They were very close to death, and had no more defense left; but when they saw the help coming behind them they were reinvigorated. The hundred were joined with the twenty, and were welcomed immediately. The peasants were discomfited. They had to abandon the whole field, and they began to flee. The Trojans continued attacking them. The countrymen, great or small, did not defend themselves, but were stricken down in the forest. Those who had assembled from nearby died by sword and violence. Tirus, their leader, departed and fled to his castle. He entered with a few followers and had the bridge drawn up. They climbed the battlements and manned the herison, for they wished to defend the house.

[3727–3748] The Trojans arrived and went down into the ditch, attacking boldly. Those within defend themselves bitterly, hurling sharp pikes at them, with which they pierce their shields and knock them down into the ditch. The assault lasts a long time, and they defend themselves stoutly, until their weapons fail them, and they find no more to throw, and no one to aid them. They do not wish to let themselves be captured. Thus they begin to descend from the parapets and the herison, abandon everything entirely, and depart through a postern gate on the side of the palisade; no one great or small remains. They all flee toward the thick woods, push into it, and at length escape.

[3749–3770] The Trojans shouted and climbed to the top of the great trench. Finding no defense, they moved up to the herison, which they smashed and threw down. They climbed up from all sides, and entered without opposition. Finding no one, they plundered the whole house, and took so many provisions that they loaded thirty sumpter horses with them. Then they flayed the deer. Ascanius took his dog, which had been put in a chamber, where the maiden had hidden it and tied it with her sash. The youth untied it and gave it some of the entrails of the deer. They cut up the deer and loaded it; one youth bore the fork with the beast's liver and lungs and another carried the head, which they had won by such great struggle.

[3771–3782] When they had finished their business they set out for home, gathering booty from the countryside. They plundered and seized everything, and they burdened a thousand sumpter horses with wheat; the squires were busied loading it. They won very great spoils that day before withdrawing to their castle. They so supplied it with one thing and another that those within could hold it and sustain a great siege for more than a whole year.

[3783–3808] The news of the battle had spread until it arrived in Laurente. Everyone in the city was saying that the Trojans had come and were putting the countryside to destruction, like a people who love war. They said that King Latinus had done very badly in receiving them. Tirus had paid for it first, since they had killed his elder son. The burghers—the most powerful in the city—assembled in confusion and disorder. They went to the court to speak with the king, and there they uttered their complaint and their outcry. The king asked them what was wrong, and they told him the occurrence, recounting the great destruction which the Trojans had inflicted that day, and cursing all their conduct: they had killed a hundred of the king's men and they had burned and plundered all the countryside. The burghers said more than had happened in fact, so that the king would be alarmed. They said that if a plan were not formed, the Trojans would conquer the whole country.

[3809–3836] Thereupon Turnus came down, and entered the hall at these words. He had already heard the news by which the whole city was agitated, and he was extremely happy over it. He stood before the king, and heard what the burghers were saying, and the complaint that they were making. He heard what the king answered to them: that he inclined towards the Trojans and greatly wished to keep them and admit them to his land. Turnus took the discussion in hand, and the citizens became quiet. "Sire," he said, "I wonder greatly how you can have conceived this desire to keep the Trojans. They do not know how to share; they have no wish to become owners of half; they have no care for dividing; rather, they want the whole. Know that this is always true: the Trojans are of such a nature that whoever receives them within his walls will be thrown outside in the fields by them; they will put themselves entirely inside. If you receive them into your country, you will soon be thrust forth from all you own.[73]

[3837–3868] "They have built a stronghold in your land, from which they are now waging a great war against you,

[73] The *Eneas* poet replaces the *Aeneid's* ceremonious opening of the gates of the temple of Janus (opened by Juno herself when the king refuses, vii. 601–25) with Turnus' long speech to the the council, stressing his feudal right. The French poet is addicted to formal speeches in councils of barons, reminiscent of the *chansons de geste*.

burning and plundering and killing, and allying your men with themselves. If they are permitted to go so far they will wish to dispossess you completely. But I think that this is what you wish. You have brought them to this country. You do not wish to share it with them, but rather to abandon everything to them, and you think you will count me—to whom you are bound by oath—as nothing. You have endowed me with your land: you have given me all of it, together with your daughter. I have pledged and promised myself to her. I have not yet espoused her, and we have not lain in one bed— this still waits through your delay—but I am enfiefed with the land and I have received the castles. I have its towers and its fortresses, and the homage of its barons; if you wish to cheat me of my right, these men cannot fail me, but all will hold with me in due order. I have long since been enfiefed with all, and you can take nothing back from me. I am unwilling to give up a single foot of it, and to take it away will not be easy: rather, a thousand knights will die over it. Know, then, that whether you like or not, I will hold to my right."

[3869–3880] The king heard what Turnus said, and shook with anger and fury, but he did not wish to speak against him or to listen to him further. He rose from among his men and went to his chamber, saying only this to them: he would leave the entire prize, to take or leave, to whoever could or would do better. Whichever one of them could gain her in battle would have the maiden, with all the land.

[3881–3896] Turnus remained with the barons and complained to them of the king, who wished to withdraw his agreements. He asked them what he could do about the Trojans, who had fortified a castle within the country without his permission, who had taken another one by force, and who were bringing destruction on the country. They advised him in council that he should have his men assembled, should call his barons and his friends and neighbors from other countries, as many as he could get; that he should go very quickly and besiege the Trojans, and, if he could take them by force, have them all burned or hanged.

[3897–3928] Turnus accepted their advice. On the same day couriers and messengers went out to summon the baronage and his followers and relatives. He sent word to many foreign peoples, assembling them from all directions. He would have revenge on the Trojans. There were numerous footsoldiers and knights, as many as one hundred forty thousand. Indeed, I can give you the names of some of their princes and barons. Mesencius came there first, bringing a thousand knights. He was a prince of his land, a very wealthy man and well instructed in war. With him came Lausus, his son, a brave and hardy knight: Nature never made a more handsome creation of living man.[74] Lausus brought with him more than seven hundred troops with their equipment. Aventinus came next, a youthful son of Hercules. He brought a thousand knights, besides his foot-soldiers and archers. His shield was made of the skin of a lion which Hercules had conquered. He carried it with very great pride, for it was a symbol of his father's victory and great strength, and a great example of good to him.

[3929–3948] The Duke of Prenestine came, and the Lord of Palestine. Mesapus, the son of Neptune the sea god, came with a great following; he brought with him a thousand knights and their arms and war horses. They had colts of Capadocia, born of a marvelous stud of the sea, which have no defects, mange, or sores, and which are very easy to arm; there are no horses under the sun more valiant, but they

---

[74] M. Wilmotte (*Origines du roman en France: l'évolution du sentiment romanesque jusqu'en 1240* [Brussels, 1941], p. 232) has noted that this is apparently the first mention in vernacular poetry of the personified Nature as creator. Bernardus Silvestris' *De mundi universitate* (c. 1150) had already been written, and one is tempted to speculate, on the basis of this lone allusion, whether the *Eneas* author had attended the school of Chartres, or been elsewhere instructed by one of its masters.

never live beyond youth: not a single one can last longer. They are born of sea-mares, which live only in the sea and conceive wholly from the wind. These colts are extremely good and wonderfully fast, and would be of very great value if they would live nine or ten years.[75]

[3949–3958] Claudius came, a rich count who was lord of the Sabines. The Sabarins came, and the Polains and the Latins, those from Naples and Salerno, and those from Volterne. I cannot enumerate more, for Turnus assembled so many of them, foot-soldiers, as well as knights, that he counted one hundred forty thousand of them.

[3959–3986] Next came a maiden, queen of Vulcane, whose name was Camille.[76] She was marvelously beautiful and of very great strength. There was no other woman of her wisdom. She was very wise, brave, and courteous, and possessed great wealth, and she ruled her land wonderfully well. She had been raised always amid warfare, so that she loved chival-

[75] Vergil describes Messapus merely as "equum domitor" (*Aeneid* vii. 691), but the French poet takes the opportunity to introduce a marvel. Faral (*Recherches,* pp. 89–90) suggests that the idea might have been inspired by the horses of Neptune in the *Thebaid* and the *Achilleid* of Statius, and that Pliny or Solinus could have given him the detail of the impregnation of the sea-horses by the wind. Dressler (*Einfluss,* p. 163) cites *Thèbes,* v. 6008, on the Arabian horse of Ptolemy, "Engendrez d'ive et de neitun."

[76] The *Eneas* poet has compressed Vergil's roll of the Italian tribes (*Aeneid* vii. 641–802) until the appearance of Camille. To her, Vergil devotes fifteen lines (vii. 803–17), the French poet, a 147-line (3959-4106) *tour de force,* hardly appealing to modern readers. "We would gladly have dispensed," remarks Jessie Crosland ("*Eneas* and the *Aeneid*," *MLR,* XXIX [1934], 285), "with the conventional description of Camilla and her ridiculous horse." And Faral (*Recherches,* p. 413) remarks: "Portrait élogieux, qui vise à émerveiller le lecteur et qui, pour nous, n'a guère d'étonnant que sa puérile minutie, la naïveté risible de ses détails, la consciencieuse et gauche ordonnance de ses parties." It is nevertheless a compelling revelation of the taste of the romancer and his audience, for whom there could hardly be a more attractive embellishment to the action than an exotic and beautiful lady warrior, virginal, provocatively dressed, and fantastically mounted. "Dorénavant," continues Faral, "dans tous les romans postérieurs, elle sera prise comme modèle et fournira la formule de tous les portraits à venir." See also the valuable discussion of the description in relation to that in the *Aeneid* by E. Auerbach, *Literatursprache und Publikum in der lateinischen Spätantike und im Mittelalter,* pp. 135–42.

ry greatly and upheld it her whole life. She had no interest in any women's work, neither spinning nor sewing, but preferred the bearing of arms, tourneying, and jousting, striking with the sword and the lance: there was no other woman of her bravery. During the day she was king, but at night, queen; no chambermaid or handmaid ever went about her during the day, nor ever in the night did any man enter the chamber where she was. She governed herself so wisely, both early and late, that no one could detect any folly in her, either in deed or appearance, or feel any envy toward her.

[3987–4006] No mortal woman was her equal in beauty. Her forehead was white and wellformed, the part of her hair straight on her head, her eyebrows black and very fine, her eyes laughing and full of joy. Her nose was beautiful, and also her face, for it was whiter than snow or ice, with color intermingled harmoniously with the whiteness. Her mouth was very well formed, not large but small, her teeth fine and closely set, more sparkling than any silver. What shall I say of her beauty? In all the longest summer day I could not tell of it, either of her beauty or of her manners—her bounty—which are of more worth than beauty.

[4007–4028] The queen was extremely beautiful as she rode toward the army. Her hair was long, reaching down to her feet, and she had braided it with a golden thread. The lady was very tightly clothed in black royal silk over her bare flesh.[77] The silk was embroidered with gold, and worked with great pains. Three fairy sisters had made it, weaving it in a chamber.[78] Each of them labored to show her best skill on it, and embroidered it with fish of the sea, flying birds, and wild beasts. She was clothed tightly in this, and over it she was

[77] The details recall the description of Antigone in *Thèbes* (vv. 4051–52): "D'une pourpre ynde fu vestue/tout senglement a sa char nue."

[78] Faral (*Recherches,* p. 88) sees in these fairy sisters an echo of the Fates of classic myth.

daintily girt with a sash embroidered in gold and finely orna-
mented with buttons.[79] She had hose of a precious cloth and
sandals made of fish skin of a hundred colors, finely varied.
Her sandal thongs were of gold.

[4029–4048] Her cloak was rich and costly, all made of
checkered squares: one square was of white ermine, and the
adjoining one of red martin. It was lined with magnificent
silk, and its clasps were of enamel. The border was marvelously beautiful, made from the throat of a bird which is wont
to lay its eggs on the bottom of the sea and to hatch them on
the water. They hatch them a hundred fathoms in the depths.
They are of such a hot nature that if they sit on their eggs
they will burn them all from the heat.[80] Her cloak was well
bordered as far as the ground with these birds. She had left
the panels of it open, so that her right side was exposed, and
she rode a palfrey,[81] which showed great spirit beneath her.

[4049–4084] Never was there such a noble beast: its head
was white as snow, its foretop black, its ears both all red. Its
neck was bay and very large, its mane blue and gray in tufts,
the right shoulder all gray and the left, wholly black. Its
forefeet were like those of a wolf, and it was all brown on its
sides. Under the throat it was like a hare, but on the crop like
a lion, and it was all black beneath the saddle. Its two forelegs
were fawn-colored, its two hindlegs, red as blood. All four feet
were white, its tail was all curly, black on one side and white

[79] Reminiscent of the description of Antigone in *Thèbes* (vv. 4059–60).

[80] The source of this marvel is uncertain. S. de Grave (*Eneas*, Cfmâ, II, 134) recalls
that Ovid (*Metam*. xi. 746) mentions the halcyons, which brood on the water, and
that Philippe de Thaon in his *Bestiaire* (v. 2759) mentions the "fulica," which builds
its nest on the water, but no source has been suggested for the birds' great heat.

[81] Cf. *Thèbes*, v. 4069. The *Eneas* author seems to have had the description of
Antigone and her horse, from *Thèbes*, vv. 4045–4084, in mind throughout his description of Camille and her horse. For details see the close comparisons and comment
in E. Langlois, "Chronologie des romans de *Thèbes*, d'*Eneas* et de *Troie*,"
Bibliothèque de l'Ecole des Chartes, LXVI (1905), 107–20. See also the interesting
conclusions of G. Angeli, *L'Eneas e i primi romanzi volgari*, pp. 134–41.

on the other, the feet light, the legs straight: it was very well formed and agile. The palfrey cantered very well. Its bridle was most handsome: its tether was of fine gold, set with precious stones and enamel work, and the reins of fine silver, very carefully braided. The saddle was good, and the bows were the work of Solomon, with an inlay of white ivory which was decorated by arch-work in gold. The covering and all the other padding were of royal silk. Both the stirrup straps were good deer hide, and the saddle girth of fine, gold-embroidered bands. The stirrups were of fine gold, and the chest-strap was worth a treasure.

[4085–4106] Camille came to the army very splendidly equipped, leading a large following. Indeed, she had with her as many as four thousand knights. When they came into Laurente there was a great tumult in the city. The burghers climbed up to their apartments, and ladies and maidens ran to the windows to look at the maiden who was so brave and so beautiful. All the people who saw her held it for a wonder that she should ever enter combat, or joust or strike down a knight.[82] She passed through Laurente and took up her lodging on the other side of the city. She had her standard set up apart, below the city, to one side. The shelters, the pavilions, and the tents of the knights, as well as the lodgings of the servants, occupied a full league in compass.

[4107–4126] One morning when Turnus saw the assembled host of the great army he had summoned, he called together all the dukes, the chief captains, and the princes of troops, and joined them in an orchard. Very briefly he explained to them his desire and his need. "My lords," he said, "hear me; I must explain my affairs to you, because of which I assembled you here, so that you may understand my right and help me to sustain it; in justice you should not fail me. If you see that I am wrong, I pray you that you bring me no assistance, but

[82] The romance *topos* of the hero's entry; see n. 18 above.

tell me that I should desist, and I will indeed accept your advice. I do not wish to begin anything wrongly, nor that you should aid me in such a venture.

[4127–4138] "King Latinus is old, a very aged man of many years, and he can no longer hold his kingdom. He has given me his daughter as a wife, and likewise all his land, without exception; all the barons have confirmed it. There is not a castle, tower, or fortress with which he has not enfiefed me long since. I have received all in my keeping, have accepted the homage of the barons, and have placed my garrisons in the castles.

[4139–4164] "At this point the Trojans came, after the Greeks had defeated them, and arrived in this country. They have fortified a castle near here, are burning and robbing the country, and have now seized a fortress. The name of their lord is Eneas; I do not know if he is a king or not. They came here to the king the other day with a large gift and a messenger to seek safety for their group. The king informed him that he granted his daughter and his land to Eneas, and made him heir to his kingdom. He is retracting all his agreements with me, and the grant which he had made me. I have since complained of it enough to him, but he has left the decision of it to us: he grants the maid and the land to him who can conquer them, and for that reason I have summoned you. Since I was the first heir and am possessed of the land, and since the king has failed me and left the decision to us, I beg that you help me to maintain my right.

[4165–4182] "I summon those who hold their fiefs of me—as indeed I should—and my neighbors who, for love of me, for their own nobleness, and for my honor, are come here at my need. I thank them with all humility for it. If, with your help, I can gain my dominion, I will serve you to the best of my ability. I know indeed that if you are willing to aid me I will overthrow the castle which the Trojans have built in this country. They have begun a very bad year: Paris never paid for Helen, for whom he was killed, more dearly than Eneas will pay for Lavine. He wishes to take her from me by rapine, but he will buy her very dearly, if you are all willing to aid me."

[4183–4210] Mesencius, a count of great virtue, answered him and said, "truly you are right. Eneas has fallen upon us unjustly. By my faith, we will never accept him, nor will we ever have a foreigner ruling over us. We would be all hoary with age before we could make his acquaintance, or before he would at length know who each one of us was. He would want to dispossess us and to give our lands to those few in our country who have known him. We would all be confounded by this: he would hold them in great honor and us in great contempt. I do not advise that we draw them to us, but rather that we send them away from us. But we should act with moderation. It seems to me that the just way is this: you should have him approached and accused of wrongdoing, and then informed that he should make due amends for it in your court, before affairs become worse for him. If he evades doing you justice, before you go against him by force, you should first have him challenged and dismissed from your land."

[4211–4236] Mesapus said, "Now I am hearing wonders. You counsel Turnus strangely, that he should have the Trojan approached and accused of all his misdeeds. They have seized a castle from us and killed a hundred of our men. I do not know what amends we should take for that, except at the points of our lances. Let us busy ourselves avenging it; there is no need for a challenge. As soon as they committed violence in this country, they began the war. They have acted arrogantly toward us; I know here no other challenge. When they committed this madness against us they knew—doubt it not—that we would wish them no good and would love them not at all; the evil came first from their side. Let us all be on our horses tomorrow, and go to lay the siege. We should not warn them of it: one should afflict one's enemy, and one should do it indeed in such a way that he is not warned until it comes to blows."

[4237–4243] All the barons who were there accepted this argument, and in the morning they went to make the assault. They never thought that in time to come the Trojans would not flee, but they were very foolhardy when they believed this; the Trojans would not depart thus.[83]

[4244–4266] Eneas had indeed heard that Turnus was assembling his army, and that there was no delay. Eneas spent night and day having work done and having his camp well fortified: he had no wish to flee. He had his parapets well prepared, his ladders set in place, and his galleries strengthened. He had polished swords, ensigns, lances and shields placed all around the palisades, and had great stones and sharp stakes set in place. He had handles placed on great double-bitted axes, hatchets sharpened, roofs built overhead, and shooting holes down at the foot of the wall. He had great dropping-weights fixed outside: whoever would come to attack, when they tried to climb up, then the Trojans would let the weights drop on them. Whoever was struck by these weights would escape from them with great difficulty.

[4267–4286] He placed a hundred ensigns on the fortress, and in the center his own pennant, of purple silk with bands of gold. Hector had captured it at Troy when he killed Proteselaus, who fought the first joust; Proteselaus was first to come there with his forces, first to joust, first to die. The pennant was very rich. A thousand ensigns—pennants embroidered in many ways with gold—fluttered

[83] This long council of feudal barons, of the type familiar in *chanson de geste,* is entirely the medieval poet's. His interest in the intricacies of feudal right and custom—contemporary legal problems, as we should say—is manifested frequently.

there in the wind. The castle seemed most proud, and was
marvelously beautiful.[84] It was well stocked with food and
well garrisoned by good men, thoroughly trained in warfare.
The castle was built upon white ground; therefore the Trojans said that it would be named Montauban.

[4287–4296] When Eneas had readied and prepared his
whole castle, he notified those who would be on guard and
those who would be within the castle. He placed his crossbow-
men, his sergeants, and his archers all about. He made ready
a thousand knights who would hold tournament outside the
castle against the army, when there was need of it.

[4297–4340] When Eneas had arrived in the land and the
war had begun, Venus, the goddess of love, was in great fear
for her son, who was shut up at Montauban. She went to her
lord Vulcan, who was a great master at working gold and
silver, iron, and steel. She embraced him closely, kissed him
a hundred times and a hundred more, and blandished and
flattered him much. He asked her what troubled her: if she
wished to ask for anything he could make, she would have it
indeed. "Sire," she said, "what will you do? I see that my son
Eneas has arrived in Lombardy with a very small company.
He has gone to the shore and built a castle on a hill. He is shut
up there with his followers, without help or defense. Turnus,
his enemy, is unwilling to agree to peace, and summons his
army, assembles his followers, wishing to do harm to my son.
He will besiege him at Montauban, but Eneas can surely
withstand the siege for a year, for he is well stocked with food.
Yet, he should have good arms, so that he may be able to do
battle, for if Turnus could provoke him to single combat, man
against man, the two of them all alone, he would need suitable
arms, well able to protect his person. I ask and beg these of

[84] Vergil's *castra* has here developed into a model castle in the twelfth-century
manner. This medieval tableau is paralleled in numberless contemporary romances,
chansons de geste, and manuscript illuminations.

you; now I have need of your craft. If you wish to enjoy my love again, now deserve it by your labor: you should serve me very much during the day, for at night you can lie with me, and if you have had any pains I will pay back the equal in pleasure."

[4341–4352] Vulcan heard his wife's request for his craft, and promised her very gently that he would act according to her desire. For that she kissed him a hundred times or more. That night he lay with Venus, and did with her what he pleased, and all his desire as best he could. Seven full years had passed by, during which he had not possessed her, or lain in one bed with her, because of the great anger between them.[85]

[4353–4374] I wish to explain very briefly the occasion for this hatred. Vulcan knew indeed and with no doubt whatsoever that Mars, the god of battle, loved his wife and she him; they hated each other because of it. Vulcan was god and master of the craft of fire and forging. He made a fine net of iron, with very slender threads, and set it in place around his bed. When Mars lay with her—while he held her in his arms—Vulcan gathered together the cords and enveloped them in the net. Then he led all the gods there and showed them publicly what had happened. This thing displeased the gods; nevertheless, there were those among them who would have wished to be tied up likewise tightly with her.

[4375–4393] For this the goddess was most angry: she hated her lord intensely, and never after showed him any love or favor until that day. She would have been unwilling to do it yet, if she had not wished that her son have a hauberk and a strong shield to protect himself from death. Were it not to get these arms made, she would hardly have taken him for a

---

[85] In the passage which follows, the *Eneas* poet expands Vergil's Venus–Vulcan episode by adding the ancient tale of Mars and Venus, drawn from Ovid (*Metam.* iv. 171–89), and obviously attractive to a courtly Norman audience.

long time to come. But she pardoned him his ill will, for in her need she reasoned that one must surely beg where one wishes to gain something: he who can do no more must blandish and flatter and plead. Thus that night the accord was reached, and Venus made a great outlay to attain her need.

[4394–4426] Vulcan sought no pretext for delay. The next day he arose in the morning, called all his workmen, and asked them to begin making and fabricating the work. They lit the fire at the forges; the furnaces burned and smoked; they hammered the iron and tempered the steel, while Vulcan began to forge. The workmen who were beating the gold and silver hammered fiercely, striving and hastening much. The hammers crashed on the anvils: I cannot describe it further, but Vulcan had not spent a full two months before he had finished the arms and given them to his wife. They were good arms—none such in the world—nor could mortal man have made them. Vulcan never after made such arms, nor took such pains. The hauberk was of silver links, very finely and subtly hammered. It was strong and wonderfully light, and iron or steel would do nothing to it. The hauberk was finely banded with gold mail, all the way across the whole body and the sleeves, and likewise on the panels below. No blow which any man might give it would make a single link give way. The knee pieces were likewise of gold and silver in bands.

[4427–4444] With the hauberk was the bright helmet, made of the skin of a sea fish. It was extremely strong and highly polished, and its value was one hundred forty besants. If anyone struck it on top with a sword, the sword would be all notched before it would dent the helmet anywhere in the least. It was strong and hard and very solid, and was banded with gold in quarter-panels. On the crest were four enamel plates and four natural stones, and the circlet above was very well made, completely of gold, rich stones, and enamel work. The nose-guard was made of a stone which would not be broken or cut or split by any weapon.

[4445–4468] Vulcan made the shield of the side of a great fish of the sea, named *cetus*.[86] There was never a shield so good, before or since. It was wonderfully strong and light, and all red by its nature, without any other color. It was very bright and very hard, so that it could not be cut either by lance or by sword. Iron or steel which struck it would harm it no more than lead. The whole shield was edged with gold, arranged in three bands with very delicate inlays and very fine embossing. By these bands were set precious stones, with good enamel-work placed between them. The boss was of a green topaz, and set above in the gold was a carbuncle, which threw out such light at night that it seemed like a summer day.[87] The harness was of very costly gold braid. Never did count or king have such a shield.[88]

[4469–4490] The sword was very highly polished, and forged with great skill. Ten times the steel was ground, and again ten times remelted. It was tempered many times, and well annealed and strengthened. The sword was very sharp and strong and bright and glittering. Iron or steel could not hold against it, nor dark marble, were it struck. Its blade glittered much, so that it might have been used for a lamp. Vulcan set his

[86] The *cetus* was repeatedly described in the bestiaries and their forerunners. See Faral, *Recherches,* pp. 91–92.

[87] The carbuncle, a legendary gem commonly described in medieval lapidaries and now usually identified with the garnet, was noted chiefly for its power of throwing out much light in the darkness. It was a commonplace wonder in romance and *chanson de geste* from the earliest period. See, e.g., *Pèlerinage de Charlemagne,* vv. 442–43; *Roland,* vv. 2632–35; *Thèbes,* vv. 663–66, 3209.

[88] The author has omitted Vergil's description of the engravings on the shield (*Aeneid* viii. 626–731), with its wealth of thematic detail from Roman history and legend. He has replaced it with a relatively technical discussion of the beauty and excellence of the arms.

mark and wrote his name on it in letters of gold. Its hilt was
all of fine gold and its grip of ivory, all tied with golden cord
and very tightly bound for better gripping and holding, so
that it would not turn when blows were struck. The pommel
was made of an emerald, all glittering at the top of the sword.

[4491–4514] When Vulcan had completed it, he tested it on
the anvil where he made his forgings, which was very large
and very hard. Its base was broad, its bulk large: thirty oxen
could not drag it. He struck the anvil and cut it, the blade
sliding through to the ground. If he had not held the sword
so well, I think it would never have been seen again. No mark
appeared on the sword: it did not bend or break. But this is
no wonder, for a god made it, who knew how to forge the
thunderbolts which Jove used to hurl.[89] With the sword was
a very good scabbard made of the tooth of a fish, all decorated
with beaten gold, and inlaid and enameled. Its belt was of
white silk. At one of the belt's ends was a jasper and at the
other a jacinth, each of one ounce, and set in gold.

[4515–4542] The lance was tipped with fine, sharpened
steel, very well made and well pointed, honed to great sharp-
ness. No steel or iron, or any shield or hauberk, would stop it.
The shaft was of sycamore, fixed to the head with two golden
nails. Venus attached there a pennon which Mars had long
owned, and which he had given her as a love gift when she had
first become his beloved. It was well woven and finely worked,
embroidered with gold in bands, and worth a hundred pieces
of other cloth. Pallas had made it out of envy. She had worked
it with great skill when Arachne had provoked her to a con-
test. They vied with each other in weaving, whence Pallas
made this pennon. Since she made the better work, Pallas
changed Arachne, who had challenged her, into a spider. She
had devoted herself all her life to making cloth and spinning;

[89] For a possible inspiration for the anvil test see Faral, *Recherches*, p. 99.

therefore, she cannot stop yet: always the spider spins and weaves, with thread which issues from her belly.[90]

[4543–4564] When Venus had received everything—hauberk and helm and shield, leg pieces and lance and sword—and when she had attached the pennon to the lance, she charged her messenger with them and sent them to Eneas at Montauban. That day the messenger went directly to where Eneas was preparing and making ready for the siege and—if it should come to great need—assigning those who would defend the fortress. There the gift was given to him. All those inside began to praise it, and each one examined it for himself. Eneas took the arms his mother had sent him: it is no wonder if he loved them. He assembled all his knights and explained to them something which his mother had told him.

[4565–4595] "My lords," he said, "in this land we are much beleaguered by war. Turnus does not wish to let us stay here, but is about to come here to besiege us. If he can capture us by force, he will have all of us burned or hanged. No ransom will be taken, nor do we expect any help. Venus my mother has told me that near here there is a city, of which Evander is king and lord. I am told that he came here from Arcadia. He has always been at war with the people of this land, and Venus tells me that I should seek his aid. If I go there I will not fail to bring back as many men to this castle as we have here now. If you think it is worth my while, I will have returned from there before Turnus attacks us, and will help you with a thousand troops. I will sail up the Tiber river with only two ships—I will take no more—for the country in which the city of Palentee lies is there. Whoever would go there by land would arrive more quickly than by water, but there is a very great war in the country, and it will be safer on the sea than on land. Tell me how this seems to you."[91]

[90] See Ovid, *Metam.* vi. 5–145.

[91] This request by Eneas for advice from his barons is the French poet's invention. In the *Aeneid* (viii. 31–65) the idea of the visit to Evander is given to Aeneas by the

[4596–4622] They advised him in council that he should go there quickly; the weather was fair, and he had good winds. When Eneas heard that they consented, and that they were sending him to seek aid, he delayed no longer for anything, but took leave of them. He embraced them and begged them most earnestly that, if Turnus should come to the castle, they should commit no disorder, nor go outside to tourney. Not a single man should go outside the gate, but they should defend themselves if anyone attacked them. Weeping, he kissed his son, went to the Tiber and boarded his ships, ordering two of them to weigh anchor. As evening began to fall, he ordered the sails hoisted, and they sailed that night by the stars. They sailed all the next day also, and the third day until noon. Then they arrived beneath Palentee. All the countryside along the Tiber was covered with woods down to the banks. They went upstream on the water, keeping to the cover of the trees, until they came close up to the city.

[4623–4646] The king had come out of the city and gone to the riverside in the woods. There he was sitting at his dinner, with a very large retinue, under a laurel tree. On that day he had made a very solemn sacrifice, in his manner, at a feast in memory of the wonderful vengeance which Hercules had once taken near there on that day, on a monster who had ravaged all the countryside. When this monster seized a man, he tore out his entrails, drank his blood, ate his flesh, and gnawed his bones; he ate nothing except men. The monster's name was Carus. When Hercules came to the land, he went in search of Carus at his cave, because of a wrong Carus had done him. He killed him there with great bravery and hung his head on a tree. On that day was established the feast of the great victory, which the king celebrated with very great magnificence.[92]

river god Tybris himself.

[92] Hoepffner (*Arch. romanicum,* XV, 258) sees in these lines (vv. 4644–46) and in vv. 4627–29 a reminiscence of Wace, *Brut,* vv. 4411–16.

[4647–4668] They were still seated at dinner when they saw the ships sailing up the river; they noticed the arms which glittered through the trees. They were all alarmed and in a great uproar at what they saw. Pallas, the king's son, took a dart in his right hand, and went quickly in that direction. On the bank he stopped and looked at them, but recognized none of them. He was about to throw his dart at them, but first he addressed them. "My lords," he said, "who are you who have come upon us here? You come armed to our land, and I do not know whether you want peace or war. If you come here to do ill, we do not wish to have you at all: before you could come ashore you would all be wounded or dead."

[4669–4688] Eneas stood upright in the bow of the front ship, and answered the youth. "We have not come here for evil. We have no desire to do violence, nor does any of us care for hostility. We are from fallen Troy, and are a distressed people, driven from every land. We come to the king to seek counsel and to explain to him our need: I have no wish to do ill. Advise us, for God's sake, good sir, if you can tell us where we may find him without fail; direct us without delay." Then he extended his arms toward the shore and showed him the olive branch, for this was at that time a sign of peace among the pagans.

[4689–4706] When Pallas heard what he said and saw the branch which he held out, he knew that Eneas had no desire for war. He asked him to come ashore, and they rowed quickly until they reached the bank beside him. There they tied up their ships. A few of them remained there, while most of them came forth and accompanied their lord. Pallas led them directly to where the king, his father, was. Eneas spoke first, greeting the king and all his knights very humbly, and the king greeted him most gently. Then Eneas made his speech, while his companions remained silent.

[4707–4742] "King, do not take offense at what I am about

to say. I am from Troy. Anchises was my father's name, and the goddess Venus my mother. When the Greeks destroyed the city, the gods commanded me that I should return with all my followers to Lombardy, the birthplace of our ancestor, who was called Dardanus, and who founded the city of Troy. We have come with much difficulty to the place which the gods ordained, and we have a castle in our possession. But Turnus forbids us the country, and has taken to war against us. He has undertaken this war against the gods, who have granted us the whole land; but whether we like it or not, it seems to me that he will drive us out. In that country we heard that he has attacked you frequently and has long made war against you. We have come here to you for strength and support, that you might succor us with your power. If you are willing to aid me a little and to give me some of your followers, I will avenge both you and us: in a short time we will be saved. If, with your help, I can win my war and capture or conquer my enemy, I will hold all my domain in fief from you, and grant you lordship over it."

[4743–4770] The king heard what Eneas said, and the request he made of him. He answered him very gently and said, "You are of a very good race. In my youth I was at Troy. I knew King Priam very well, and all his sons and his barons. I know well the names of many of them. I also knew Anchises your father well. He gave me a dog, a bow, and a good quiver of gold, and ten arrows and a horn; he honored me more than all the others, and gave me much from his possessions. For the sake of your father, whom I hold very dear, and in order to destroy your enemy, I will provide you with twenty thousand men.[93] I am an old man, and will remain behind, but you see here my son Pallas, whom I love greatly. You will take him; tomorrow I will make him a knight. Now be secure, and come

[93] The romancer's enlargement of the 400 horsemen provided by Evander in *Aeneid* viii. 518–19.

dine and rejoice with us, for this day is very glorious. We are now celebrating with a feast how Hercules cut off the head of a monster who was here, and who was killing all our men."

[4771–4790] The king called for water, which was brought in golden basins. Eneas and his men washed, then dined very splendidly. I cannot give an account of the dishes which came thick and fast, or of the good wines, plain and spiced, but everyone had enough of them. Eneas rose from the dinner, called a knight, and had his acrobats, his players, and his singers brought. He had them perform the entertainments of Troy before the king, to whom they gave great pleasure. The people of that country watched them and marveled very greatly at the customary entertainments of the Trojans. They praised the gods above, who had led the Trojan people to their feast and their joy.[94]

[4791–4809] When they had sung for a time and had passed the day in joy, the king saw that it was nightfall and led his people into the city. On the way Eneas told him, and explained all in order, how he had come from Troy, how the battle there had ended, why Turnus had begun the war against him, and how he was withholding his land from him. Thus he talked and recounted to him until they entered the city. It was very small and unfortified, and there was yet little wealth there; but later, Rome, which held the whole world in its power, was located in exactly that place. She was queen of the whole world, and all lands were subject to her. That night they slept in the city.

[94] The romancer has altered completely Vergil's account of the hero's visit to King Evander. For example, Aeneas' tour of the site of the future city of Rome, full of allusions dear to Augustan ears (*Aeneid* viii. 310–69), is omitted completely. Eneas' entertainment of the Palenteans at the dinner, with "ses tumbeors,/ ses geus et ses anchanteors" (4781–90) is the French poet's addition, perhaps inspired by Vergil's lines (*Aeneid* viii. 285–88) on the sacred songs and dances of the religious ceremony, perhaps, as Hoepffner suggests (*Arch. romanicum*, XV, 259), by Wace's *Brut*, vv. 4442–44. For an amusing, if harsh, comment on the French poet's debasement of Vergil's pastoral episode see J. Crosland, *"Eneas* and the *Aeneid,"* p. 285.

[4810–4824] The next day when they rose in the morning, the king had his son called forth, and had arms brought for him. There Pallas was dubbed knight: Eneas girded the sword on him. Then the king summoned his men, and they came quickly. On the third day they were assembled, to the number of twenty thousand. The king had a hundred ships equipped, and placed in them food to last thirteen months. Eneas took his leave and started back with a great army. He began his return, for it was needless to remain longer.

[4825–4850] Turnus had heard the news: the day after Eneas' departure he had learned through a spy [95] that Eneas had gone away, and was not at Montauban. He was most delighted when he heard it, but he did not know with any certainty in what direction Eneas had gone. He summoned his captains and commanded them quickly to lead his army to the castle. He had his trumpets sounded, and the army began to move. They went to the castle and besieged it, throwing those within into a great uproar. The Trojans ran to take their arms, readied themselves for defense, mounted the gangways and the parapets and the towers. They raised the bridge, closed the gate, and prepared their equipment very well. Nevertheless they feared greatly because of the large army which they saw. They feared that they would not be able to hold out, and they did not know where to flee, nor did they have their lord with them; it is no wonder that they were afraid.

[4851–4869] Turnus departed from the army. He chose a hundred knights from it and went to the castle with great noise, for he wished to begin tourneying. He would have been happy if he could have done it, but he could not draw a single person out to joust. When he saw that they could do no more about it, he rode around the castle twenty times and more to examine it, to discover in what way it could be damaged. He was in sorrow and anguish that he could find no weak place

[95] Not, as in Vergil, from Iris, Juno's messenger.

where he might make an assault against them. They began
to shoot arrows at him and he withdrew a little. Since it was
evening he did not wish to do more, and he began to return
to the army.

[4870–4888] When he saw the Trojan ships down on the
beach he spurred in that direction, and said to his men,
"These cowards who do not dare to come out of their castle
will never be able to flee us by sea. Now I intend that we burn
their ships for them, and they will be forever in our power; for
they have no other recourse, nor other hope of saving themselves, except—if they can escape—to put themselves all to
sea. If we do not guard them well tonight, surely we will not
find them in the morning; but if they escape us thus, then we
are forever disgraced." With that he had fire brought, and the
ships all ignited. The ropes and the masts and the sails
burned, and in a short time the ships were destroyed.[96]

[4889–4905] When Turnus had avenged himself on the
ships, he prepared those who would guard the gate to prevent
a sally, and placed his guards all around to watch during the
entire night, so that those within the castle and fortress would
not flee away secretly. Fires were lit throughout the army,
where they carried on great merrymaking. They sounded the
tabor and made much noise; wine was there in plenty; they
drank so much of it that they were all overcome, and lay next
to their fires without moving. Toward midnight they were all
asleep. But those who were above in the castle were thoroughly awake; they did not sleep.

[4906–4936] At the gate Eneas had placed as guard a knight
named Nisus; he valued no man more. Nisus was very brave,
and had complete charge of the castle. This knight had a
companion named Euryalus; they loved one another with
such a love that they could have none greater. There was

[96] Vergil's tale of the metamorphosis of the Trojan ships into sea nymphs (*Aeneid*
ix. 74–122) is characteristically rationalized. The ships simply burn.

never a truer love than that between them, as long as they lived. Neither of them knew anything, or had any joy or desire, without the other. That night these companions stood guard, watching at the gate. Nisus had heard the merrymaking, the dancing, the noise, and the outcry which were taking place in the army. He saw that they were all asleep, and thought of a wonderful thing. He whispered it to his companion: "There outside, the army is asleep, all drunk and unconscious. They have drunk so much they are all dead drunk, and the fires are all lit. Anyone who would wish to harm them now could surely accomplish much there; a single man might kill a thousand of them; surely none would escape it. I would like to go and make trouble in the army, and then I will return to you very quickly."

[4937–4954] When Euryalus listened and heard that Nisus wished to do such brave deeds, he was most happy and joyful over it, but he was desirous of going with him, and said, "I will not remain here, and you will not go about this business alone. How will I remain without you, or how will you go without me? For are you not I, and am I not you? I think you have lost your senses: we are one soul and one body, and one-half will go outside; how can the one remain without the other? From now on I can complain about you that you deceive me, and do not hold any love or true companionship with me. You will not go against the army without me, nor will I remain behind without you."

[4955–4985] Nisus answered the youth: "I am not angry that you wish to go there with me; rather it seems good to me. I am very delighted, and I agree to it, if we can achieve something and take vengeance on our enemies. Indeed, we will be able to go on and get Eneas to return. I know the way to Palentee well; it is not more than a day's journey. When we are accustomed to going in the woods, we can pass very near there, and will bring him back from there before the third day. Our men here are in great alarm, and find no one to send to him, either for promise or for pay. If we can supply this need and return from there in the manner that I plan, we will be talked about forever." With that they stopped talking, for they were eager to go. They went together to the fortress. Ascanius and the barons were not sleeping: that night they were awake, holding very serious deliberations. They were in fear and dismay, since they did not have their lord. They did not know at all what to do, for they found no one to send to him; no one dared to go after him.

[4986–5010] Then these two youths came, willing to undertake the brave deed. Nisus spoke first. "My lords," he said, "hear me. Our king is nowhere here, and Turnus has besieged us; outside he has laid his siege. If they can capture us by force, all of us here will be burned and hanged. If Eneas were here with us, and our enemy knew it, we would be feared much more, and I know in truth that we would be able to defend ourselves mightily if we had him among us to obey when we were afraid; what he commanded we would do. You will never see a company so large that without its captain it will not be very quickly scattered, defeated, and wholly destroyed. If Eneas were here with us, we would be the more courageous for it. We would heed him in everything, and I think we would be the stronger for it.

[5011–5024] "If you will counsel us to do it, we wish to go after him. You will be able to hold the castle until we have him come to you. If we can, we will depart very soon. We will go easily through this army, for the guards are all asleep, and there is no more noise and outcry; they are all drunk and sick, unconscious around the fires. If we can pass through the army we will then know the way ahead well. We will strive to bring Eneas to you by the third day."

[5025–5042] Ascanius heard the news, which seemed wonderfully good to him. A hundred times and a hundred more he nodded agreement. He thanked them very gently for what they wished to do, and said to them, "If my father returns, he will repay you well for this service, and will never hold anything against you. If you can supply this need and I come to hold the land, we will always stand together as three. You need never fear anything from me." They delayed no longer, but took leave of the barons. Ascanius conducted them as far as the gate, and embraced them; they parted from him with great sorrow. Never again after that hour did they see the Trojans.

[5043–5074] They descended from the castle and went secretly among the army, stabbing and beheading the first whom they found. They killed more than three hundred of them, for they surprised them sleeping. They struck and stabbed with their swords, and the wounded gave up their souls. They struck many blows and made great swordplay all along the way that they passed. The companions went until they came to a tent where Rannes lay, a man who was very wise. He knew all the languages of the birds, and knew very well how to divine and to cast lots and utter spells; there was no better diviner under the heavens. But that night he had drunk wine until he had muddled all his senses and forgotten his wisdom: he who divined of others knew nothing of himself, that his death was so close to him. But indeed he had said that week, he knew without fail that he would not die in battle. And he did not—he had spoken the truth—for he was not there, and did not see it. I do not know whether he might have died there, for before the battle took place Nisus made his head fly: this he could not forsee at all.[97]

[5075–5092] Euryalus went ahead, and entered a tent where Mesapus was lying asleep among his men. Nisus ran after him, seized him, drew him close, and whispered to him. He

[97] This ironic incident is elaborated from Vergil's few lines (*Aeneid* ix. 325–27) describing Rhamnes as Turnus' favorite augur.

said softly into his ear that there was no more time to remain: day had begun to dawn; they should set out on their way before anyone of the army might see them. Euryalus did not wish to depart. He saw a bright helmet near the fire, and said that he would not leave without it. He seized it, carried it off, and then laced it on his head. They delayed no longer, but began to travel, for they feared daybreak.

[5093–5109] A count whose name was Volcens was coming toward the army from Laurente, riding at daybreak when the moon had risen. He was bringing with him a large following— well over a hundred knights—and he noticed the two from a distance as they were leaving, because of the helmet which glittered, flashing in the moonlight. Volcens saw them and was much surprised. "Speak now," he said. "Who are you? Stand and talk to us. I wish to hear news from you, for I see that you come from the direction of the army. How are our troops conducting themselves? Are those within the castle still holding out? Tell us the truth of it."

[5110–5126] The two did not stop, but began to flee when they saw the men come toward them. Thus they fell into anxiety and fright and doubt; for if they had answered boldly and with all assurance, and had let themselves be seen, the strangers would never have doubted that they were from the army. But they took to flight too soon; hence Volcens saw this and pursued them. Nisus was very fleet of foot, and soon was so far from them that if he had not waited for his companion they would never have captured him.

[5127–5144] Euryalus, going behind, enters a sort of thicket. They surround it: it is no wonder if he is afraid. He does not remember to take off his helmet, and they see it glittering brightly. He cannot get so far away from them that they do not see it flashing. He runs into a sort of underbrush, where he cannot go forward. There they seize him. Nisus was so far from them that he would never have been captured. Then he

remembered his companion, stopped, and looked around: he
did not hear him or see him. His sorrow was not small but very
great. He sighed bitterly, beat himself with his fists, and tore
his hair.

[5145–5184] "Alas, wretch, what will I do now about my
friend, whom I have lost? I have kept very bad faith with him,
since he is captured or dead without me; like a coward I
abandoned him. I feared death too much, and fled; but I
thought he would follow me, and did not see what he was
doing. Most certainly I should have remained. I would not
have felt too much cause to lament if I had died and he had
lived. Euryalus, sweet friend, for love of you I will lose my life:
I will never live longer than you. Ill-fated was your youth! I
have given you my affection, and have lost you very quickly.
Now I think I am delaying too long, for my soul is not joined
with yours, which is suffering; it will be there quickly. But I
think in good truth that my friend is not yet dead. I feel my
heart and it is wholly alive. If he had felt the mortal pangs,
my heart would likewise have felt them. It may well be that
they have captured him, but they have surely not killed him.
They would never do such cruelty as to lay hand on him with
evil intent. Who would touch such a creature? Ah, wretch,
what an evil turn that I have escaped their hands, if he has
suffered while I am well! I will return to where I was when
I parted from him. If I do not find him I will value my life
little. If there is no one else who will kill me, I know well that
I will kill myself. I will outlive him only a little."

[5185–5210] He ceased to lament and began his return,
going back the whole way as far as a light pine forest. He
stopped, and heard the noise and the outcry of those who had
seized the youth and were putting him to questioning. Euryalus would not answer them anything. Nisus went close to
them, in hiding, and saw his companion captive among them.
He did not dare address them, but instead drew to one side,

then threw a dart into their midst. He did it to separate them, to see if his friend might escape them. The dart struck a knight in the midst of his breast, which was all naked and unprotected, and felled him dead on the ground. The men began to seek the direction from which the blow had come, but Nisus was not noticed. When he saw them recovered, he let fly another dart. It struck another knight in the body, and he fell dead among them on his shield.

[5211–5224] Volcens saw his men dying and did not know the source of the attacks. He was very angry, and seized the captured youth with rage, saying to him, "Whoever may have killed my men, I will take vengeance on you. You will indeed pay dearly for it; on you I will avenge myself. I will have the price from you, whoever may have done it." He was very angry. He drew his sword and readied the blow to strike him; then Nisus could not contain himself, but gave himself up to death. He leaped forward and cried out to him.

[5225–5239] "Hold, now," he said, "Do not touch him, but take me and avenge yourself! This man has done no wrong, small or great, but I alone have done all the evil, and I alone should pay for it. Let him go, and take me. Whoever would touch him has a very hard heart; whoever wishes to kill him has never loved; whoever would touch such a creature has no care for true love. I will offer my head for his: if I die for him it will be most agreeable to me."[98] Volcens payed no heed to what he said; it touched his heart very little. He cut off the youth's head.

[5240–5258] Nisus saw it: it was most painful to him. He saw a javelin lying on the ground, seized it, and went after Volcens. He gave him a great blow on the shield, knocked it

[98] The comments of Jessie Crosland ("*Eneas* and the *Aeneid*," 286)—who resents the absence of Vergil's humanizing and pathetic touches from the *Eneas* episode—are perhaps too unkind: "Certainly the author of *Eneas* did his best to make Vergil unpopular when he substituted such sob-stuff for the true pathos of the original." Notably absent is the description of the grief of Euryalus' mother.

down from his neck, and pierced one of his sides, but did not wound him to the death. And then he drew his steel sword for his friend, whom he wished to avenge. He killed ten of them in a very short time. But they ran upon him from all directions, surrounded him, together seized him, and there dealt him such blows that they killed him. Thus they reunited him with his companion. They took their heads and carried them off. They carried their lord on a stretcher, a little wounded, and took once again to the road. They arrived at the army easily by morning.

[5259–5278] They found the men of the army in great mourning, weeping over those who had been killed. They did not know who had killed them until Volcens arrived with his forces and told them, and related how they had found the men who had killed them all. Volcens' men said that they had taken their heads, and showed the heads to them by the hair. Mesapus, who was among them, recognized his helmet, which he thought he had lost, but which Euryalus had carried off. But the youth had paid for it dearly. Those in the army were somewhat more cheerful when they knew that they had been avenged, and they all agreed together that they themselves would avenge it very harshly. If they have the power and the opportunity, they will make the men of the castle pay for it.

[5279–5302] Turnus had the heads taken and hung in front of the gate. He commanded his men to arm themselves, and then had the trumpets sound, so that the whole countryside echoed with them. They said that the castle would surely be taken. Seven thousand pennons fluttered there, as they called upon the Trojans to tourney outside, provoking them very strongly; but they would not come out for anything that was said. They climbed up on the gangways and the parapets and the towers, but were much dismayed when they saw the heads which were hanging outside; they knew that the messengers were dead who had gone secretly to obtain their lord's return. Most of the Trojans knew them well and were greatly dismayed by their deaths. They did not think that they would have help, that Eneas would return in time, or that they would hold the castle until they could get aid—not even from morning until evening.

[5303–5330] Mesencius, who was very well equipped, attacked from the right with his following, and Mesapus from the left. Turnus and his men went in front of the gate at the head of the bridge; they surrounded the castle from all directions. A thousand trumpets, which give heart to the most cowardly, sound the assault. Javelins, rocks, and darts fly, barbed arrows and javelots and great lead shot fall like rain down into the castle. No one can stay at the battlements, nor do they dare show their faces: the archers make them hide. But the Trojans who are armed thrust downward toward the moat from above. They do not wish to hurry too much or to waste their weapons in vain, or shoot at random from a distance, before it should be necessary. But when they saw the need, and the enemy troops were drawing very near and coming together at the palisade, so that they thought that they would most surely all be quickly captured, then they threw themselves into the battle.

[5331–5354] The Trojans are above, the enemy below. Forthwith they strike into the crowd and thrust at them through the loopholes, breaking shields and piercing armor belts. They let the weights drop down, knocking over three thousand of the enemy, who fall back into the trench at the bottom. There they kill them from above. Whoever falls down there can only get up again with great difficulty. The enemy makes three such assaults that day, but always has the worst of it. When Turnus sees that nothing avails, that he cannot take them by assault, although he has made three attacks against them, he orders the Greek fire thrown at them. This they surely will not escape. He truly believes that they will not escape from this peril. But they were provided with vinegar, and with this they extinguish the fire quickly. No other help avails at all against Greek fire, and nothing will extinguish it except vinegar; it will burn in water.[99]

[5355–5369] With this, again Turnus can do nothing, and he orders his troops to withdraw below. He is very sorrowful in his heart, for much harm has been done to his men. More than three thousand of them are dead—and this is surely just, for they are in the wrong. But also more than two hundred of those within the castle have died from the three assaults. In front of him, Turnus sees his enemies, whom he had expected to capture quickly. He can scarcely shoot or thrust enough to harm them. He goes all about, studying and examining the whole castle, in order that he might see where it is the weakest.[100]

[99] Although the last-resort use of fire might have been suggested by Wace, *Brut,* vv. 333–34, it seems, rather, that the *Eneas* poet, with his "feu Griois," is bringing Vergil's firebrands (*Aeneid* ix. 522) up to date. Greek fire was frequently employed in medieval sieges, and was used with great effect during the twelfth century by the Moslems against the crusaders, in whom it aroused considerable terror. Although incendiary mixtures were used several centuries before the Christian era, the term *Greek fire* was first applied to an incendiary substance used by the Byzantine Greeks against the Saracen fleet in the successful defense of Constantinople, A.D. 673–79. This incendiary was said to ignite upon contact with water, though the evidence for this is unclear. In Western writing the term first appeared in a ninth-century Latin treatise by Malchus, translated from the Greek, and came to be applied to a variety of long-used incendiary mixtures, which were thrown by *ballistae* or arbalests in earthenware containers, which clung to whatever they struck, and which resisted extinguishing by water. Vegetius (*De re militari* iv. 18) gives a formula for such an incendiary: sulphur, asphalt, resin, and an incendiary oil. Twelfth-century incendiaries were probably of similar composition, with the oil a petroleum naptha.

Though there is no scientific ground for considering vinegar appreciably more effective than water in extinguishing this sort of incendiary, the idea was prevalent among the old authorities. As early as 360 B.C., Aieneias, in his *Polyorketikon* (33–35), when describing an incendiary mixture, noted that it was not extinguishable by water, but only by vinegar. The belief persisted throughout the Middle Ages. Jacques de Vitry and Gossuin de Metz, among many others, both remark that Greek fire or its constituents could be extinguished only by vinegar, urine, or sand. It is possible that early vinegars contained salts which, after the liquid was evaporated by the heat, might tend to blanket burning materials. See F. Lot, *L'Art militaire et les armées au moyen âge* (Paris, 1946), I, pp. 62–63, and esp. J. Partington, *A History of Greek Fire and Gunpowder* (London, 1960), pp. 1–41.

[100] In this account of Turnus' unsuccessful assault on Montauban, esp. vv. 4291–93, 5310–15, 5346, 5343–44, 5355–56, Hoepffner (*Arch. romanicum,* XV, 265–66) finds

[5370–5390] Turnus acted exactly like the wolf who is in the fields and comes to the sheepfold of the peasant. Around it he goes most hungrily, watching the sheep which he covets. He hears the lambs bleating within, and looks for a place where he may be able to enter. He sees his prey close by before him, so that they are not even three fingers apart; but he grinds his teeth, and cannot taste them. The peasant calls his dogs, which chase him as far as the woods, tearing now and then at his skin. The wolf comes and goes there so often that he loses his skin, when he is at length captured. So likewise is Turnus acting. He sees his enemies before him, but cannot harm them at all. They have him thrust at and shot at. If he does not leave the castle in peace, he will very soon lose his skin there.[101]

[5391–5414] Outside the castle, at the foot of the bridge, was a little round hill; a parapet was built there for defense near the gate. Within it were seven knights, ten sergeants, and five archers. These were defending the bridgehead and inflicting the greatest damage. Turnus attacked them immediately, turning all his attention there. He ordered the best of his army there, and had the parapet assaulted. Those within defended themselves sturdily, and did marvelous battle against them. They would never have been captured by assault, but the enemy set a fire beneath the parapet, burning the bridge and the fence. The lashings of the work all came apart, and half of it burned and flamed. The defenders withdrew to the other part; but the beams failed, the planks fell, the weight was thrown on the part where they were, and everything fell backward in a heap, crushing all those within it.

---

echoes of Pandrasus' assault on Brutus early in Wace's *Brut*. See esp. vv. 305–6, 325–28, 333–34, 337–40.

[101] The essential part of this extended simile—unique in *Eneas*—appears in *Aeneid* ix. 59–66, at the burning of the Trojan ships. Its latter half, with the threat of Turnus' destruction, is the romancer's expansion.

[5415–5433] Of all of them, none could escape death except two; one of them was Licuz, the other Elenor, who was formerly Hector's squire. They jumped up, and Licuz ran off, but Elenor drew his sword and killed and cut up ten of the enemy. Turnus killed him and avenged them. The other was fleeing directly toward the castle. They could not admit him quickly enough, for an archer from the army saw him, standing on high next to the palisade. The archer saw him, shot, and struck him through the body, so that the arrow pinned him to the fence outside. More than a hundred others shot likewise, killing him there where he hung. This emboldened the army greatly.

[5434–5452] They then attacked a fourth time. Many within the castle died from that assault. It was only by a little that those outside failed to gain entry. They might have succeeded, were it not that Ascanius gave the Trojans heart, crying out and encouraging them strongly, so that they fought there most fiercely. They killed so many of the attackers who were close to entering inside that the moat was all bloody from them, and one could not stand there. They let the dead roll down below to the bottom, which was full. Turnus had ten thousand fewer men after tierce than he had that day at dawn. On the other side, many of those within were dead and wounded.

[5453–5478] Turnus had a very brave brother-in-law, named Remullus, a wealthy man of high lineage and very great valor. He harried the Trojans greatly, insulting them with his speech. "Come, now," he said, "give yourselves up, you evil race, and believe me. Repent, cry mercy, turn and flee from here. If you are willing to beg for mercy, we will grant you pardon. Each one of you will lose either an eye or a hand, then he will go. If you are not willing to do this, and surrender as I say, then you will all be taken by force and killed before nightfall. You will not turn this into a game. Do you think that these men are Greeks, against whom you can defend yourselves for ten years without being captured? It is not Diomede here outside, or Protheseleus or Ulysses; rather, it is Turnus, who will capture you before the next day passes."

[5479–5492] Ascanius, who was in the fortress above, heard him speaking. He shot an arrow through a window at the knight, who was standing below. He struck him over the border of the shield, in the mouth, so that the arrow which struck him came out the back of his neck. Remullus fell down from his horse dead, and said no more to them, either good or bad. The Trojans, who saw the shot rejoiced over it throughout the castle; but the attackers were coming up, throwing spears from a distance and dealing sword blows in close.[102]

[5493–5516] At the bridge the onset was very great. There were two brothers in the fortress above, of the lineage of the giants. Pandarus was the name of the elder and Bicias that of the younger. Eneas trusted in them very greatly, and had given the two of them a share in his control and rule. These men descended from the fortress more fiercely than any lion. They came down, opened the gate, and divided the crowd. Pandarus was on the right side, and Bicias was on the left. There they defended the entry: they paid for it very dearly. Those of the enemy who saw the gate open wished to get ahead of one another, and thought that they would enter immediately. These two killed them by the hundreds, and did marvelous damage there. So many of the enemy lay dead on the bridge that the living could not pass them. These defenders made them all stand back.

[5517–5546] Turnus was on the other side when he heard the news that the gate was open to them and that there was great destruction of his men, for there were two giants there

---

[102] The entire episode of the death of Remulus is found in *Aeneid* ix. 590–637, but an instructive example of the freedom with which the romancer adapts his source may be observed by contrasting the taunting speeches of Remulus in the two works.

within, who were killing them by the hundreds. Turnus went there very quickly, leading a thousand knights, and came to the bridge with his force. They passed over the top of the dead until they came to the gate. The two brothers, who were defending the gate mightily, had great power and were putting up a wonderful fight. The men from the castle had run in that direction and come to the brothers, and were helping them. They were putting up a very great fight, and many died from it with great pain. They cried out and made the enemy fall back very far to the rear, beyond the bridge. They did not pursue them far, but returned to the gate. Turnus rallied his troops and attacked them again, more bitterly. By sheer force he entered inside the gate, with more than two hundred of his troops. A great crowd of those from the outside went in. The two brothers closed the gate behind their backs, so that they were shut up with those inside.

[5547–5584] Now Turnus is much taken by surprise, shut up with his enemies and in very great need of help: he will have none from those outside. He attacks those within in a powerful assault, and holds them in great battle. The two brothers, Pandarus and Bicias, are both killed immediately, with the first blows. This dismays the Trojans. The outsiders cry out and attack fiercely, the Trojans draw back to the rear; the enemy pursues them, the Trojans flee. Ilioneus comes down from the fortress and approaches, crying out to the Trojans: "What are you doing, proven cowards? Will you then be completely conquered by these few men? What are you doing? Turn around; spare them not; let each man strike now!" He cried out "Troy," their battle-cry, and then not one of them hesitated to deal blows forthwith, until the enemy was withdrawing backward. Then Turnus would have been killed on the spot, and never recovered by his men, when one of the Trojans ran to open the door, and rescue those who had been shut outside. Turnus came up behind his back, there where he was holding the bar, and gave him such a blow on the neck that the man fell dead. Then Turnus went out, but he left most of his men behind. He escaped with great difficulty, and was very glad of it when he was outside.

[5585–5601] Then night began to fall, and Turnus ordered his army to withdraw. He returned to his lodgings and readied the guards who would watch that night, begging them to guard better than they had done the night before. They made a very great noise in the army, and the sound of horns and trumpets and flutes echoed loudly in the castle. The next day, early in the morning, Turnus did not rest until he had returned to the castle and done battle with the Trojans for a very long time. The men defending the castle held out with very great difficulty; most of them were nearly dead of wounds.

[5602–5623] The defenders looked down at the harbor and saw ships arriving and hauling down their sails and their yards; they realized that Eneas was coming, and would help them at the castle. They were most joyful, and cried out. In this they acted very wrongly and were too hasty, for if Eneas and his men could have arrived in peace, to disembark and arm themselves, and could have come secretly upon the army under cover, so that they had their horses at the enemy's backs, the enemy would have been trapped between them and totally defeated. But this harmed them greatly for when the men in the castle cried out, those in the army looked, and saw ships near the shore, coming to land under oars. If the enemy are not there at the landing, Eneas' men can hurt them indeed.[103]

---

[103] The romancer has characteristically scrapped the entire opening (vv. 1–259) of Book x of the *Aeneid:* the long council on Olympus with its quarrel between Juno and Venus, the catalogue of Aeneas' Tuscan allies, and the warning of Aeneas by the sea nymphs, formerly the Trojan ships. In their place he confines himself to a comment on the tactical disadvantage under which the allies found themselves when they were detected before their landing.

[5624–5640] Turnus sees them and leaves the castle, though he has not yet made an assault on it. He spurs toward the ships with all his men; there is no one left in the army who does not rush there with great speed. Surely there will be destruction there, there will be shields pierced and three thousand lance shafts scattered. There will be a thousand jousts, for there is no wall or ditch between them. Turnus has arrived there first and has killed three knights with his lance, and another with his sword. He has begun the melee. All of the army has arrived, and Eneas' men have come out of their ships. They begin to do battle on the beach by the sea.

[5641–5666] It would be very hard to name all the men and to recount the jousts, the feats of prowess which each one did, or who died there and who killed him, but a marvelous number of them did die there; the sea was all red from it.[104] Through the battle went Eneas, doing very great destruction. There he tested his sword well—the one which Vulcan had forged. Whoever was struck with it once, if he were squarely hit, would never after recover from it. On that day Eneas shed three hogsheads of blood; no one who saw his blows would not willingly give way before him. Eneas conducted himself most bravely, and Pallas also laid on very well. No man of his youth ever gained greater honor for his prowess, nor was any his equal in valor. He did wonders there that day, meeting no one who did not regret it, or who remained in his saddle. He thrust well with the lance and better with the sword, and thoroughly cleared his path.

[5667–5693] Pallas looked up and saw Trojans who were fleeing, with Turnus striking them on their backs from behind, letting them have no rest. They were throwing them-

---

[104] The *Eneas* poet replaces Vergil's long epic list of single combats (*Aeneid* x. 308–425) with this *occupatio*. The entire battle is rehandled with great freedom, the jousts of mounted knights replacing the single combats of footsoldiers or chariots.

selves into the sea and swimming. Turnus had set thirty of them to swimming there, and was cutting them up in heaps. Pallas rode in that direction and called to the Trojans from a distance: "You are very fine in our great need! The man who led you to a new land can conquer great things with your help! You would not commit cowardice or baseness even at the risk of losing your life! Nevertheless a thousand of you are in flight because of a single one of the enemy, all alone. What are you looking for in that sea? Do you want to go back to Troy? You will not get there very soon. Now return back to the army. If you run into that sea you can perform no brave deeds there, and you will have no strength there at all. Now show your prowess here! If you want to swim in the sea, first come and avenge yourselves, and do not die in such shame!

[5694–5708] "I do not know how it can be, or what it means, that you would escape one death by throwing yourselves into a worse one. Do you prefer to feed the great fish of that sea with your carcasses, with your bodies, rather than to feed the birds out here? Stay there then, do not come out; men do not fight bravely by fleeing. Your help is of no value if a single man chases you all. If he came toward me, I think I would not flee a single foot because of him. Hold me for a coward if I do not face him from the front."

[5709–5730] Turnus heard him, drew up his reins, turned, and rode toward him, asking him who it was that was thus provoking him. Pallas told Turnus who he was, and said that Turnus would find him completely ready for battle if he wished to offer it. To one of them it will bring great harm. Both knights were on the level beach, and each spurred his horse toward the other. Pallas struck Turnus on the shield, breaking and splitting it completely, and tearing the links on his hauberk. The iron passed close to his ribs, but the blow slid past outside so that it did not wound him in the body at all. Turnus gave him a great blow in return, and both fell from their horses. Turnus got up immediately, and Pallas was on his feet as soon; they had both broken their lances, and went on with drawn swords.

[5731–5752] They strike each other with great blows and make splinters of their shields. Pallas strikes Turnus on top of the helm, knocking to the ground thirteen of its precious stones and a quartering with all the enamel, so that he is completely staggered and almost falls under it. Turnus feels the great blow, and knows well that this man has great strength. If Pallas can strike him thus again he will never recover from it. Turnus covers himself and goes to attack, but Pallas stands so sturdily against him that he does not give away a single foot. But Turnus, lying in wait, surprises him and drives his whole sword beneath his shield through his body. Pallas falls wounded, throws up his sword, drops his shield, stiffens, and sobs. His soul parts from his body.

[5753–5774] Pallas is dead. It can concern him no longer who gets the woman, Turnus or Eneas. He has paid dearly for it. Never before or after that day was he in battle or combat: he came to it too soon. But he sold himself very dearly, for first he killed well over a hundred of those in the army. Turnus sees him dead before him and notices on his finger a ring which Eneas had given him. A lion cub carved of a jacinth was set in it very handsomely, and it had well over an ounce of gold. Turnus bends down, draws it from his finger, and places it on his own. He does this in folly. Later there would be a day—if he could have known it—when he would never have taken it if he could have repented of it, for because of that ring he was to die.

[5775–5802] Turnus was standing before the dead man. In a ship in the port was an archer who saw him. He shot at him and pierced four of the mesh of his coat of mail, wounding him a little, beneath his loin. Turnus felt himself slightly wounded, looked where the shot had come from, and saw the man holding his bow. At great speed he went straight for the ship. On the right side he saw the gangway by which he climbed aboard. He found the man hiding down in the hold and took his head. But meanwhile, the rope by which the ship was held had broken. The wind was blowing from the shore, and drove the ship out to sea. When Turnus had killed the archer he wished to return to his men, but he found this very hard to do. The ship was moving, getting more distant from shore, and the waves were carrying it out to the high seas more rapidly than any swallow. Turnus did not steer or row, for he was so sorrowful that he was almost mad: he saw his men dying on the land, but he could not reach them in time.[105]

[5803–5836] When he saw that he could not return, he began to lament. "Alas," he said, "what will I do here? I will never have joy or peace. They will say that I fled. Sorrowful wretch, how unluckily I acted when I boarded this ship! The gods hate me—I know it well—and are fighting for the Trojans. They have long upheld them, and will give them this land. I was foolish when I began the war against them. The very winds fight for them, which have swept me away suddenly and have brought me far from the land. I will never have a single foot of it, nor will I even be permitted to die there. I think I will never return, for I am lost to sight on this water. I have lost my whole land. I want to leap into this sea, or strike myself through the body with my sword: one of these two I must do, for there is no hope of my returning. Since I shall never reach shore I do not understand how I can live. But nevertheless it could well be that if this wind could blow a little from my left, I might be able to return. I might yet arrive in time to discomfit the Trojans by tonight. I might still kill forty and eight of them with my sword before nightfall."

[105] Again the French poet has rationalized the narrative. In *Aeneid* x. 606–88, Turnus is lured aboard ship by a phantom Aeneas, fashioned by Juno in order to protect Turnus from imminent death.

[5837–5846] Turnus lamented bitterly, but he was not to return soon. Rather, he will see the third day pass before he drifts to shore beneath the city whose lord is Daumus, his father. He is most sorrowful and angry. His army will have no help at all from him before the third day: let them do the best they can, for he will never return earlier.

[5847–5860] Eneas soon came upon the place where Turnus had killed Pallas. There was very great sorrow in his heart. "Friend," he said, "it is pitiful that you have been killed for me. I led you here from another country, but our love has been short-lived. I have been a poor protector to you. I will avenge you if I can: Turnus is dead if I find him now." With that Eneas departed and went over the battlefield seeking Turnus. He did not find him, for Turnus was not there, but he met no one who did not pay for it.

[5861–5877] On the other side, Mesencius was in turn wreaking destruction on the Trojans. Eneas spurred against him, and they struck each other violently. Mesencius attacked him well, striking a great blow on his shield, but his lance glanced off, without damaging or piercing it. Eneas did not move from his saddle. He carried his lance low and struck Mesencius in the thigh, knocking him off his horse. The followers of Mesencius ran to his rescue—a hundred of them were helping—and carried him away on his shield straight to the Tiber. There they washed him, for the wound was bleeding heavily.

[5878–5908] Lausus, his son, was filled with sorrow when he saw his father knocked to the ground, and went to seek out the Trojan. If his father, whom he saw wounded and battered, could not defend himself against Eneas, Lausus hoped to make Eneas pay very dearly for him. He set his shield in front of him, each spurred his horse against the other, and the knights struck. Lausus struck high on the shield, above the boss. But what did this matter? The lance did not enter at all, or split or pierce it. Eneas struck him in turn on the shield with great force, so that he split and shattered it, and tore and unmeshed the hauberk. He drove the spearhead close to his side beneath the arm. It did not touch him in the body at all, but knocked him out of his saddle over the tail of the horse, throwing him to the sand. Lausus had hardly touched the ground when he drew his sword and went to fight him. The one was on foot, the other on horseback; it was not divided at all equally. Lausus struck the horse, cutting him through to the teeth and causing both the lord and the charger to fall down in a heap.

[5909–5920] Eneas jumped to his feet, furious with anger. He gave Lausus such a blow on the helm that the sword cut down to the teeth. He struck one blow and felled him dead. He went to the charger—that from which Lausus had fallen—jumped on it from the level ground, and went on in search of battle, leaving the other lying dead on the ground. Lausus had hoped to avenge his father, but paid for it very dearly.[106]

[5921–5943] Lausus lay dead on the battlefield. His followers came around him, full of great sorrow, crying out and weeping very much. They all said that he was unfortunate, and that the battle had gone most badly for them. They carried him straight to the Tiber, where his father was lying badly wounded and calling for him often. He was about to send for him, for the youth was wonderfully dear to him, and he was in very great fear for him, worrying more about him than about himself. He heard the lament uttered by those who were carrying the dead youth, and was told that they were lamenting for Lausus, who was

[106] Notably lacking from the romancer's version of the death of Lausus is the pathos introduced by Vergil, who accompanies the death with Aeneas' expressions of sad regret (*Aeneid* x. 810–32).

dead, killed by Eneas. Lausus had sought him out in battle because he had wished to avenge his father, but had fallen woefully from it.

[5944–5958] When Mesencius heard that his son was dead, he had very little strength, for he was most greviously wounded. He sat with his back against a tree. He was in very great sorrow: he had never felt a greater. He did not think of his pain, his wound, or his illness, but called for his good horse. He was armed, and did not delay longer, but had himself lifted onto his saddle bows and said: "If I find the stranger now, I will surely avenge my son, as well as the great blow he gave me; one of us will pay for it. If I can bring the matter to combat, either I or he must die."

[5959–5986] Mesencius sat on his horse and spurred down along the beach, going straight into the battle. He saw Eneas there where he saw the greatest swordplay. Eneas had just struck down a knight. Mesencius came before him very speedily, and addressed him most fiercely. "You must joust with me," he said. "Let all these others be. You have killed my son and wounded me: now you will have to pay dearly; now we will both be avenged." With that he charged toward him, spurring the charger with one foot, because he could not make use of the other. The horse ran with the spur, but charged with only a little force. Mesencius struck a light blow on Eneas' shield, for he had lost much of his strength and was thoroughly enfeebled from the wound in his thigh. Eneas in turn struck him on the shield with his lance, driving it through the body so that he struck him down dead from the saddle-bows. Mesencius has hardly avenged his son; he has uttered all his threats in vain.

[5987–5998] The battle lasted, and the thrusting and jousting and swordplay, until nightfall separated them. The Latins returned to their lodgings, carrying their bloody wounded, and the Trojans—who had not all had the best of it—went to their castle. Pallas was carried inside. Eneas did not wish to abandon him or leave him with the other dead. That night he had him very well guarded.

[5999–6020] The enemy army did not have its leader. On the next morning their counts and dukes assembled and decided in council that they should send to Eneas, requesting a fifteen days' truce, to have the dead buried and the wounded treated. The messengers departed, each one holding an olive branch; in that day this was a sign of peace, accord, and love. In the morning the messengers came to Montauban. There was not a gatekeeper who dared forbid them the gate when he saw them carrying the branches. They went into the castle without interference until they climbed up to the fortress, where Eneas was lamenting over Pallas, whom he had lost so soon. It had been a very unhappy event for him.

[6021–6046] The messengers came before him holding the olive branches in their hands. Aventinus, whom they held to be the wisest of them, spoke the message. "Sire," he said, "hear me a little. I will tell you very briefly why we have come here. We are very worn with battle. We have assaulted this castle and have yet failed to capture it, and also we have yesterday done much battle with you down on the beach. Whether for right or for wrong, many of our people are dead— both many of yours and many of ours. Of Turnus, who assembled the armies and summoned peoples from other countries, we do not know whether he is dead or alive. All the barons outside have discussed it in council and have sent us to you, that you might grant us a fifteen days' truce, in which we will have our dead burned on pyres, cremated, and buried. We should not leave them on the ground: one should not make war against the dead.

[6047–6067] "If Turnus does not come meanwhile, it is finished with him—I know no more of it—and if he never returns, you will have a good peace from us. We seek a truce from you for the dead. It is surely right that you take one: take pains to bury your dead, who are lying there outside, dead for you. We grant you your free choice of the wood from all our forests for your pyres, and your men may go in all safety together with ours."

Eneas heard him and smiled a little, then said to the messengers: "You ask a truce for the dead. I do not wish that the wrong in this be ours; we would indeed have granted it to the living, if they had wished it, for all time. No evil will come to you through us. We will grant you a firm truce." On both sides they swore their oaths.

[6068–6092] The messengers returned and told in the army what they had done, that they had sworn to the truce. They had it announced throughout the army that the men should build funeral pyres very quickly, that all the dead should be carried there, and that they should be burned and buried. When it is announced through the army, they delay no longer. Some hasten to build pyres and others to carry wood. Still others go for the dead. They all work with great energy. They bring in ten thousand dead on carts, place them on the pyres, and burn them there, putting their ashes in the ground according to their faith and custom. The men of the castle do likewise, cutting wood together, carrying the dead, and building their pyres. They burn and bury the dead, and celebrate very solemn rites, according to their faith and custom. At the burial they rejoice greatly, according to the custom of Troy.

[6093–6102] When the men from the enemy army had done everything, they withdrew to Laurente, saying that if Turnus did not return within eight days, they would remain there no longer. But he traveled so that he arrived there before the fourth day, and thus kept them. He was highly annoyed at the truce which was lasting so long, and said that when it was over the Trojans would pay for it.

[6103–6124] Eneas had caused all his dead whom he could

find to be buried. He said that he would not keep Pallas, but would send him to his father. He had a very rich and expensive bier prepared, whose shafts were of ivory set with gold as far as the head. The bars were likewise delicately encrusted. The webbing was of silk, the lacing very well made.[107] He placed on it a Tyrian pad and a Galacian coverlet. On the top was a quilt of cloth which Paris had brought from Thessaly, embroidered outside with gold lace, with four enamel plaques in the four corners. They clothed Pallas in a robe woven in masterly fashion with gold, which Dido had presented to Eneas when she loved him.

[6125–6146] Eneas had Pallas placed on the litter, with four chargers drawing the bier. Over him he placed a coverlet (never did any king have a better one: Priam had given it to him with his daughter), and he had a canopy placed above, made of a filmy covering, arranged all around like an awning. To call to mind Pallas' prowess, he wished to have carried before the bier whatever he had won before Turnus had killed him. Then he ordered to mount their chargers as many as three hundred knights, all of whom went with the dead youth. There was no one carrying a candle, and in order that they might go more safely he did not have them carry arms. When they had prepared everything, Eneas kissed the dead youth and spoke to him very gently—though Pallas did not hear or listen to him.

[6147–6166] "Pallas," he said, "flower of youth, never will there be a day when I do not repent that you came here with me. I have taken poor care of you, since you received your death in my absence. I bear the guilt and the wrong of it, and will yet take vengeance for it with my sword or my lance on the traitor who by felony and treachery took your life. Fortune has been too harsh. If there had not been an unhappy

---

[107] In striking contrast with the simple litter of woven osier and willow, shaded with oak leaves, in *Aeneid* xi. 64–66.

accident, I think you would never have been defeated by him, or killed or captured. You had much courage and greater worth in arms; but Envy would not suffer that you escape the loss of your life, nor that I conquer the land or end the war with your help.

[6167–6184] "When I had conquered it all, I would have divided the country with you. Now the earth has lost you; your part of it is small. Your father will feel deep sorrow, and your mother will hear cold news when your death is announced. On the day when I took leave of them, I assured them that you would not be killed in battle or tourney without me. Now you are dead, and I am alive; quite plainly I have lied to them. They will be forever in sorrow. I have set their life in sadness, and they will never have any joy. They will always complain of me that I brought them to evil over you.

[6185–6208] "Friend, I do not know what I should say to you. This life is extremely fragile. Yesterday morning you were so handsome that there was not a more seemly youth under the heavens. In a short time I see you changed, paled and all discolored: your whiteness is all darkened, your color all turned to perse. Handsome creature, seemly youth, as the sun withers the rose, so has death quickly undone you, and withered all, and changed all. My heart sorrows so much the more, since you do not hear or listen to me, and will never answer me. I do not know what more to say to you. May your soul have no pain or suffering, but rather may it go to the Elysian Fields, where the good men are, beyond the great, deep hell.[108] It was only a short time ago that I was there, and saw my father, and spoke to him. May your soul be united with his happiness."

[6209–6228] With that he was silent: he could say no more. There was sorrow and very great anguish in his heart. He fell

---

[108] Faral (*Recherches,* p. 117, n.3) suggests that this allusion to the Elysian Fields was inspired by Ovid (*Amores* iii. 7. 59–60).

over the dead youth in a faint, and, when he revived, he kissed the corpse, all weeping. He ordered the bier to go forward, and thus set them on their way. He accompanied them outside the castle, going on foot after the bier for an entire long league. His followers made him stop, and he let the corpse go forward. When he came to the parting he uttered many laments and many sighs. He could never turn back as long as he could see the bier moving. When he lost sight of it he departed with very great regret, and returned with much difficulty, leading his followers back to Montauban.

[6229–6251] Those with the dead youth went quickly straight to Palentee, traveling night and day until they came to the city. They saw the fortress and the tower in the morning at daybreak. There, as the sun rose, the bier entered the city. The news was quickly heard, and the city was in a tumult from it. The burghers ran to meet the bier. The ladies cried out and wept, and everyone lamented over the youth. The king was up in the castle. When he heard the great noise in the town, he sent there in great haste to know the cause of the noise, and why the people were causing a tumult. He whom the king sent returned and announced to him that it was his son Pallas: Eneas was sending him back to him, dead, and the burghers were giving vent to their sorrow over it.

[6252–6276] When the king heard the news, he tore his white and hoary hair with his two hands, plucked at his beard with his fingers, and fainted more than twenty times. He beat his head and struck his face. Weeping, he went out to meet the bier. When the queen heard the news, she tore at her face and breast, came out of her chamber in the palace, and went running, all pale and disheveled, to meet the body. There on the portico in front of the hall the father met his son. His mother came from the other direction. They swooned over him a thousand times, and accused and blamed all the gods, for each day they had prayed to them, and sacrificed at their altars, that the gods might protect their child and defend him in battle. At the entrance in front of the hall they took the body down from the bier. They carried it into the palace, and lit there a thousand candles.[109]

[6277–6298] The Trojans came forward and made a great gift to the king. They led him five hundred bound captives whom Pallas had taken, and showed him the arms and war-horses of more than two hundred knights whom he had killed in battle. They recounted to him how brave the youth had been, how he had acted as a knight, and how Turnus had wickedly surprised and killed him. They showed the wound which Turnus had made, tightly bound in a large bandage. The king was doleful when he saw it, and his mother could not look at it. When they heard tell of the knightliness of their child, of his prowess and heroism, it was no wonder if the father and mother felt sorrowful, for they loved him greatly. The more brave he was, the more grieved were those who loved him most.

[6299–6314] The king stood before his son and lamented, weeping. "Fair son," he said, "I have lived too long, when I have seen the time and the day that you are dead and I am alive. Who will now sustain my country, my realm, all my domain, to which you would one day have been heir? I have no other child to have my kingdom nor any baron who will remain with me, for they all know well my power— that I am an old man and have no heir. They will never have a king of my lineage, who would be lord by inheritance. Because of you, I will fall into great contempt all the remaining days of my life."

[6315–6352] The father lamented bitterly, and on the other side the mother wept. "Fair son," she said, "I bore you in an

---

[109] This episode—the return of Pallas' corpse to Palentee—is greatly altered and expanded from *Aeneid* xi. 142–81. In the *Aeneid* (xi. 158–59) King Evander is a widower.

evil hour, for your life has been very short. Unhappy the day when I ever saw the Trojans! I can complain of them for ever more. Never did I hear anything of them except evil and wickedness and treason. Cursed be their coming, for I have lost all my life from it! Son, you have paid dearly for it. They have shown you their bad faith. They came here to seek help, for they were much troubled by war. Evander did not wish ever to believe me, but hastily sent you with them, and they led you away with them. They have shown you bad faith! Alas the day I knew them, and alas the day I saw them! It is only a little while since you left here, and now they have sent you back dead. They have given us poor comfort for it: they send here a present which is little help. This booty and these conquests and these prizes of prowess in battle, the knights whose arms and war-horses I see, these show even more how much you helped them: Turnus was much weakened from it. You are dead in their service. I cannot in any way understand what use this comfort might be; rather, it makes us much more sorrowful, for now we know the heroism which was in you, and the bravery. The more we hear you praised, the more burdened we should be by it.

[6353–6370] "Never more will I pray to our gods, or do them honor; they will never have more service from me. I have done wrong to sacrifice to them, which I did every day very solemnly, with great honor. Either they have been asleep so that they have not heard my prayers, or else they cannot save a man, or protect or defend life. They have shown me very evilly that they are not omnipotent.[110] Son, they have given you very poor help, and guarded your life very little. Alas, I will never have comfort for my sorrow until death; always I will lead my life in sorrow. My wish is that death might take me."

[6371–6390] The queen lamented, and the king swooned again and again. Whoever saw such sorrow could never have

---

[110] Faral (*Recherches,* p. 117, n.3) sees in this agnostic outburst an echo of Ovid (*Amores* iii. 7. 33).

kept from weeping. The king had his servants come, and ordered his son buried, according to the custom of their faith, as one would bury a king. First they stripped him of all his clothes and removed his shoes. They washed the body and the wound, first with plain, then with spiced wine: it was somewhat blackened and dark. They dried him well with a silken cloth, and cut his blond hair. Next he was embalmed. He was most handsome, and had no beard. They anointed him well with fresh balm, so that he would not decay, nor any bad odor come forth from him.

[6391–6408] They dressed him in clothes of fine linen which the mother gave her son; they dressed him in a tunic of purple which three of their goddesses had made, and had woven all with gold.[111] He had sandals of embroidered silk and spurs of gold strapped to his feet with good orphrey. They equipped him wholly like a king; they put a ring on his finger with a good stone, an expensive onyx. Over all they clothed him with a robe, and on his head they placed a crown. The king gave him his alms purse. When they had prepared him completely, they carried him to the temple of the gods, where they made a great sacrifice and offered a great service, according to their faith.

[6409–6436] Outside, on one side of the temple, the king had made with great care a vault for his own burial, which was rich far beyond measure. The place was extremely beautiful, and the tomb was all ready: there the king had thought that he would lie when he died, but his son was placed there first; for this the king was the more sorrowful. The vault was completely round: there was none more beautiful in all the world. It had no window of glass-work except a single one in the rear. The frame was all of jacinth and beryl and silver. Outside, the whole wall was of good marble, whole and entire. The stones were of a hundred colors, carved with beasts and with flowers.

---

[111] Faral (*Recherches*, p. 88) sees here an allusion to the classical Fates.

The covering over it was made all of ebony. A spire was raised over it, all covered over with copper. On it were cast three small balls, and on these sat a bird, cast of fine gold, which could not be shaken by wind or by storm.[112]

[6437–6459] The vault occupied little space. It was painted within with powdered gold. All around it there were pillars and alcoves and arches and also works in painting, and very good carvings. There was much gold and good enamel and many precious natural stones. Pillars, railings, and capitals were of filigree and black enamel, and the floor beneath was all of iris-stone and crystal. The king had the casket which he had prepared for himself placed under the vault, directly in the center. One could not seek a better casket for a king. It was very rich and very costly, entirely of a precious green stone. It was most noble and bright and beautiful, and sat on four lionets cast of fine gold, well polished and enameled in black, seated at the four corners.

[6460–6484] There within was placed the corpse—the noble, the brave Pallas—all arrayed in royal clothes, with both scepter and sword. They raised his head and placed a pillow beneath it, to bring his face forward a little. They took two straws of fine gold and placed the tops in his nostrils, with the other ends in two vessels. One vessel was of gold, marvelously beautiful, and held no less than a gallon. This was completely filled with balm. The other was of sardonyx, and was all filled with turpentine. The vessels were stopped—sealed with good coverings— so that the odor would not go outside at all, except through the tubes into the body. The odors of these

[112] Faral (*Recherches,* p. 163) identifies the *Letter of Prester John* as the source of this detail of the tomb's spire. Aeneas' mourning for Pallas, the preparation and embalming of the youth's corpse, his burial, the description of his tomb, and the record of his epitaph are all carefully balanced later in the narrative by similar details for Camille. These two young victims stand as representatives of the price paid by the opposing sides in the war. The description of the tomb exhibits well the *Eneas* author's addiction to architectural marvels. Cf. O. Söhring, "Werke bildender Kunst in altfranzösischen Epen," *Romanische Forschungen,* XII (1900), 534.

spiced liquids went within him and always protected him from rotting, and from corrupting, and from stinking. The body would never decay unless water touched it.

[6485–6494] When they had accomplished these things, they placed over the casket the covering, which was all of a single amethyst. On its head was a plaque of fine gold, with two verses on it. The letters and the writing read:

> HERE WITHIN THIS TOMB
> LIES THE BRAVE, THE HANDSOME, THE NOBLE
> PALLAS,
> WHO WAS THE SON OF
> EVANDER THE KING.
> TURNUS KILLED HIM IN SINGLE BATTLE.[113]

[6495–6518] The tomb was somewhat high. There was bitumen from the Asphalt Lake to seal the vault. Asphalt has this nature: when it has dried a little, then it will never after be broken except by one thing. It is not polite or well or good to name this thing openly, but only secretly, in private.[114] The tomb was very rich, and was most excellently suited to the

[113] The exact source of the tradition of Pallas' embalming and burial is unknown, but the story was recorded by William of Malmesbury, writing between A.D. 1125 and 1135. His account of the discovery of Pallas' uncorrupted body (*De gestis regum anglorum,* ed. W. Stubbs, 2 vols., Rolls Ser. [London, 1887-89], I, 258–59; II, 206), with an epitaph and an eternal, inextinguishable flame, is close enough to the *Eneas* episode to deserve quotation: "Tunc corpus Pallantis filii Evandri, de quo Virgilius narrat, Romae repertum est illibatum, ingenti stupore omnium quod tot secula incorruptione sui superavit. . . .Hiatus vulneris quod in medio pectore Turnus fecerat, quatuor pedibus et semis mensuratum est. Epitaphium hujusmodi repertum:
> Filius Evandri Pallas, quem lancea Turni
> Militis occidit more suo, jacet hic.
. . .Ardens lucerna ad caput inventa arte mechanica, ut nullius flatus violentia, nullius liquoris aspergine valeret extingui. Quod cum multi mirarentur, unus, ut semper aliqui sollertius ingenium in malis habent, stilo subtus flammam foramen fecit; ita introducto aere, ignis evanuit. Corpus, muro applicitum, vastitate sui moenium altitudinem vicit; sed procedentibus diebus stillicidiis rorulentis infusum, communem mortalium corruptionem agnovit, cute soluta et nervis fluentibus."

[114] The author perhaps had in mind the description of bitumen in Isidore of Seville, *Etymologiae* xvi. 2. 1, "Bitumen. . . .neque aqua neque ferro rumpitur, nisi solis muliebribus inquinamentis," which explains his rather ostentatious reticence.

knight, who was great: it needed nothing more nor less. It did not go without light. It had a lamp hung above it, whose whole chain was of gold. The lamp was full of balm, of marvelous richness. Its wick was of asbestos—a stone which one lights. Asbestos has this nature and property: after it is lit it will never be extinguished, nor at any time will it be consumed.[115]

[6519–6536] The king had the lamp lit. It was never again necessary to renew it. He kissed the precious stone on the outside a hundred times. He swooned often at the parting, and the queen made great lament. She left with very great difficulty. When they had all gone outside and left the corpse within, the king had the entrance stopped so that no one could ever enter. The Trojans took leave of the king and returned home. They arrived at Montauban exactly on the day when the truce which had been sworn came to an end. Now they are about to wage war, to do battle, and to tourney.

[6537–6572] King Latinus was at Laurente, where he was complaining and lamenting bitterly that he had lost his people through great folly, and to no purpose. He summoned all his barons, assembling them in his palace; Turnus was there with them. The king spoke his opinion. "My Lords," he said, "this war, which is bringing my country to destruction, and in which our men are being killed, and many men from other countries—know that it is not because of me: it is not good in my opinion, nor do I agree to it. I never wanted it, and still do not want it; it was begun in great arrogance. Those who take arms against the gods will find themselves wholly wretched from it. It has long been well known that the gods are defending the Trojans. They are related to their lineage;

[115] This description of asbestos, like that of bitumen, appears to derive directly or indirectly from Isidore of Seville (*Etymologiae* xvi. 4. 4). Faral (*Recherches,* p. 86, n.2) notes that asbestos plays a part in some of the contemporary descriptions of the monuments of ancient Rome.

one should not do violence against them. If they suffer evil or
pain, do you think then that it could not concern the gods?
This you can know with certainty, that the gods truly support
them. They aided them against you on the day that the
Trojans were besieged. There were four of you against each
one of them and, when you came to combat, for each one of
their men who was killed there, you lost fifteen of ours. I will
advise indeed henceforth that we seek peace from them.
Enough evil has been done; the fear is that it may be still
worse.

[6573–6594] "There is a land in this country which has
always been waste and which was never inhabited, tilled or
worked. It stretches from the stream of Tuscany as far as the
river of Sicane. It is a broad land, extending without interruption for four days of travel. It would be an extremely beautiful country, good and rich, if it were peopled: it has great, full
forests, and prairies and rivers, and beautiful slopes for growing vines.[116] Surely we can place them there. The land has
never done us any good, nor have we ever had anything from
it. If we can agree on it, I advise very strongly that we give
it to them, that they build walls and towers there, moats,
castles, cities, and towns, that they hold everything in common with us, that their people and ours be one.

[6595–6632] "If they do not wish to remain here to take the
land I have spoken of, if they wish to go elsewhere, let us
provide for restoring to them their ships which were wrongfully burned where they were in port. Those we will return
wholly at their choice, for we have forests in plenty; they will
not put us to great expense. We will have everything built by

[116] There are relatively close parallels between the king's description of Latium and
King Gurguint's description of Ireland in Wace's *Brut. Eneas*, vv. 6573–76, especially
parallels *Brut*, vv. 3357–58, and *Eneas*, vv. 6581–85, parallels *Brut* vv. 3368–70. The
Eneas author deliberately departs from the authority of Vergil (*Aeneid* xi. 316–19),
who declared that the territory was cultivated by the Auruncians and the Rutilians.
Cf. Hoepffner, *Arch. romanicum*, XVI, 164–65.

our people. Let Eneas have at his desire gold and silver, silks and cloths, horses and mules and palfreys. I have thought about it many times. Let us consider how we may make peace with this people whom we know that the gods love, who have a claim on this country through them. But know this: I will do nothing about it, either good or bad, except through your counsel. I will by no means seek the accord of which I spoke unless you wish it. Whatever you venture to advise me, I will carry out in full; know this. I am not one who does not accept advice: he who seeks counsel should follow it. A man should not take counsel in anything in which he is unwilling to abandon all his desire for another when he hears someone speak better than he. I will follow all your counsel about making peace with this people." All the barons said among themselves that the king was quite right in wishing to keep the Trojans, for if they wished to be his men they could do it very well, if only he could hold them.

[6633–6652] Drances rose to his feet, a rich man, very eloquent, and of very high lineage. No one in the court was wiser, or knew better how to speak in court or to give important counsel, or argued more reasonably, or made a better judgment. He was very clever with words, but he was not soldierly. "Sire," he said, "I will answer for all these others, but I know well that Turnus hates me most unjustly; I will bear it as best I can, and will recover from it quickly, for I hardly value his pride. His power does not extend over me, nor will I ever once flatter him, or because of him keep quiet about what I know and think of this business.

[6653–6692] "You have said—and it is good sense —that you will offer peace to the Trojans. You wish to give them part of your land if they will remain here. But I think you are offering too little when you merely keep them in your country. Give your daughter to Eneas, their lord. You granted her to him when his messengers came here, and you can not better bestow her. We strongly advise this marriage: there has been great destruction indeed because she has not been given to him. Many men have paid for it, and there will be still much worse done if you fail in your covenant with him. Turnus does not want him to take her; he wants to have her and claims her. He says that he should have the girl and that you have made him heir to the land; that you have sworn an oath to him, and cannot give her to another; that if you have made any later grant of her to the Trojan, it is unjust, and he will not suffer any loss because of you. Indeed, he makes himself lord and king, and says that he will by no means lose her, unless she is sold very dearly; rather, fifteen thousand will die for it, footsoldiers, as well as knights. He holds them lightly, for they cost him nothing at all. It means very little to him, I think, if we are all killed for it; it is agreeable to him if we should all come to that, and he would grieve handsomely enough over it; but let him have the land in peace, and the girl, and he would think no more of it. It would not concern him who had died over it, but only who would then have the rule.

[6693–6706] "We say here among ourselves that it should not be thus; but since he wishes you to give him your daughter and make him your heir—if he wants her so much and loves her so much—since he sees that Eneas claims her against him, let him do battle against Eneas. Let the two dispute her between themselves. Let each of them be there in his own behalf, and let us stay far away from it. We will see who conquers, and will then adhere to him in due form. Let him conquer her alone and let him have her alone. It will never be well if it goes otherwise."

[6707–6728] Turnus heard what Drances said, and burned with anger and ill will. He jumped forward and said to him: "We are winning little with your help. Your shield is still untouched: it was never seen in time of need.[117] If we had to hold court, you would make yourself much heard there, and would make speeches to us all, and there you would be very bold; but you do not wish to hurry off to the place where you would have to do battle; for one wins there only what one earns. Your mother has no other children besides you; you consider that; very sensibly you stay far away. You are not simple or foolish: if you did not fear the blows you would go forward very quickly. You would lay on heartily, if he who was fighting with you had his hands entirely bound.

[6729–6752] "Your arms are dearly purchased, and should be well kept; if your shield were pierced it would put you to too much expense, but so long as you keep it whole, you will not have to pay another penny for it. You have a horse so fleet-footed that there is none as fast in the whole army, but you have taught it so well that it becomes very balky when it sees arms; yet it is very skilled at fleeing. Then no one can keep up with it. If you fall into a little trouble, you trust more to your speed than to your sword; it will never be bloodied by you. In talk you surpass; you fight with your tongue. I will conquer nothing through you. I will be poorly aided by your shield and lance.[118] I have such confidence in you that I will never seek to conquer the maiden or the land with your help."

[6753–6790] Drances heard the words which Turnus spoke spitefully, accusing him of cowardice. He said to him, "This is indeed the truth. I never gave myself to heroic deeds, nor will I do it now.[119] A man should be good in an undertaking when he expects to take all the profit of it, or have all the loss fall on him. But I am gaining or losing nothing from this. If I can protect my person, I will not let myself be killed. If I

[117] Faral (*Recherches,* p. 113) finds the source of this taunt about the undamaged shield in Ovid (*Metam.* xiii. 117–18).

[118] The taunt may have been suggested by Ovid *Metam.* xiii. 9–10.

[119] The *Aeneid* (xi. 296–467) account of the debate in council allows no rebuttal speech to Drances.

should lie all cold and dead from the battle, you would not sorrow over me at all. Now look at you, making great lament, complaining, weeping, tearing your hair over those who are all dead for you; a fine comfort you are to them! And you would willingly enough display the same sort of sorrow over me. If I were killed for you, and you had the country and continued to show your insolence, my soul would be very happy indeed! If you got the king's daughter, you would feel a fine sorrow for me: you would have very quickly forgotten me! I have protected myself in the past and will continue to do so in the future. In faith, it is not Drances who now wishes to give his all for you. I do not seek to flatter you by wishing to die for you; I do not wish to come to that. For my part, I will tell you truly: since you want to have everything—first the girl and then the land—then I will leave them for you to conquer."

[6791–6804] He turned toward the king. "Sire," he said, "hear me. We have here reached a conclusion, and it should be clearly announced. All these barons present hear it; they agree to it, and it is right. You will give your daughter to the Trojan and make him heir to your land, and if Turnus wishes to defend her, he can indeed take up battle against him. If he can win her, man against man, then let him have the girl and all the land. We assure you that we do not consent that one man more die over it except one of these two"

[6805–6828] Turnus jumps to his feet, approaches the king, and holds out his gage of battle there in sight of all the baronage. He says that he will end it all by himself alone, if he conquers her; and since the king's court wills it, it is well to bring the affair to an end. The king sees him hold out the gage, but does not yet wish to take it, and says that he will first send to the Trojan and inform him that now there will be an end to the war, if he can win the girl in his own person. If he consents to it, he will have battle. Let the day be chosen when he will appear on the island outside the city, and let

only the two be there. Whoever conquers the other in battle
will have won all without fail. To this Turnus has consented,
and the king considers—there is nothing else to do—what
messengers he will send, what he will inform him, and by
whom.

[6829–6848] While they were considering what they should
send to the Trojans, a messenger came running into the hall
crying loudly that the Trojans had come, that they were
spread over the countryside, and that they intended to assault the city. The council had lasted too long. There was
great excitement in the hall, and all of the council departed.
They all jumped up and remained no longer, but ran to take
arms as soon as they could. All the decision which they had
reached in council was forgotten. Turnus and Eneas will not
fight alone, in their two persons; instead, they will all fight
together. The whole city murmured and roared. The fighting
will be heavy indeed; there will be a good thousand frays.

[6849–6870] The Trojans were approaching the city, and
the burghers were mounting the walls, carrying rocks and
sharp spears, swords, lances, and shields. Ladies, townswom-
en, and maidens went to the temples and chapels, sacrificed
on the altars, and prayed to all the gods to defend the town
and prevent the Trojans, who were outside and all ready for
battle, from seizing or burning it. Turnus was armed first of
all and had twenty thousand knights; he went ahead and they
after him. He saw Drances unarmed, and said to him, "Exceedingly great joy and much profit will now come to the
Trojans, since your arms are in pawn today; else you would
have done great damage indeed. They would have paid for it
in men slain: you would have wrought great destruction."

[6871–6904] Drances said to him, "Indeed, I am not seeking
to draw my sword for your affair, or carry my shield or lance,
receive or give blows. End the war yourself, you who wish to
conquer everything. But you do not wish to do this at all; you

wish to do it through other people. You put twenty thousand of them in front of you, whom you will certainly not save. You have done well: this is no joke, for men have died for you in many places. As long as you can entice men who will let themselves die for you, you will not come forward in time of need, but will be far behind them. You never harangue your men in vain. You are like the peasant who urges on his dog where he would not dare go himself for anything; and you do likewise, for you urge on your followers where you are unwilling to go yourself. Eneas waits for you outside there, wishing to claim the girl. Go! Now you can avenge yourself! Spur your Castillian charger! But no, you wish to pull the serpent out of the brush with another man's hand. I regard as a great fool and a blockhead the man who serves you with such folly. Know you that I will not do it at all; I will not beat the brush so that you can eat the sparrows from it".[120]

[6905–6934] With that, Turnus spurred his horse and went as far as the gate below. There he found Camille where she was waiting for him, fully armed. She had with her a good three thousand knights, all equipped, on their chargers. There was none who did not have a heraldic device—blazons of many kinds. Camille had a very fine following. She was handsomely clothed, and sat upon a gray charger which was worth a thousand others. Its covering was ermine, and the bordering around it was of a red silk. It was wonderfully well made, as was her blazon. She was leaning on her lance, with her shield hung around her neck. Her shield was of ivory, with a boss of gold, and its grip was of orphrey. Her hauberk was white as snow and her helmet glittering and bright, all quartered with fine gold. The cape of the hauberk was made in such a way that she had drawn her blond hair outside, so that it covered

[120] The final verbal skirmish between Turnus and Drances, with its rare simile of the villein and his dog, and its proverbial taunts, is the romancer's addition.

her whole body. It fluttered down behind her as far as the horse's back.[121]

[6935–6946] Turnus saw her and went in that direction. The maiden drew near him and addressed him, smiling: "You come to us too tardily; the scouts are outside now, and here we are delaying all day. If I had not waited for you, we would have gone outside against them, and already would have killed three hundred. They have us shut up in here. It seems almost cowardice that we delay here in such a manner."

[6947–6978] Turnus answered the maiden. "Lady," he said, "I wish to tell you some news which I have heard. I know well from one of my spies that Eneas is far to the rear, and will pass along a cartway which runs beneath a fir wood. The road is very difficult. I have never seen a better place to attack one's enemy. I will go into ambush in the woods above, to lie in wait along the road; if he enters the cartway, he will never turn back, and he will not move forward without first losing his life. One man may kill a hundred of them there, for defense is worth nothing. If I can surprise him there, I think I will give him an extremely hard battle. I will lead a thousand knights with me. You will remain here at the tourneying, and let Mesapus remain with you. You will have in your company well over twenty thousand knights, besides the footsoldiers and the archers." Camille agreed to this, and Turnus took leave of her. He set out on the way with his men and went into ambush in the fir woods: if now he falls upon Eneas there, there is death in that pass.

[6979–7006] Camille rode out to the tourneying, leading a hundred maidens with her, well clad in mail, each in a different armor; it was an extremely beautiful company. When they were in the midst of the field, the Trojans gazed at them,

[121] There is no further description of Camille in this part of the *Aeneid* (xi. 489–521). The romancer on his part omits Vergil's lovely sketch of Camilla's childhood, and Diana's preparations on Olympus for the approaching death of her devotee (*Aeneid* xi. 532–96).

and feared them immensely. When they spurred on at great speed the Trojans thought they were goddesses who were defending the city. They were all thoroughly frightened. They did not dare defend themselves against them, or even await them at all: they feared them much. The maidens pursued them, and since the Trojans did not defend themselves, it is no wonder that the maidens struck them down. The maidens laid on very well there, and left them lying on their backs. They shed much blood in a little time. Orsileus, a Trojan, saw the maidens thus giving battle, striking, and felling knights. He drew and struck a damsel. Her name was Larine, and she was very beautiful. He knocked her from her horse and she fell down dead in the dust.

[7007–7034] The Trojans, who saw the blow, were much elated, and all laid on, since they knew that these were women who could die. They attacked them vigorously, beating them back as far as the streets, and drove them into the city. The Trojans laid on so fiercely there that they blocked the gate with the dead. If the entry had then been clear, they would have entered together into the city, without opposition, but the dead were lying about so thickly that they could not go forward, and those in the towers, on the walls, and on the galleries shot arrows, threw spears, and tossed great rocks on them. They had come too close, and many of them were killed. They had drawn back a little, when Mesapus and Camille, who was with him, charged them. Thus they were driven back to the open fields, and the tourneying and jousting began anew. Four times they drove forward in that manner, striking back into the city, but the others always drove them out into the fields where they were tourneying.

[7035–7060] Camille spurred among the ranks, jousting often with the Trojans. She brought down two hundred of them there who could never after rise up again. She struck well with the lance and better with the sword, and was wonderfully feared. Her blow did not fall in vain; he who was struck down by her hand did not languish long: medicine was of no value to him, for death always followed her blow. She struck with such great strength that there was no defense against her in a good hauberk or a strong shield. The maiden laid on well there, making the Trojans leave their saddles. She upset many knights, whose horses went wandering. On the field lay the shields, the pennons embroidered with gold, lances, swords, torn hauberks, coverings of green samite. In whatever direction the maidens went, the Trojans gave way before them. They could not withstand them long, and began to flee.

[7061–7080] Tarcon, a Trojan, saw them and spurred straight in that direction. He began to shout at them: "Where are you fleeing, wretched warriors? Return back to the field! Do you know who is chasing you? These are women! Now may he be shamed who out of fear of them flees in time of need! Do not run off, but stay back here. Fear them not. Let each man lay on!" He turned to Camille and addressed her very haughtily: "Lady," he said, "who are you, that you do battle against us here? I see you striking down our knights, but a woman should not do battle, except at night, lying down; there she can defeat any man. But a bold man with a shield will never be defeated by a woman.[122]

[7081–7106] "Let this arrogance be. Put down the shield and the lance and the hauberk, which cuts you too much, and stop exhibiting your prowess. That is not your calling, but rather to spin, to sew, and to clip. It is good to do battle with a maiden like you in a beautiful chamber, beneath a bed-curtain. Have you come here to show yourself off? I do not want to buy you. But nevertheless, I see that you are fair and

---

[122] Tarcon's long, unhandsome taunt does not appear in Vergil though his reproaches to the Etruscans are there (xi. 732–40). Nor does Vergil's Camilla kill Tarcon. Faral (*Recherches,* p. 117) shows that the figure of the love combat in bed is an Ovidian commonplace.

blond. I have here four Trojan deniers, all of very good fine gold; I will give you these to have my pleasure with you a little while. I will not be too jealous of it, but will share you with the squires. Indeed, I wish to offer you my deniers; if I lose a little by it I will not complain. You will have a double profit from it: the one in that you will have of my gold, the other in that you will be doing your pleasure; but that will not suffice you at all, unless there are a hundred of us; you may become tired, but you will not be satisfied."

[7107–7125] Camile was full of shame and very great anger at what she heard him say. She dug and spurred her good horse, letting it charge at Tarcon, and attacked him. She struck him with great strength below the boss of the shield. She shattered it from one side to the other, tore his hauberk, and stripped off its mail, throwing him dead from his charger. Then she said to him in reproach, "I do not come here to show myself off, or to indulge in debauchery, but to practice chivalry. I want none of your deniers: you have made a most foolish bargain. I know better how to strike down a knight than to embrace him or make love to him; I do not know how to do battle on my back."

[7126–7138] Then two knights charged at her, striking her from the side. She did not move or leave her saddle from the two lance blows. Tarpege, one of her damsels, spurred in that direction to her rescue. She struck one of them, withdrew her lance, drew her sword as she turned, and made his head fly. Camille in her turn struck the other knight: he paid very dearly for the blow he had given her. Both knights paid most dearly for their blows.

[7139–7160] A Trojan named Arranz did not fail to observe how Camille was fighting, how she jousted, how she struck, how she rode through the tourneying. He did not have so much faith in himself that he dared joust with her or face her alone, but he followed her from behind at each turn she made.

He was always ready, watching to find a place or opportunity where he might strike her by surprise, either close in, or by throwing from a distance. In whatever direction the maiden went, Arranz was always lying in wait, all prepared to strike her if he could find the opportunity for it. She did not know this or see him, and hence took no care to prevent him from lying in wait behind her or following her in such a manner.

[7161–7184] Cloreus, a Trojan of great valor and one of the priests of their religion, was in that tourney. There was not a single man of them there who was armed so richly, for he was entirely gilded. His armor and his blazon and his covering were all of gold, and he had a helmet so bright that none could gaze upon it as it glittered in the sunlight. Beneath the crest it had a stone of a good seven colors, set in fine gold carved with flowers. All the helmet's rims and its nose-guard were made of precious stones and enamel. Camille saw the Trojan's helmet, which was rich. She thought to herself that if she did not get it, she would value herself poorly. She spurred her horse, sought Cloreus out, struck him on the gilded shield, ripped his hauberk, and tore off its mail, and threw him dead on a hillock.

[7185–7212] She drew in her reins, got down from her good horse, went to where he lay on the ground, seized the helmet, and unlaced it. She was occupied with a great deal of nothing, but thus it goes with covetousness: men covet many things from which they will gain nothing but their deaths. She could well have left the helmet, and not let herself be drawn to it: her harm and her death lay there.[123] While she stood there over the dead man, Arranz was lurking on the other side, lying in wait for her, holding a dart. He threw it with great strength. It flew over the handle of her shield and struck her in the

---

[123] The *Eneas* poet develops his moralizing digression from a brief comment in *Aeneid* xi. 781–82: "caeca sequebatur totumque incauta per agmen/ femineo praedae et spoliorum ardebat amore. . . ."

heart near the left armpit, below the breast. She fell dead. The Trojans who saw this blow were very glad. Arranz was delighted with what he had done, but was afraid and ran in flight. One of the maidens who saw him spurred her horse to him and struck him, knocking him dead. Then she said to him, "This joy has lasted little; I have taken vengeance for my lady: you will never live to boast."[124]

[7213–7224] Camille lay on the earth, dead, and her followers were disconsolate. They abandoned the jousting and went quickly to the place where she lay. Her maidens suffered great sorrow. Her hands, which were so beautiful, were darkened in a short time, and her color all turned to perse, her tender flesh completely changed. They carried her into the city. Those within felt great sorrow. The tourneying was forgotten.

[7225–7239] Turnus was in his ambush when a messenger came to announce to him that the damsel was dead. When he heard the news of it he thought that he would surely go mad with sorrow. He would not linger any more, but came out of the ambush in the fir woods. Eneas had meanwhile gone through the forest by another route, and had come out onto the plain. The two saw each other well—the enemies rode close—but they did not wish to approach one another, to joust or to tourney, for it was well toward evening.

[7240–7256] Turnus went straight to Laurente and found the maiden dead. The king and the queen were weeping, and burghers, ladies, and servants; the lowly and the great all made lament. They all mourned the damsel, who was so brave and so beautiful, and they all said that her death was sad. It was a heavy misfortune to them: they had lost a very great ally, and their party was weakened. Turnus

[124] In *Aeneid* xi. 836–67, the death of Aruns is accomplished supernaturally by Opis, messenger of Diana.

swooned repeatedly, and said that he had no care to live longer, since the maiden had died for him. He took comfort in nothing that he heard or that men said to him: he had no regard for his life.

[7257–7280] Eneas was outside Laurente, and said that he would put all his efforts to the capture of the city, that he would by no means cease until he had finished the war. The great majority of the knights of the area, the peasants, the nobles, and the barons had come to his aid, for they feared much the power which Turnus would hold over them if he could gain the dominion. All the countryside allied itself with him and promised him very great aid. Evening began to fall, and the sun to set. Those in the city sent to Eneas and asked that he grant them a truce of seven days to bury their dead and to refresh themselves and their horses, for they were fatigued. They said that Eneas should in turn do likewise. Eneas granted them the truce without more ado.

[7281–7310] In front of Laurente there was a hill which had been formerly the site of a castle. The moat around it would be good if it were repaired a little, and some of the fortifications remained. Within the moat, the level ground extended a good four long shots of the arbalest. Sir Eneas stopped there, for the place was defensible. He called his Trojans and asked them to set up his tent so that it might be seen from Laurente. They worked that night in the moonlight and lined the whole moat with a tent which belonged to Eneas, made of different colors of cloth sewed in bands and blocks, with parapets and crenelations. It was all squares set in rows, in the manner that a wall is built. From a distance it seemed as if it were a castle, and it was marvelously beautiful: it was not at all made for strength, but for beauty and richness. It was supported all around by stakes, ropes, and poles. Their castle was raised very quickly. When they had finished the outside, they pitched their tents within, fifteen hundred of them of many kinds.

[7311–7330] In the center, Eneas spread his own tent, which he had captured from a Greek: he had killed him very near Troy, and taken his tent and his arms from him. The tent was of a hundred colors, decorated with beasts and with flowers, with tassling and rectangles, with stripes and checkering. It rose above all the others, and seemed like a fortress, for it was large. It had a golden eagle on its peak, which could be seen throughout the countryside. All night long the Trojans worked until they were completely ready, their tents pitched in rows, the ropes all tightened, and the camp well ordered, all around on the moated hill. Thus was their castle very quickly built; it was not strong, but it was most beautiful.[125]

[7331–7364] When the next day dawned, the Laurentians who were in the tower and on the wall at the battlements saw the camp and tents of the pavilion. Because of its size they thought it was a fortress. Everyone throughout the city heard how the Trojans had worked much and had built a castle during the night. Everyone who heard went running to the top of the wall to see. They all declared that it was truly stone and mortar and that the Trojans were very good workmen; they had built so much and worked so much in one short summer's night that four times as many other men could not have done it in three years: it was very mistaken to war

[125] From this point (the opening of Book xii) the action of the *Aeneid* moves rapidly to a conclusion in fewer than 1000 lines. The French poet has almost 3000 yet to write. He halts the narrative first for this description of the marvelous tent city of Eneas, which looks like a castle, then with the mourning of Turnus for Camille, with her funeral rites and the description of her marvelous tomb, and finally with the extended romance between Lavine and Eneas. Faral (*Recherches,* p. 89) suggests that the idea for Eneas' tent may have reached Western romance from the Arabs' custom of surrounding their grouped tents with a wall of fabric. Part of the description of the tent appears to derive from the description of the tent of Adrastus in *Thèbes,* vv. 2921–62. See Faral, *Recherches,* p. 98.

against them, and they would not be easy to conquer, for they were most accustomed to enduring hardship. The Trojans were showing no signs of fleeing, but those in the city were feeling great fear. They were all much frightened, and blamed the king—they could do no more about it—for not making peace with the Trojans. In the morning Turnus had it proclaimed that they would go to bury the dead. The Trojans likewise prepared their dead there. According to the custom of their country, they burned them and placed them in the ground.

[7365–7387] Turnus was in the city. He felt deeply hurt over Camille, who was dead, and he lamented sorely over her. "Alas," he said, "what an evil fate! My fortune is wholly overthrown! Never can any good come to me from continuing this war. Camille, you should not have suffered from it; it should have turned back on me, never on you, gentle maiden. You were so courteous and beautiful, and you so loved chivalry, that you have lost your life for it. There was never a woman of any lineage who did such heroic deeds or who so gave herself to chivalry. The man who killed you has hurt me grievously. By your death I have lost my joy and my pleasure. You came to serve me, and are now cut off from everything: you have been badly paid for your service.

[7388–7426] "Pallas—a knight of theirs whom I killed—is very dearly bought. Now they have repaid me well for him; they have paid me off in kind. Through you they have completely confounded me; through your death I have lost all my life. My party, which you sustained, is weakened, and I know not by whom I shall be saved. You were always ready at my need, whether it were near or far. Unhappy your valor! You were the flower of all women; never, I think, did nature join together two better qualities: such great prowess with such great beauty. If anyone would tell the truth about it, it would seem like a lie, so wholly different was your valor from your youth, your judgment from your heart. You were a courteous and gracious and beautiful damsel, and you were also brave and strong. The coward who killed you would never have dared even to look at you, if he had seen you coming toward him. He struck you by surprise, he did not come at you from the front. Alas, sorrowful wretch, in what an evil hour I left you! Where was I, since I was not with you? You should not have been thus killed; greater care should have been taken of you. You would not have died near me at all, for I would have protected you faithfully, as my dear friend. I do not know what more to say to you, but I am so sorrowful over your death that I never expect to take comfort."

[7427–7458] Turnus lamented bitterly and swooned very often, grieving over the damsel. Then he called Camille's followers. He had the maidens come and uncover their lady, who was all caked with blood. They washed her with rose water, cut her beautiful hair, and then embalmed her. There was plenty of balm and myrrh, and they prepared the body well. They shrouded the maiden in a cloth of the silk of Almeria, and then placed her on a very rich and costly bier. The bars and the two shafts were of the tooth of a fish, all inlaid with gold and decorated with precious stones. All the lacing beneath was of silken cords. The bed was filled with cotton padding, and on top was placed a carpet which covered the whole litter. On the bier was placed a covering, whose silk was worked finely with gold. The fabric was very costly—there was no finer silk. This covering was long and wide, embroidered with purple Caffan silk.

[7459–7478] A cushion of tricolored silk was at her head, raising it up, and on top of the cushion was a pillow. Its case was of a very expensive cloth, and was all stitched with decorations. Its feathers were from a sort of bird which lives in the highlands of those countries. The kings have them in their palaces. These birds are called *calade*. They have a nature such that a sick man can test by means of them whether he is about to die or to recover. When one of the birds is led in front of him, if the sick man is going to live on, the *calade* knows and sees it, and looks straight into his face. If he is going to die of that illness, it gives a deadly sign of it: it turns its head in the other direction, and does not look at the sick man at all.[126]

[7479–7494] Within this bier lay the maiden. Over her was a covering of sable, finely bordered, edged all around with imperial purple. Over the bier was a covering of green and red sendal for shade from the sun. After they had made everything ready, they harnessed four good mules to carry the bier gently. When they were ready, they went forth from the hall. Turnus accompanied the body, walking behind the bier weeping, lamenting, and making great sorrow.

[7495–7516] The king also accompanied the bier, and the knights and burghers, ladies, townswomen, and servants followed, showing great sorrow. Through every street which the bier entered people wept and cried out after it. There was very great sorrow in the city, and men were deeply stirred. When they had brought her outside the city they felt great sorrow at the parting. The king returned, weeping, but Turnus went a long distance farther, after all others had returned, a long league away from the city. At the parting he kissed a hundred times the outside of the bier where the body lay. He swooned thirty times.[127] Only with great difficulty did he return to the city. Those who

---

[126] This marvel of natural history is the *caladrius* of the *Physiologus,* and a commonplace of the bestiaries in the vulgar tongue. S. de Grave notes (*Eneas,* Cfmâ, II, 135) that the bestiaries usually describe how these birds, when they see that the sick man will live, help in his cure by drawing the illness to themselves.

[127] The *Eneas* author, like other romancers and epic poets of the period, enjoys fixing his hyperbole with specific numbers. The device appears throughout the romance. Cf. S. de Grave, in *Eneas,* Cfmâ, I, xxvi. Hoepffner (*Arch. romanicum,* XV, 265) notes that in this habit he was preceded by Wace.

were taking the corpse went on and devoted themselves wholly to traveling until they entered her country. They took a good fifteen days for the journey.

[7517–7530] When they arrived at her city, everyone renewed the mourning. When the news was heard, the townspeople were completely shaken by it. They ran out to meet her, weeping. Both the lowly and the great made sorrow; the whole people was disturbed. They brought their lady to the temple, where her knights and her burghers and her barons and her vassals guarded her for three months, until they had made ready the sepulchre where she would lie: in truth, there was none so beautiful in this world.

[7531–7560] There are a hundred marvels in this world, but among them all there is none greater or more unusual or better than this tomb. Near the temple was a level place which was enclosed by a circular wall. The area within was large and was paved with marble. There were four stones there, carved in the shape of lions, very artfully placed. Above them were set two arched vaults in the form of a cross, with a cornice above like a canopy, completely round. They were joined together exactly in the center, united very masterfully. Above, exactly over the juncture, was placed a handsome pillar of many-colored marble. The base which was set beneath it was six large fathoms in height. The pillar was completely carved with flowers, beasts, and birds, and the capital was carved likewise. High above on the cornice there was a part which widened out; it projected out beyond the pillar equally all around in a circle. It extended symmetrically twenty feet in every direction.[128]

---

[128] Camille's tomb is the *Eneas* poet's architectural triumph, an obvious delight to him and probably to his audience, whatever the modern reaction. It is the extreme example (except perhaps for Camille's horse) of the poet's delight in the exotic and bizarre. Faral (*Recherches,* pp. 81–82, 161–67) argues persuasively that the idea of a tomb mounted on a column, with successive stories expanding from base to top and surmounted by a magic mirror, is derived from the description of the temple of Diana

[7561–7589] On top of this flare was built a beautiful entablature. The wall was set there directly above in such a way that on the inside it was all solid: it had no window or glass. On the outside there were sixteen pillars, and arches were built all around. This upper wall was ten feet high and no more. On the outside it was all arcaded, and over it was a vaulted ivory covering. Above that was flooring with a very large overhang, which extended out all around more than did the first. The wall which was placed on top of that was well constructed, in a manner wholly different from the one beneath. It was twenty feet in height, and had thirty pillars set around it with arches of very fine workmanship. Another vault was likewise set on top of that, on the roofing. It projected all around to a greater extent than the first or the second. It was made symmetrically all round, of work of yet another type.

[7590–7614] On top was set the third wall, which was thirty feet in height, with pillars placed all around it. Atop the third wall was a ceiling, vaulted and round. Above, this entablature was adapted most artfully to the roofing over it. This was very sharply pitched, a hundred feet high and more. The roofing was of adamant, the slope made in many sorts of panels and squares, and at its peak was placed an eagle with three gilded balls around it. Over that was a mirror, in which they could see very well when someone was coming to attack them, whether by sea or by land. They would never be conquered in war; whoever was seated at the foot of the tower could see in the mirror their enemies coming toward them. Thus they could supply

---

at Ephesus in the *De septem miraculis mundi,* almost certainly with the help of the version given in the *Letter of Prester John,* which already combines the magic mirror and the temple. The temple was said to have been built by the Amazons, a detail which would naturally associate it with Camille. On the *Eneas* poet's description see Söhring, *Romanische Forschungen,* XII, 507.

themselves well and prepare themselves for defense; they would not be easy to surprise.

[7615–7637] It is useless to look for a greater wonder (for there was none in any land) than the two slender arches which supported such a great work, and the pillar set on top which in turn carried that building, which extended out so far; and on top of that, another which projected more than the first, and a larger one on top of that. The topmost one was surely three times as wide as the others beneath: as the work went higher it spread out more by projections. It seemed a great wonder to everyone that the building was larger above than below, and most people also considered the mirror a great marvel. Up in the last vault—above, in the highest one, which was painted in many colors, with golden borders all around them—there the tomb was placed.

[7638–7658] They clothed Camille in a gown with a fine tunic of Bagdad silk. On her head she had a crown of fine gold, and in her right hand she held the scepter. Her left hand was placed on her breast. In the center of the vault was set the tomb where Camille was placed. The whole casket was of electra. Beneath it were four golden images, which supported it at the four corners. Next to the body were placed vessels full of balm and other liquids to freshen her with their odors. The cover was placed on top, and cemented on very subtly. It was entirely of chalcedony, of jacinth and of sardonyx. The mortar with which the casket was sealed and put together was made of other precious stones, finely ground, soaked in the blood of a serpent.

[7659–7684] There was a golden plaque on the tomb, with letters of enamel, on which her epitaph was written. The lettering and the verse read:

HERE LIES
THE MAIDEN CAMILLE,

WHO WAS VERY BRAVE AND VERY BEAUTIFUL,
AND LOVED CHIVALRY GREATLY,
AND UPHELD IT HER WHOLE LIFE.
SHE GAVE HERSELF TO THE BEARING OF ARMS,
AND BY ARMS WAS KILLED BENEATH LAURENTE.

Over the tomb, directly in the center, hung a chain of gold swung from a pulley overhead, and descending with great art. At one end of the chain hung a lamp, full of a very rare oil so that it threw a very bright light. It will never fail in its fire, but will always burn, and last forever. This lamp was lit, and will always burn, everlasting, if it is not broken or struck. It was made of a garnet-red jacinth. There was not such a costly vessel of its size in all the world, nor one so beautiful.

[7685–7718] The other end of the chain, which held and supported the lamp, went across to a pillar. There a golden dove, fixed to the cornice of the pillar, held it in its beak, wholly at rest in the tomb. The lamp would never fall as long as the dove held it; and it would hold the chain forever if it were not for a single thing. There was an archer in another part of the room, sculptured with great care, and facing the dove on a block of dark marble. He held his bow stretched and looked straight toward the dove. The arrow was nocked and was so directed that it would strike the dove immediately, as soon as it left the bowstring. The archer could look long, and forever stretch the bow, but he would not shoot the arrow unless the noose of a snare were first moved. The snare was set above the archer and held the bow always bent. At a breath all would be lost: if someone blew the snare it would loose the bow immediately, and the archer thus would shoot straight at the dove and hit it. Then the chain would be broken and the lamp wholly destroyed.[129]

[129] William of Malmesbury, *De gestis regum Anglorum,* II, 169, details the tradition from which this fantastic guardian statue of the archer is imitated. About the year 1000 Gerbert, who was then Pope, discovered a huge buried treasure of gold in Rome, a room full of golden utensils and golden statues, one of which was a boy with

[7719–7724] When Camille had been entombed, the door-way was blocked up, and all the passageways by which Camille had been brought there were taken down from the heights. They departed from the tomb.

[7725–7752] While this was being done, King Latinus wished to send a plea to the Trojans to make peace with him. Turnus knew it, and came to the king. There was a great assembly at the court. Turnus spoke his thoughts to the king, and expressed his desires completely to all the others as well.[130] "My lords," he said, "I know and see well that you do not all hold with me. Most of you are deceiving me; but never from this day forward will I ask that any of you aid me. Indeed, I offer to give the battle which was debated the other day. It is agreed on my part that I will do battle against Eneas. Let the day be set; if I violate the agreement by being unprepared and failing to give battle, then I will have lost everything, and you will hold me forever as defeated. Never after will I raise difficulties about it. I will give up my claim to the things I most love, the rule and the land of Italy, as well as Lavine. If I default without a challenge, I hereby surrender entirely the inheritance and the possession of it.

[7753–7784] "Eneas has attacked me strongly, with great wrong, and I will offer him the chance of two outcomes: either I will kill him or he me; let each one of us defend his cause; I do not wish one person more to die for it. Through one of

---

a bow bent and arrow nocked. The room was brilliantly lighted by a carbuncle. When anyone attempted to touch the gold, the statues appeared to jump forward to prevent the theft. Finally, Gerbert's servant attempted to snatch a knife from a table; but, William's narrative continues: "Verum mox omnibus imaginibus cum fremitu exsurgentibus, puer quoque, emissa arundine in carbunculum, tenebras induxit; et, nisi ille monitu domini cultellum rejicere accelerasset, graves ambo poenas dedissent." The passage is quoted by Faral (*Recherches,* pp. 84-85). The tradition recorded in it was perhaps inspired by the Byzantine automata.

[130] Here the *Eneas* poet returns for the moment to the Vergilian narrative. The speech of Turnus which follows, with its slightly mournful and elegiac tone, contrasts instructively with its short, angry counterpart in *Aeneid* xii. 10–17.

us there will be peace, whichever of us—both, if needs be— must die for it. Now it will be seen who is stronger, or who is right and who is wrong. If I should die over it, I will not then be disturbed if he possesses what I cannot have, and if I come out of it alive, I will then be your friend as you deserve it from me. And you, sire," he said to the king, "set a date for the battle. Do not think that I will default on it. Send certain word of it to the scoundrel who would do battle for this domain, that I will defend it against him; I do not care to wait longer. It can be brought to an end yet tonight, or in the morning. The truce ended last evening, and he has drawn near to besiege us; but I will end the war. If I can win there in my own person, there will be no man in the Trojan band who will not lament it. I will treat them badly enough then; they have claimed Italy from us wrongly."

[7785–7812] The king heard what Turnus said, offering battle, but he did not wish him to do it. In the hearing of all his barons he spoke to him. "Friend," he said, "hear me. I made an agreement with you about my daughter—whom I granted to you—and about my land—of which I made you heir—well over seven years ago. But I cannot be your guarantor against the gods, who grant all things: they have given all to Eneas. We will never conclude this war successfully against him. All our diviners say this, that the gods have brought him here and made him heir to Italy. Since the gods will that he have it, you are about to undertake a very foolish cause when you wish to do combat with him. You will miscarry in it, I believe. I feel very great pity for you; let this battle be, and believe me; you can choose enough other women at your pleasure. Let him have this one in peace. Take half of my possessions, and let this turmoil be. I feel very great pity for you."

[7813–7828] Turnus answered, "Now I am hearing childishness. You are not troubled about me. It means nothing at all to you whether things go well or badly for me. I do not ask that you have any care over it. You are failing me completely in justice: you wish to take away my wife, and you ask that I choose another, and renounce my troth. But I would thus be a thorough coward. Let it be known to Eneas that if he wishes to have battle, he will find me all ready tomorrow. Whoever may die from it, there is an end to it; let him who defeats the other have all. Send word to him by whomever you please."

[7829–7841] The king heard that Turnus wished to do battle without fail, that he wished the date to be set soon, and that he did not seek to delay long. It grieved him greatly that Turnus wished to do it. When he saw that he could not dissuade him, he made ready his messengers and sent them to the Trojan, to inform him that the battle between the two would take place on the eighth day, on an island beneath the tower. Turnus will do battle with him all alone, and whoever wins will have everything forever.

[7842–7856] The messengers departed in the morning, went to Eneas, and found him outside his tent. They told him that Turnus wished this: through their two persons—and there should be no more—let this war be brought to an end: "You will find him ready for battle on the eighth day in the morning." And Eneas said that without fail he would do battle with him on that day, and whoever won would have the domain. The date of the battle was set and agreed to on both sides. Meanwhile they swore a truce and a firm peace for eight days.[131]

[7857-7887] The queen was in her chambers. On that day she held a conversation with Lavine.[132] "Daughter," she said,

---

[131] There are some marked similarities between this agreed single combat and that between King Arthur and King Frolle of France, beneath the walls of Paris on an island in the Seine, in Wace's *Brut. Eneas,* vv. 7837–41 is especially similar to *Brut,* vv. 10259–64, and *Eneas,* vv. 7853–56 to *Brut,* vv. 10270–75. See Hoepffner, *Arch. romanicum,* XV, 266–67.

[132] The romancer has arrived at the *pièce de résistance* of his adaptation, the most

"I know and see well that this evil, which has brought the country to destruction and for which so many men have been killed, has come because of you. Turnus, who loves you, wishes to have you, and Eneas disputes you with him and wishes to conquer you by force; but he does this more for the land than for love of you. He will never love you at all, and you can know that love of you will never in any way be important to him. You should not love him at all, but should turn your heart away from him and desire that Turnus have you. For love of you, Turnus has left his own land, for you alone, whom he wishes to have. You should be very grateful to him for it. Do you not love him in your heart? In faith, you are of such an age that you should know well about love and its ambushes and its skills and tricks and glances. You should draw gladly toward him who loves you deeply; but him who claims you by force you should hate with all your heart, for he wishes to take your lord away from you. Turnus is noble, and you should love him."[133]

---

important of his own contributions, and one which was to revolutionize courtly narrative. The romance of Eneas and Lavine—especially the love of Lavine—dominates the remainder of the narrative, far overshadowing the final battle between Eneas and Turnus, and occupying some 1600 lines of the romance. It was a bold step for the French poet, who elsewhere cleaves with reasonable fidelity to the main outlines of Vergil's narrative, and we may speculate that it came to him as a late inspiration, for he has done nothing to prepare his readers for it. Though the hand of Lavine has become an important prize in the Eneas–Turnus conflict, we never meet her before this crucial conversation in the queen's chambers. Vergil allowed his readers only two glimpses of Lavinia in the *Aeneid*, the first as she silently accompanies Amata to the temple to pray Athene for aid in resisting the Trojan assault (xi. 479–80), the second as she weeps and blushes in maidenly fashion, while Amata pleads with Turnus to avoid single combat with Aeneas (xii. 64–70). Vergil describes her merely as "virgo,/ causa mali tanti," and the French poet uses this hint to open the conversation between mother and daughter. Cf. A. Adler, *Romanische Forschungen,* LXXI, 73–91, who offers an interpretation of the contribution of the Eneas–Lavine love affair to the *sen* of the romance, in its relation to other episodes.

[133] From this point in the narrative Ovid has thoroughly defeated Vergil in the inspiration of the romancer. What follows is a tissue of echoes, imitations, and

[7888–7901] "I hardly know how to make my way in this."

"But you will learn."

"Tell me, what is love? I don't know what it is."

"I can't describe it to you at all."

"How will I know about it then, if I don't hear it talked about."

"Your heart will teach you to love."

"If I hear no other talk of it?"

"You will never learn it by words."

"Then I think I will always be ignorant of it."

"Yet you will be able to learn it quickly."

"How, if I am not directed?"

"Begin to love; then you will know enough about it."

"And I should begin, when I find no one who will tell me what love is?"

[7902–7916] "I will tell you what I know of its sorrows and its nature. I remember well when I used to love. One who has not loved or felt love can hardly speak of it at all. If you had an illness, you would know best the truth about the anguish which you felt and the pains which you had from it. If someone then wished to ask you about them, would you not know better how to explain them and would you not be more sure of them than I, who were completely healthy?"

"Yes, I would speak much better; but is love then an infirmity?"

[7917–7942] "No, but it is not far short of that: it is as good

---

translations from Ovid's major works: *Metamorphoses, Heroides, Amores, Ars amatoria,* and *Remedia amoris.* "Une fois conçue l'idée de l'épisode," remarks Faral (*Recherches,* p. 126), "il a traité son sujet en suivant Ovide pas à pas." The constituents of the love narrative as they are assembled by the *Eneas* poet—the stichomythic conversations on love with mother or confidante, the imagery of Cupid or Amor, the long detailing of physical symptoms, the lover's probing of his own psyche, the stichomythic internal arguments between Heart and Head or Ideal and Real, the extensive use of oxymoron on love—all these were apparently enormously successful and popular with the poet's audience, and quickly became the staples of romance.

as a quartan fever. Love is worse than an acute fever; there is no cure for it but to sweat. From love one must perspire and in turn suffer chills, shake, tremble and sigh and gape, lose all desire for food and drink, toss and quake, change color and grow pale,[134] moan, lament, blanch, brood and sob, lie awake, weep. Whoever loves well and feels it deeply must do all these things often. Such is love and its nature. If you wish to concern yourself with it, you must often endure what you have heard me tell you, and much more."

"I will have nothing to do with it."

"Why?"

"I can't turn my heart to it."

"But this evil is good; don't avoid it."

"I have never heard tell of a good evil."[135]

"Love is not of the same sort as other evils."

"I have no interest in it."

"And surely it is such a sweet thing."

"I have no care for it."

[7942–7956] "Rest assured, you will love yet—this I believe—and you will not do it at all on my account. You will never be able to deceive me about it. If I can know or see that you are able to move your heart to love the traitor from Troy, you must die at my two hands; that I could never suffer. Turnus loves you and wishes to take you; you should give yourself over to love for him. Love him, daughter."

[134] Cf. Ovid *Ars amat.* i. 729. For the Ovidian parallels these notes are heavily indebted to Faral, *Recherches,* esp. pp. 125–54. Faral (p. 17) notes the parallel between the physical symptoms of love here listed in *Eneas* (vv. 7921–27) and those described in the Old French *Piramus et Tisbé,* vv. 218–20, 369–71, 439–42.

[135] This oxymoron and those which follow (e.g., vv. 7957–74) are characteristic of the genre, are found as early as Ovid (e.g., *Fasti* i. 11; *Rem. amoris* v. 138) and lived on through the love poetry of the Renaissance. For the popularity of the antithesis of love as a delightful illness, see P. Meyer,"Mélanges de poésie anglo-normande,IX," *Romania,* IX (1875), 382–84.

"I don't know how."

"I have explained it to you."

"And I am frightened."

"Of what?"

"Of the evil, the sorrow which always comes in abundance with love."

[7957–7974] "And yet this is all sweetness. He who is accustomed to an illness bears it easily. If there is a little evil in love, the good follows after it in equal measure. Laughter and joy come from weeping; great delights come from swooning; kissing comes from yawning; embracing from lying awake; great pleasure comes from sighing; fresh color comes after growing pale. There follows a great sweetness in your body which quickly cures the ills of love. Without any potion of herbs or roots, Love makes his medicine for each ill. No ointment or balm is necessary: he heals the wound which he makes. If he would wound you a little, he knows well how to heal you later.

[7975–8001] "Look in the temple, how Love is painted there alone, holding two darts in his right hand and a box in his left; one of the darts is tipped with gold, which causes love, and the other with lead, which makes love alter.[136] Love wounds and pierces often, and is thus painted figuratively to show clearly his nature. The dart shows that he can wound, and the box that he knows how to heal. With him it is not necessary that a doctor come to treat the wound which he heals. He controls death and health; he cures after he has wounded. One should indeed be willing to suffer much from Love, who wounds and heals in a single day. Indeed, you should be one of his following. If you are approached by him, you will love his service

[136] The image of Love with his two arrows is found in Ovid *Metam.* i. 468–71, but, as Faral remarks (*Recherches*, p. 144), its popularity, at least until it found its way into the *Roman de la rose* (vv. 907–85), seems largely due to the influence of *Eneas*. H. Laurie ("*Eneas* and the Doctrine of Courtly Love," *MLR*, LXIV [1969], 284) finds the groundwork for the image in Propertius ii. 12. 1–12.

very much; in a little while he will have taught you what you do not wish to do for my sake. If you lament and sorrow from it, yet it will please you well. Do you understand it at all yet?"

[8002–8024] "Since I haven't heard about it, I don't know how."

"Did I not tell you the nature of love?"

"It seems to me very fierce and bitter."

"But after that comes great sweetness; one feels more of that than of pain. Love heals when he has wounded."

"Rather love seems very dearly bought."

"With what?"

"With suffering evil."

"One must pay dearly for the good before one has it."

"He is a fool who knowingly does what he expects to cause him so much ill; know indeed that I do not seek Love's acquaintance. Now I am in peace and repose: I will not place myself—I do not dare—in such straits. I have no care for it. Its evil is immeasurably great. I will not now become involved in love, from which I expect to have ill and pain." The maiden was very stubborn. With that the queen left her. She did not wish to force her any further, since she saw that it was of no avail.

[8025–8046] There was a good truce and security between those of the city and those outside, of the other party. None of them feared that the others might seize or attack him before the day of the battle. Eneas left his tent and went to look at Laurente, all unarmed, with a large company. He was on horseback on a plain down below the tower. Most of the townspeople were climbing up to the battlements of the wall to gaze at the Trojans. They all agreed in saying that there was not a more handsome people under the heavens. The Trojans were all well dressed and equipped, but Eneas, their lord, surpassed them all in beauty. Everyone who saw him praised him highly. They said that he was very noble and handsome, and gave him great praise along the battlements.

[8047–8072] Lavine was up in the tower. She looked down from a window and saw Eneas, who was below. She gazed intently at him above all. He seemed most handsome and noble to her. She had heard well how everyone praised him throughout the city both for his prowess and his beauty, and she took good note in her heart. There where she was standing in her chamber, Love struck her with his dart. Before she moved from the window she changed color a hundred times. Now she has fallen into the snare of love: whether she wishes it or not, she must love.[137] When she saw that she could not escape it, she turned all her desire and her thought toward Eneas: for his sake Love had wounded her severely. The arrow had struck her as deep as the heart beneath her breast. The damsel was all alone. She went to close the door of her chamber, then returned to stand at the window where she had received the mortal blow. From there she gazed on the knight.

[8073–8100] She began to perspire, then to shiver and to tremble. Often she swooned and quaked. She sobbed and quivered; her heart failed; she heaved and gasped and gaped: Love had indeed placed her in his service! She cried and wept and sighed and moaned. She did not yet know who was doing this to her, who was so agitating her heart. When she recovered and could speak, she said, "Alas, what is the matter with me? Who has taken me by surprise? What is this? Before now I was entirely healthy; now I am all pale and weak. I feel a burning within my body, but I do not know for whom I am

[137] Cf. Ovid (*Ars amat.* i. 263–70). Lavine's first view of Eneas and her falling in love seem obviously patterned on the beginnings of Scylla's love for Minos in Ovid (*Metam.* viii. 32–54). In connection with this scene, Auerbach (*Literatursprache und Publikum,* pp. 157–62) offers valuable comments on the manner in which the *Eneas* poet transformed the spirit of Ovid in adopting his love casuistry, working material from the courtesan books into themes on the epic level.

so inflamed, who is moving my heart, why I am so distraught, from what I am feeling these mortal pangs—unless this is that evil wretch of whom my mother told me yesterday, about whom she wished to teach me. I know Love only as a name, but he is doing me nothing but utter evil. I think—as far as I can tell—that I love. Henceforth, I will come indeed at his call. I feel the evils and the pain of Love, of which my mother told me.[138]

[8101–8126] "Where then is the alleviation, the box with all Love's ointment? The queen told me yesterday that Love carries his own medicine and that he quickly heals his wound. I do not think that I am getting any help from him. Since he is withholding his medicine from me, I do not know, alas, who might help me. I think that his box is lost, or the drug used up. I know well by what I feel that he has wounded me sorely. If he does not in turn cure the wound quickly, then his help is bad. Alas, how unhappily I have changed! I avoided him, but he has indeed taken his vengeance: he has thrown my heart into great turmoil. I must become one of his following. He seized me here at the window from which I was gazing at the Trojan; I had no thought of loving at that time. Now I am tormented for him; now I pant and now I quake. In a little space of time I have both chills and fever.[139]

[8127–8148] "I must love the Trojan, but it is most important that I hide it, so that the queen, who restrains and threatens me, does not know it; she does not want me to feel love for him. Alas, what can I do about it but weep? Now I love him; but only today he meant little to me."

"Foolish Lavine, what have you said?"

"Love for him torments me very much."

[138] For a discussion of these symptoms see Faral, *Recherches*, pp. 133–35.
[139] Faral (*Recherches*, p. 17) notes the close parallel, both in content and antithetical structure, between these lines (vv. 8124–26) and *Piramus et Tisbé*, vv. 202–3.

"But you will escape it if you flee."

"I cannot find it in my heart to flee."

"You were not so wild yesterday."

"But now Love has completely overcome me."

"You have protected yourself very poorly."

"He meant very little to me this morning; now he is bringing me to a bad end. I cannot live long like this."

"Why did you stop here?"

"To look at the Trojan."

"You could well have refrained from that."

"Why?"

"It was in no way wise that you came here to look at him."

[8149–8172] "I have looked at many of them from here and it never meant anything to me. One doesn't love everyone one sees. I would be in very bad straits indeed if I could not look at a man without having to love him: I may either love him immensely or think very little of him. Have I forfeited my life for this? Will Love have no mercy on me? He has wounded me with a glance. He has struck me in the eye with his dart, with the gold one which causes love: he has struck me to the heart. But I think that I alone was wounded, and in this Love has dealt with me wrongly. The Trojan does not feel love at all; my life is hardly anything to him; he does not deign to look in this direction. Love has pierced him, I think, with the dart of lead which makes one hate; thus I must die of sorrow. Alas, how can I love if I do not find my partner in love?

[8173–8194] "It seems to me that I am mad, if I wish to love him and he does not love me: it takes two to make a pair, and each should be submissive to the other, and do his will. Now I know enough about love; my mother spoke the truth indeed; I could not learn about love from anyone else as well as I could from myself. I am very learned in it; I see it well. Love has sent me to school, and in a little while has taught me much.[140] Master Love, I know my lesson very well: until now you have read me nothing but the bad; you should in turn read me the good. Now you have wounded me; now be the physician. Love, now heal my wound. Your help is very feeble. I don't know how to pray to you so fairly that you will be willing to help me at all. You have thrown me into great confusion, and I must complain against you.

[8195–8217] "To whom will I make my complaint? Who can do me justice in love? Under whom does Love serve? Under what law? I cannot conceive the extent of his lordship.[141] There is no lord anywhere over him, and he holds his fief very lightly, mistreating whomever he wishes. He will do nothing, either right or wrong, for others. Love, you have brought me low; Love, lighten this illness! Love, you are showing me too much haughtiness in this new affair. Love, you have put the madness into my body: relieve it only a little, so that I can be reassured. Then I will be better able to endure the ill. I am only a foolish maiden, and you have me newly in your school, but I have learned in less than a day all the ills, the pain, and the sorrow. Bitterly I complain, grievously I lament. Love, turn over your page, make me look in another place!

[8218–8232] "Henceforth I should taste the good and the sweetness. You have placed in me a bitterness worse than soot or gall. Love, now give me some honey, and soften my sorrow by some pleasant taste! I know well the ill which you can do, but I have hardly felt your good: you have shown me none yet. What have you done with the ointment which you once used to carry to cure your painful sorrows? Love, you have troubled my heart: relieve it, if only a little.

[140] On the image of Love as a schoolmaster, repeated twice again in *Eneas* (vv. 8213, 8431), see Faral, *Recherches,* p. 146.
[141] This appears to be the true meaning of v. 8198, "Ge ne sai pas sa manantise." The characteristic feudal image of the lordship of Love should be noted.

[8233–8256] "It seems to me that I am all changed and pale and discolored. My mother knows much of such things, and she will perceive clearly from my face and my color that I have been wholly overtaken by love. If she asks what is wrong with me, and if I love, what shall I say to her? How can I hide it from her? She will see me change color, quiver, tremble, and swoon and sigh, moan, grow pale. If I conceal it from her, she will know it well from these appearances which she will see. I do not want to lie by denying that I love; I will not hide that from her at all. But if she then asks me whom, how shall I name to her him whom she has so forbidden to me, so that she will know the truth of it? She will kill me, but what does that matter to me? Will any other medicine help me? I do not expect to have any other relief from this anguish but death.

[8257–8278] "I have begun this very foolishly, and should have acted otherwise: I should not have given my love wholly to Eneas, but should have let Turnus share in it equally. Neither of them should have come first, nor should I have loved one of them more than the other. I should have put on a fair appearance to each and acted so that however it might come out—whichever of the two won me in battle—I could not feel unhappy because I had not loved him more."

"I do not know what would happen if I divided my love, so that each would have it equally."

"That would have hurt me not at all. I should have been drawn to both of them. Then I could have done well, if I had loved them both thus. I would not have lacked a lover: whichever of them were killed or defeated, I would yet have one of them as my beloved."[142]

[8279–8307] "Foolish Lavine, what have you said? Now surely you know little of love. Can one then thus divide one's love? Now admit that you are a fickle one! He who loves truly

---

[142] Though the figure of a second lover plays an important part in Ovid (*Rem. amoris* vv. 441–88), the *Eneas* poet develops the idea in a wholly different manner.

cannot deceive; he is loyal and cannot change. True love flows all alone from one individual to another, singly; as soon as one wishes to attract a third, then love has nothing at all to do with it. Let him who wishes to love firmly and well have his companion and partner. I know nothing of a third after that; that seems more like merchandizing. One can laugh indeed at the thought of having many loves; but those loves are not true either, with which one pleases even two or three. He who would love more than one does not satisfy Love's precepts or laws: Love does not wish to be thus divided.

"In faith, I do not love thus. It is Eneas I regard as my *ami*. I love him. I will never act so as to divide my love. I do not wish to deceive him in love: there will be no one to share it with him. Whatever may happen to me, I will never seek to divide my love. I am not yet a lover of variety.

[8308–8334] "Yesterday love was very strange to me, but now I know much of its nature. I will devote my attention and my care to it. Now it suits me well, and I wish it; presently it will be grievous, and I will sorrow from it; but now my heart is feeling, now I wish to love, now I would like to speak of it much.[143] If now I should find someone who would listen to me, and who would hold my words in confidence, I would know how to speak many good things about it. If now it makes me cross or angry, in a short time it will again be good to me. My eyes have never spilled tears over it for which I will not be wholly recompensed. I will have joy and laughter and pleasure from it; I will have no mortal sorrow which will not later be repaid by goodness and sweetness. It will please me much when all is done. But alas, I do not know when this will be. They have settled on a battle, and whoever wins is supposed to have me without challenge. But I think I know one thing

[143] The antithesis followed by anaphora, glorifying love, is a common device of the *Eneas* poet, and later romancers under his influence, to introduce something approaching lyric feeling into their love passages.

very well: if Turnus wins he will never have me. I wish to lose my life if Eneas is killed there, rather than take Turnus for my lover."

[8335–8352] The damsel was thus occupied in debating about her new love until Eneas turned away. He departed without speaking to her. Then she thought she would die of sorrow, and gave a very profound sigh; she fell back in a swoon. When she had revived, she said, "Alas, sorrowful girl, what is he doing? Is he going away? In faith, yes, and he did not speak to me; he took no care for that. I do not think that he will come back."

"Wretched fool, what does it matter to you?"

"It matters much, since he has killed me."

"How?"

"He is carrying off my heart; he has stolen it from my breast."

"Then you have guarded it very foolishly."

[8353–8380] "My heart is going away with him. He has taken it out from within my breast. Beloved, will you never return? Your friend means very little to you. Can I not have a gentle look or a sweet glance from your direction? My life is all in your hands. But how can it matter to you, since you are not certain that I love you with a true heart? I will not trust a messenger, by whom I might make you know that you can have my love. Nevertheless, I would find a way to tell you, but I fear that you would hold me to blame for it if I sent you my love first, and since you would have me without resistance (for that would be less than a little), you would say that I might later make elsewhere such an advance as I had made toward you, and that I was fickle in love. Do not think this at all, my love: I shall be your love forever. I will never change my love for you. Be secure; if I have you, I will never love any man but you. Never be jealous of me."

[8381–8398] The maiden stood at the window. She could not

express all her condition, nor what she felt toward her beloved. When she saw that he was thus going away, she
followed him with her eyes as far as she could, gazing
motionless after him until she could see him no more. All
day until evening she stood there and gazed at the place
where he had departed: the road seemed very beautiful to
her. The damsel was so occupied with gazing and lamenting and weeping and suffering that she would not move
from there until she could see no longer. At last she left
regretfully. She was very sorrowful and sad and dejected.

[8399–8424] She went to bed to no purpose at all, for all
night she had to lie awake and quake and tremble, uncover
herself and then cover herself again.[144] She turned on her
side in the bed, and then face down, then on her back; and
then she laid her head at the foot of the bed. The night
offered little for her pleasure. She tore her hair and beat
her breast; the maiden was suffering great pain. She felt
pain enough sleeping; it was not a bit better waking. When
she closed her eyes—which were always damp—then it
seemed that he was holding her. From the joy of it she
turned over in excitment and embraced her blanket; but
when she realized that he was not there, she swooned.
Within her was a fire which burned her. She turned on her
other side, got up, then sat down, and then went straight
to bed and called the Trojan very softly, so that no one
would hear it.

[8425–8444] She said prettily between her teeth, "Love is
treating me harshly; I feel bad in the day and worse at
night. Love takes hardly any care about killing a tender
maiden who cannot defend herself against him. Love, you

---

[144] Cf. Ovid (Amores ii. 1-2). A number of echoes of this elegy appears in vv.
8399-8441. Faral (Recherches, p. 18) notes the close parallel between the dream
illusions described below (vv. 8409-18) and those described in Piramus et Tisbé, vv.
547-61.

have taught me a great lesson: every line of it was of ill. Now heal me with your medicine."

"Rest, foolish Lavine; you must learn this lesson very thoroughly."

"I can remember it only too well."

"Pay close attention to it, and retain it."

"I know all of the bad, but little of the good. Love cares nothing for threats; he leads me at too great a pace. I must tire of the great burden with which he loads me, unless I drop it. I am much afraid to undertake the burden and the chase."

[8445–8469] The maiden suffered much ill that night. On the next day, when the queen saw her thus discolored, her face and her color changed, she asked after her health, and Lavine said that she had a fever. The queen knew well that she was lying, that it was otherwise than she said. She saw her first tremble, and then immediately sweat and sigh and groan, blush, darken, change color. She knew well that Love had seized her and had her in his power. She asked her if she was in love. Lavine said that she did not know what love was, nor what it could do. The queen hardly believed it when she told her that she did not love, and said, "I know well this lament and these sighs which are so long: they come from love, from very deep within. Plaints and sighs which come from love are very long, and are drawn from close by the heart. Daughter, I believe that you love."

[8470–8488] "I have never concerned myself with love."[145]

"You are feeling distressed from it."

"I don't know what it is, and I don't care about it."

"Whether you wish it or not, your face is pale and discolored. Daughter, you love, I see it well. You are hiding it from me, I know not why. If you wish to love, it is very well with me; you should not at all hide it from me. Turnus loves you,

---

[145] Cf. Ovid (*Heroides* xi. 34). Other echoes of this epistle are scattered through vv. 8470–8535.

and has for long; I think it only good sense if you love him: you should love with a true love him who loves you honorably. I am not at all displeased with you; indeed, I have instructed you thoroughly and set you well on your way in it. It pleases me now to see you captured. Now take care that he knows that you love him."

[8488–8513] "May it not please God that he have my love! He will not have it."

"Why, don't you love him?"

"No."

"But I see it well myself."

"*You* love him well."

"But *you* love him."

"He is nothing to me."

"He is surely handsome and brave and noble."

"He touches me little in my heart."

"Your love is very safe with him."

"I will never love him."

"Then with whom have you fallen in love?"

"You have forgotten too quickly the first question, which is to know whether I have a beloved or not."

"I know it well; I have proven it."

"You know more about it than I know."

"You don't know? Surely you are feeling its pains."

"Then does one always become ill from love?"

"Yes, ill enough; but nevertheless it can be seen with certainty that you are pale and weak, that you are dying and are yet healthy, that you love indeed; you have no other illness. It is not at all a mortal illness: one has pains and sorrows from it, but one lives long on love. I know well that you are afire with love."

[8514–8536] "You have yet to prove it to me."

"I need no other proof; I see it very openly."

"Do you say this because of my pains? Does one have such anguish from love?"

"Yes, and many pangs yet stronger."

"I do not know what you are telling me, but I do feel great sickness and great sorrow."

"Have you a desire for no man?"

"Not I—except for one. For the others I have no care, but it pains me much that that one is so far from me."

"How does it seem to you? What would you wish?"

"That we would be together always. It does me great harm that I do not see him and that he does not talk with me; when I do not see him, then I feel pain from it."

"In faith, you love him *par amour*."

"What, is this the way one loves?"

"Yes."

"Then I know in good certainty that I love indeed, but I did not know this morning what was the matter with me. Mother, I love; I cannot deny it. You should advise me well."

[8537–8564] "I will, if you will believe me; but since now your heart is so distraught, you should surely tell me for whom."

"I do not dare, mother, for I think that you will be very angry with me for it. You have dispraised him to me much, and often warned me against him; hence I have been the more drawn to him: love has no care about warnings. If I were to name my beloved to you, I fear that it would trouble you."

"I do not think that anyone who has truly loved wishes to punish any lover."

"I love, I cannot deny it longer."

"Then is Turnus not the name of your love?"

"No, mother, I promise you that."

"And who then?"

"He is named E——." Then she sighed, and added, "ne——," then after a while, "as——." She spoke it softly, all trembling. The queen thought and assembled the syllables.[146]

"You tell me E, then ne, and as; these letters spell Eneas!"

"True, mother; in faith, it is he."

"And you will not have Turnus?"

"No, I will never have him as my lord, but I grant my love to the other."

[8565–8595] "What have you said, foolish madwoman? Do you know to whom you have given yourself? This wretch is of the sort who have hardly any interest in women. He prefers the opposite trade: he will not eat hens, but he loves very much the flesh of a cock. He would prefer to embrace a boy rather than you or any other woman.[147] He does not know how to play with women, and would not parley at the wicket-gate; but he loves very much the breech of a young man. The Trojans are raised on this. You have chosen very poorly. Have you not heard how he mistreated Dido? Never did a woman have any good from him, nor do I think you will have, from a traitor and a sodomite. He will always be ready to abandon you. If he finds any sweet boy, it will seem fair and good to him that you let him pursue his love. And if he can attract the boy

[146] Faral (Recherches, pp. 28–29) believes that Lavine's difficulty in naming Eneas is inspired by the episode of Myrrha and Byblis in Ovid (Metam. ix. 569–70; x. 419–30). Whatever its source, the episode was influential, and even in the fourteenth century Chaucer's Troilus has difficulty in confessing to Pandarus the name of Criseyde (Troilus and Criseyde, i, 871–75).

[147] On the popularity of the sodomy theme among twelfth-century writers, see Faral, Recherches, pp. 131–32, and the references there cited. For an example of a nearly contemporary attack on the vice, see Alanus de Insulis, De planctu naturae, esp. Prosa V. This work is conveniently translated by D. M. Moffat in Yale Studies in English, XXXVI (New York, 1908). Faral believes that the idea of Trojan homosexuality in particular was derived from the Phrygian Ganymede, mentioned in Ovid (Metam. x. 155–60; xi. 754–56).

by means of you, he will not find it too outrageous to
make an exchange, so that the boy will have his pleasure
from you, while in turn sufficing for him. He will gladly let
the boy mount you, if he in turn can ride him: he does not love
coney fur.

[8596–8621] "It would quickly be the end of this life if all
men were thus throughout the world. Never would a woman
conceive; there would be a great dearth of people; no one
would ever bear children, and the world would fail before a
hundred years. Daughter, you have completely lost your senses, since you have taken as your love such a man, who will
never have a care for you, and who acts so against nature that
he takes men and leaves women, undoing the natural union.
Take care that you never speak to me of him again. I wish you
to give up the love of this sodomite wretch. Turn your heart
in another direction: love him who will love you, and who has
loved you for seven years, who has given you all his devotion.
Take care that he does not repent it. If you wish to enjoy my
love, then let this traitor be. Turn your love toward him of
whom I spoke, and leave this other one, who would be a
stranger to you."

[8622–8662] "I cannot make this change."

"You would not love him whom I wish?"

"I cannot persuade myself to it in my heart."

"Has he wronged you?"

"Me? Not at all."

"Then love him and cleave to him."

"I have chosen another; I cannot do it."

"And you cannot withdraw yourself from love?"

"No; in faith, it is no joke.[148] Is it not Cupid, the brother
of Eneas and the god of love, who has conquered me? He has

---

[148] The pages which follow are full of Ovidian echoes and borrowings. For specific
references see Faral, *Recherches,* pp. 130–31, 140–43, 148–49. Faral (p. 16) finds a
close parallel to the lines on the power of Love's arrows (vv. 8633–40) in *Piramus et
Tisbé,* vv. 27–30.

inflamed me much for his brother. What defense have I against Love? Neither castle nor tower avails at all against him, nor high wall, nor deep moat. There is no stronghold under the heavens that can hold against him or endure boldly his assault. He would shoot his dart through seven walls and wound on the other side: one cannot protect oneself from him. He has made me love the Trojan, and has put me in great distress for him. Do you think, then, it is pleasant to me, and that I love with my own consent? It is against my will. Love holds me in his power, and I do not know how to resist doing what he wishes me to do, despite my distress or your threat. I always hear it said that he who kicks against the goad pricks himself twice. I dare not anger Love at all, for I am wholly under his domination. Love, I am in your power: you have placed me under your rule. Love, henceforth I proclaim myself yours. Love, do not wreak such destruction! Love, treat me a little gently!" At that word, she lost her breath and swooned. The queen departed and left her alone.

[8663–8682] The queen went into another room. Lavine swooned seven times, for she could not endure her pain, or be at rest. She went again to the window where love had seized her, singled out Eneas' tent, and looked at it longingly, turning her face straight in that direction. She could not take her eyes from it. Could she have flown, she would have very soon been with him in the pavilion. She could think of nothing but him. At last she spoke again to herself: "I have turned my love in a mad direction. I never thought I would have had the heart for it. Answer me, and speak wisely."

"Foolish Lavine, be moderate. Do not turn your attention to this. You will not be able to escape from love until you are willing to repent of loving."

[8683–8711] "But who could love in such a manner, or turn thus back? Since Love has seized me and holds me in his power, he will never let me escape or depart at my will. Love is of a very bad disposition, and is loath to release anyone he seizes. I have let him gain too much ascendancy over me, and cannot free myself from him; he can do whatever he wishes with me. I did not act wisely in succumbing to him, but surely he should in turn be easier with me and strike a little the proud man for whom I am in such distress. Love is doing me no justice at all, when I lament and Eneas laughs over it: I am dying and it means little to him. But what do I know of his thoughts? Though he has not shown it to me immediately, yet he still may feel the same as I, or more so, and is not showing it. He is a wise man, and will wait for the right time and place. But—sorrowful girl—what will I do meanwhile? For me the wait is difficult. I cannot do without him or suffer pain or grieve so long: I do not wish to suffer pain at length."

[8712–8742] "Then how would you wish to act?"

"Indeed, I wish to let him know."

"What messenger could you use?"

"I seek none other than myself."

"Will *you* go there?"

"Yes, in faith."

"It will result in your great shame."

"What does that matter? If I accomplish my will, it matters little to me what is said about it."

"Hold, now! Do not utter such vile thoughts, that ever a woman of your lineage should undertake so base an act as to go to speak to a strange man in order to offer and present herself.[149] Consider a little. Surely he will have you. And then you will be forever more vile, and he will value you much less in his heart when he has had you."

"What shall I do, then?"

"Hide it from him. It is not good that he know it thus."

"And what then?"

"Wait a little. The time is approaching when the battle will

[149] Cf. *Piramus et Tisbé,* vv. 223–43 (Faral, *Recherches,* p. 19).

take place, and if he wins he will take you; then you will go there indeed, forever. Suffer a little, and it will be good sense. If he were killed and defeated, and Turnus came to the point of taking you as his wife—if he then discovered or understood that you had loved Eneas, he would hold you forever in contempt."[150]

[8743–8775] "I have no fear of that, for I will never have him as my lord. If Eneas is defeated there or killed by mischance, I will kill myself: I know no more of it. Turnus will never have me alive. I will not seek to conceal on his account that Eneas is my love. I have chosen Eneas and will hold with him. I will never cease to love him. But I do not know how I may arrange that he know of it, that he know how love for him has me in great distress; for before the battle takes place, I wish first to make him know, and he then will be more fierce in battle for my sake. If Eneas is assured of my love, Turnus will find him much stronger; he will derive very great bravery from it, if he knows anything at all about love. He should rejoice much because of me, unless he is of that evil trade of which the queen accuses him; if this is true, let him go his way and do as he wishes. I think I must know that he will love me as I love him. I will write everything in a note, and tell him on one page all my feelings and all my desire. I will obtain a sufficient messenger by whom to send the letter. He will know well before long—before tomorrow night—the state of my heart."

[8776–8797] Then she rose from the window, quickly sought out ink and parchment, and wrote down everything, in Latin. The writing in the letter said, first, that she sent greetings to Eneas, her dear love, and, next, that she loved him so that

---

[150] In this love episode the focus is largely on Lavine. As in Ovid, remarks Faral (*Recherches,* pp. 126–27), the woman plays the central role, is the first moved by love, and makes the first declaration (see, e.g., Echo–Narcissus, Byblis–Caunus, Myrrha–Cinyras, Venus–Adonis, Circe–Glaucus, Circe–Picus, in the *Metamorphoses*, together with the epistles of the *Heroides*). From this Ovidian pattern, perhaps, originated the preoccupation of twelfth-century romance with the woman's love psychology.

nothing at all meant more to her, nor would she ever have repose or comfort if he did not feel likewise. She revealed all her desire to him and described well in the parchment how love for him was torturing and distressing her greatly, so that she was dying of it. With very great sweetness she asked that he take pity on her, and she granted him her love. When she had written what she wished, she folded the letter very tightly, and began to consider in whom she could trust—by whom she would be able to send it to him.

[8798–8822] She could not think of a good plan. She went back to the window, put out her head and looked toward the army, and saw that Eneas was coming toward the city, as was his custom. She was very joyous and happy over this. He stopped within arrow shot, near the tower on the other side, without fear, because of the truce. The damsel took the letter and placed it around the shaft of a barbed arrow, turning the writing toward the inside and tying it tightly with a thread. She called one of the king's archers and said, "Friend, shoot this arrow quickly for me at the men of the enemy army who are down there beneath the tower. They are always on the watch here, and I think that they are spies. If the truce ends, they will have examined thoroughly and seen where there are the fewest defenses, and what is hardest to defend, and through that place they expect to capture us."

[8823–8844] "My lady," he said, "there is a truce, and whoever breaks it will be killed. They have no fear of us, nor we of them: the barons have sworn to it faithfully."

She said to him, "You can surely do it. I do not ask you to shoot at them in order to strike any of them, but only to make them depart. Shoot in front of them so that they see it. It cannot matter if they are frightened by it, so long as it does not touch anyone: otherwise we would have acted most wrongfully." The archer drew his laburnum bow and shot the arrow from the tower so that it fell on the edge of the moat where they had stopped. It fell near them, but did no harm to man or horse. They drew back a little, and said among themselves that Turnus had broken the truce which they had sworn.

[8845–8860] Eneas spoke to his men. "My lords," he said, "I will send quickly to the city from which we have received surety and truce in good faith. Since they have broken the truce against me, I will inform them that I will no longer keep truce or peace toward any one of them; and if they wish to argue that they have not done the first wrong and broken the truce against us, let the arrow which was shot at us be shown, and we will thus prove it. If they deny the treachery, we will indeed show them that they are wrong. One of you go and carry it to me."

[8861–8899] One of them ran and took it, and placed it in Eneas' hand. He saw the letter and untied it. The damsel watched him. Eneas looked at the writing, and saw all that the letter said. He saw and understood from the writing that Lavine loved him deeply, and that he was sure of her love, for she would have no other lord. He saw everything that she had sent, and was most happy over it, but he concealed it well, for he did not wish his men to know it, or any of them to notice the letter. He turned back toward the tower. Lavine saw that he was gazing at her. She kissed her finger, then extended it to him, and Eneas understood well that she had sent him a kiss; but he did not feel it, nor did he know of what savor the kiss was: he would have been very glad to know. She sent him hundreds of them that day, there where she stood in the tower, but he never knew how they tasted, for they did not reach him. He looked at her very gently, but because of his men he did not linger, or look at her with a direct glance. She thought that he was proud, and did not deign to love her. When he wished to look at her he turned in the other direction, then let his gaze wander until it came to her; he held his eyes at that point, and stared at her as long as he could; thus he looked at her in passing. They both gave many semblances of love there.

[8900–8934] When evening came and Eneas turned back, he rode toward the army at a very slow pace, looking back often at the city. Then he would repeat to his men that the tower was extremely beautiful: he said it more because of the maiden than because of the masonry. He went back to the pavilion and dismounted in front of his tent, but his heart was all at Laurente: love for the king's daughter had thrown him very quickly into great confusion. He did not care to eat, and went to bed early in the evening. He delighted much in thinking about her, and recalling in his heart how the maiden had looked at him and sent kisses to him. He had noted well in his heart her appearance and her face. Pain touched him in his heart. Cupid, the god of love, his blood-brother, held him in his power; he did not let him sleep that night, but made him sigh many sighs. He tossed and stretched, turned over and then back very often. He had no sleep that night. Love had thrown him into great agitation; Love was making him brood; Love was making him sweat, and then grow chilled, and swoon, and sigh, and quake.

[8935–8960] Love goaded him and excited him, and he trembled so that he could not rest. He remained sitting upright, very gloomy and pensive, and said in his heart, "Love is doing me a very great wrong, treating me in such a manner. There is no vile chambermaid under the heavens whom he would treat with more insolence or more basely than he is treating me, though I am his brother, as he is mine. Good should come to me through him, but, instead, he does me every ill, and utterly kills me; truly, his friendship is dearly bought. Love, I have no defense against you. You let me have no rest; no stranger, by my faith, would have fared worse than I do with you. You have wounded me with your golden dart. The letter which I found around the arrow has poisoned me badly. Like a fool I read it; to my harm I took it. Indeed, I should have cried out and accused the enemy of breaking the truce by that arrow which was shot."

[8961–8988] "Be quiet, Eneas; now you are wrong!"

"Why? I am wounded to the death! Why should I keep quiet? How can he who has been thus stricken live without lamenting? The arrow which was shot has struck me badly in the body."

"You lie; it fell very far from you."

"It carried my death with it and wounded me painfully."[151]

"You do not know what you are saying. It did not touch you."

"Not actually; no blow or wound shows, but the letter which was around it has wounded my person sorely."

"Your skin is all sound on the outside; why the letter?"

"Indeed, it showed me what Lavine sent me."

"Then you are not otherwise wounded, except by the letter which has shown you that Lavine wishes to love you?"

"Not I."

"You should not make an outcry about it. Who will give you justice over a leaf of parchment? Let this be; do not occupy yourself with it, and think instead about your battle. I do not know what this love avails you, for if you win, you know that then you will surely have her; if you are defeated, then you have lost her and another will bear away your love."

[8989–9009] "This is all true, but nevertheless it has given me great hardiness: I do not think that a single knight

---

[151] On the influence of Eneas' "wound" see A. Micha, "Eneas et Cliges," in *Mélanges Ernest Hoepffner,* p. 241. Faral (*Recherches,* p. 16) sees a close parallel to these lines (vv. 8965–73) in *Piramus et Tisbé,* vv. 31–34.

could ever win her from me by battle. I should be most grateful to her that she first sent me word of her love, and I will set myself to great feats, rather than lose or abandon her."[152]

"Nevertheless, woman is very clever at devising evil in her heart; it can well be that Turnus has as much or more of her love than I, and that she is certain of him. They can both talk together. Perhaps she has offered her love to him all openly, just as she has to me. She makes us believe the same thing: whichever of us may happen to take her, she loved him first. Whoever may have her, she wishes to have his gratitude. Woman is most evilly cunning."

[9010–9027] "Now I have thought a great wrong. She has told me all her desire privately by her writing, and has shown me the pain which she is suffering for love of me. I think that if she did not feel such anguish she would never say it: he who does not love and does not feel it cannot speak at all of love. I noticed well in the letter which she sent so cleverly, that she sorrows and laments greatly. I do not believe at all that she does not love me. She does, in faith."

"But I am not certain; for does she not perhaps love him whom she can see every day? And what she feels for love of him, she makes me understand that this is for me."

[9028–9056] "Now would she do that? I know not why. I surely do not think that if she did not love me she would ever tell this to me. I can well believe after the other day, when I was first beneath the tower, that she loved me, because she looked at me with so fair an eye. From that time forward I would have understood it, if I had not been stupid about love; I did not know what it was. Never before was I in such distress. If I had had such feeling toward the queen of Carthage,

---

[152] The idea in this statement, and in Lavine's complementary statement (vv. 8758–68), that love makes the lover more brave and hardy, quickly became a romance commonplace.

who loved me so much that she killed herself for love, never would my heart have parted from her. I would not have abandoned her for my whole life, if I had known so much of love as I have learned since yesterday morning. This land is now much more beautiful to me, and this country pleases me greatly; yesterday became an extremely beautiful day when I stopped beneath the tower where I gained that love. Because of it I am much stronger and more high-spirited, and will very gladly fight for it. Since she gives me the gift of her love, I will now become very careless either of death or life. My beloved gives me boldness.

[9057–9076] "If Turnus wishes to do battle for her, I think I will challenge him very strongly. I expect to give him a great battle, for Love has given me four hands. Love makes a man very bold; Love inflames him most quickly. Love, you grant many feats of bravery! Love, you increase men's courage much! Love, you are very firm and strong! Love, you are of very great power! Love, you have most quickly conquered me![153] In a brief time you have so overcome me that I cannot have rest. How will she be able to know that I have granted her all my love service and my friendship? Shall I send her word?"

"Quiet, fool; don't do it. You should not draw her to you, or make such a show of love that you may one day repent it."

[9077–9099] "I do not expect ever to repent it."

"But a man should protect himself very well; he who would love a woman should not show all his heart to her. Let him be a little proud toward her, so that she may feel the power of love, for if she were to manage it so that she were uppermost, then he would lament. One should make a woman doubt, and should not show her completely how one is suffering for her: she will then love one so much the more."

[153] This type of lyrical anaphora, in which the knight or lady celebrates the virtues of love, soon became a staple of romance.

"This is all true, but nevertheless if she does not know of my feelings, and that I love her in such a manner, I fear that she will draw back. If I lose her love through my fault, I will indeed have deserved death. Sweet love, beautiful creature, love for you fills me beyond measure: for this I lament, for this I sorrow. Yesterday you looked at me with such an eye that it pierced my heart completely!"

[9100–9118] Then he recalled her to memory, and fell back again in a swoon. All night he was in such a state that he had no pleasure or repose, nor did he close his eyes to sleep. All that night he was in pain, nor did it improve for him in the day. If he had suffered pain during the night, on the next day, worse came to him. He could not mount his horse at all, and told his men that he was ill. Everyone around him wept, and there was no pleasure in the army that day, or laughter, or joy. They were all extremely fearful, for the day of the battle was near. They feared that he might fail, and not be able to help himself when he had need of it.

[9119–9146] Lavine was up in the tower. Early in the morning, at daybreak, she returned to stand at the window, and began to gaze at the army, to learn if she would see her beloved. She waited very long to see if he would come to look at her, there where he was wont to stop. When she saw that he was not returning, she was most sorrowful, and did not know what to do; she feared that her love was rejected. "What my mother told me is the truth," she said: "women mean very little to him. He would like his pleasure from a boy, and will love no one except male whores. He has his Ganymede with him, and a very little of me is now enough for him. He is very long at his passion, and is enjoying his delight with a boy. Since he has enjoyed his passion with boys, no woman matters to him. Happily born will be the lady who is married to such a man! She will have much good comfort and fair love and fine pleasure indeed from him! He will spare her for a long time, and will not long take his will with her.

[9147–9164] "I see well that he has no care for women, and no need for such pleasures. Never since he knew that I would love him has he deigned to look in this direction. Since he saw me at the window where I have made my feelings known to him, he would not stop there for any price: he is sick at heart at seeing me. Eneas would have prized me much more if I had split my clothes and if I had hose breeches and tightly tied thongs. He has plenty of boys with him, and loves the worst of them better than me. He has their shirts split. He has many of them at his service, and their breeches are often lowered: thus they earn their wages.[154]

[9165–9188] "May that sort of man be cursed today, who has no care for women; and he follows that custom completely. The practice is extremely evil, and he who leaves women and takes men is wholly mad in his judgment. I would have loved him if it had seemed good to him, and it would have been very beautiful to me if that had pleased him. Since it does not please him, I will leave him, and if I can do it I will hate him—if in my heart I can hate him. Or at least I will love him very unwillingly, for often we may love someone who makes us very heavy hearted. If he did not wish to love me, he yet might have looked at me, and permitted and granted that I love him. Alas, wretched girl, he is unwilling to permit it, nor does he wish to share my domain with me, nor can he permit me to love him alone. Thus, alas, I am the more sorrowful. I will never give myself to love. I would love him only as long as I thought he loved me."

---

[154] The *Eneas* author, in common with numerous of his medieval successors, both in romance and satire, places the grossest of thoughts and language in the mouths of his female characters—in this case a young and innocent maiden of high birth. But on this see the comments of A. Adler, *Romanische Forschungen*, LXXI, 74–75.

[9189–9204] The damsel suffered great pain for her love all that day. She did not know what Eneas was doing: how his love was torturing him, how he was pale and wan and all changed and stricken, how he could neither drink nor eat. But to cheer his followers somewhat, he arose after nones and mounted a gray charger. Taking many of his men with him, he went again to the shore. He rode straight toward the city, and there stopped where he was accustomed, directly beneath the tower, there where he had received love.

[9205–9229] The maiden saw him coming. She began to repent of her accusations, and said, "I have acted very badly, and spoken too much like a madwoman. I think that Love has become angry with me because I spoke so wrongly. Now I repent: I have slandered him too much. Fair, sweet love, take my pledge: I have spoken great outrage against you, but I will give you justice and do all your pleasure. I should indeed repent that I have placed such blame upon you. Ah, alas, I delay too long in letting him take his justice of me. Fair, sweet friend, if it would please you, I would go barefoot to your tent. It would be very fair and sweet to me if I suffered evil and pain. I spoke wrongly, in great folly. I have blamed you most wrongfully. My love, I have indeed deserved death: if you wish, my life is forfeit, or if you wish, I will be spared." Then she gave him a sweet look.[155]

[9230–9252] Eneas looked in that direction and noticed that she was gazing at him; then he sighed so that he could not have sighed more deeply. All the barons, who saw him, noticed it very quickly. Many of them said among themselves, "There are such glances in that tower that—if their messages might be believed—the Latins will soon receive us in the city: if all the others think as she thinks, they will surrender themselves very quickly. Sire," they said to their lord, "look; the

[155] For a parallel to this outburst of repentance cf. *Piramus et Tisbé,* vv. 450–70 (Faral, *Recherches,* pp. 19–20).

tower is most beautiful, but it has a pillar up there which leans a little down toward you. See how level the wall is, how straight the pillar, how well built the work. That window by the pillar is very beautiful, over there on the right, but there is an archer standing there who would be very happy to shoot here. Sire, draw back so that he does not shoot down at you."

[9253–9274] Eneas, who understood their jokes very well, smiled a little; nevertheless he looked so that he did not turn his eyes to see her, but in the passing, when his men were paying no attention to him, he made her a sign that he loved her. Thus both of them were able to exchange glances and make signs. When he set about to return, he began to sigh, and the maiden to tremble. The parting was very painful to them. He looked back often at his love, and she stretched her hand toward him. They both made signs: one could not forget the other, nor could they separate without the one thinking of the other. Neither of them was at all in doubt—neither he of her nor she of him—that they loved one another.

[9275–9298] Then the truce came to an end, and there was a great tumult in the city. They had no care to wait longer. Twenty thousand men took up their arms—hauberks, lances, shields. King Latinus went forth, carrying with him all his gods, on whom those who were about to do combat would take their oaths, just as they had agreed, so that there would be no other than Eneas and Turnus; no others would take part, except to see who would win. Turnus was all unarmed, and stood close by, beneath Laurente. He had his charger led, and his arms and equipment carried after him. Eneas came from the other direction. To him the hour when he would win or lose seemed marvelously slow in arriving. The Trojans came there, and the mountains glittered with the arms which they bore.[156]

[156] The author has forgotten that the single combat was to have taken place on an island (v. 7838).

[9299–9312] King Latinus had the field laid out, and made everyone draw back and enlarge the ring well. Then he had it proclaimed to all that none of them should move because of anything which he might see, good or bad. He had a silken cloth stretched out in the meadow where the gods were brought, and the idols in which they believed. Both Turnus and Eneas were about to take oath on them. The king, and his barons with him, were repeating the oath to him who would swear first.

[9313–9342] Lavine was up in the tower, where she suffered great sadness for her lover, for she saw that he was about to do combat near her. She does not know how it will turn out, and she is in anguish and great fear. In her heart she has decided and firmly proposed that if Eneas is killed there, or conquered by his enemy, she will throw herself down from the tower: she will never live an hour longer than he. She laments and weeps much, and often calls on all the gods to protect him whom she loves. "I have had very bad sense," she says. "I am not of good providence, since my beloved does not have my sleeve; he would have struck much better with his lance because of it. Or if I had sent him my wimple, it would have been well employed; he would have cut much better with his sword because of it. Turnus would have received a blow for it. I have bethought myself too late. He should have had a sign from me in his time of need; but if he cares for my love, he will see me here at the window, and he should become much more hardy for it."

[9343–9366] Before either of them armed himself or swore his oath, Eneas spoke his thoughts; the king and the barons became quiet. "My lords," he said, "I wish to explain my right to you, so that you do not accuse me of wishing to conquer, out of pride, another domain or another land by force. My ancestor, who was called Dardanus, was born here. He left this land and established himself in ours, where he was a very

strong man, and conquered much. From his lineage issued
Tros, who founded Troy and its fortress, and who gave it his
name; my father was of his lineage. Troy lasted long, with
great power, until the Greeks conquered her. The gods took
me from there and sent me here to this country where my
ancestor was born. They have granted me all Italy, which is
as it were my grandmother and great-grandmother.

[9367–9394] "When I arrived in this country I sent my
messengers to the king, who admitted me to this land; I never
would have waged war against him. He told me in his kindness that I should know this with certainty: that he would
grant me the land, and would give it to me, together with his
daughter. Here I claim it. I have come hither thus all prepared
to do battle for it. I see that Turnus challenges me; let him
be assured, he may do what he can. If I am defeated or killed
here, let my son withdraw safely with all his forces. Let him
have no kind of harm, but let my whole company depart
without fear or doubt. And if I can defeat this man who would
take the land from me by force, I promise you indeed," he said
to the king, "that as long as you live you will never be debased
in any way by me: continue to hold your land well, but after
consideration give me, with your daughter, one part of it,
where I can build a city. After your death, let me have the
inheritance."

[9395–9424] The king and those present assured and granted him that if he were killed in battle on this day, Ascanius
with his force could depart in all freedom and safety to Montauban. He would have one month, if he wished, to stay there,
after which he might remain no longer. While they were talking and arranging this agreement, a knight of the city heard
what they had discussed. He went to the others and said to
them, "We can value ourselves very little, when Turnus offers
himself for all of us, while we are as many as those on the
other side, or more. This is a very bad settlement. Our for-

tunes are placed on one man, and if he is killed or defeated, we are all in short vanquished and fallen into shame. If Turnus is defeated here, and Eneas the victor, we will have to deal with an evil people; we will be tributary forever more. Noble lords, do not allow it; let us do battle against our enemies, and not place our fortunes to such an extent on the action of a lone man."[157]

[9425–9438] With this, he spurred his horse and struck a Trojan, knocking him dead. This was immediately avenged, and the tourneying had begun anew: much was undone there in a short time. From both sides men rushed to the attack, exposing themselves to the iron of the lance-heads. They died there by hundreds and by thousands: I could never name them all. It would be very hard to relate who jousted there and who fell, who was killed there and who struck him down, but they raged very fiercely against one another, and spared each other not at all.

[9439–9448] The king saw the affair turn to battle. In short, he had to abandon completely the agreement he had discussed, and he began to flee. In his arms he carried his gods: he did not consider them at all so great that they could be of any help to him, or that he could have any protection through them. His faith was more in swift flight than in the gods he carried.[158]

[9449–9461] Eneas was all unarmed when he saw that the affair had turned into battle. It angered him much, and he sorrowed over it. His shield hung at his neck. He spurred quickly toward the fighting, crying out and shouting to his followers that they should all draw back and that there should

---

[157] In the *Aeneid* (xii. 229–37) the speech which arouses the Laurentians to break the truce is delivered, at Juno's behest, by the deified Juturna, sister of Turnus, who disguises herself as one of the Latin warriors.

[158] Rationalist though he is, this is the one place in which the *Eneas* poet permits himself a civilized sneer at the superstitions of the ancients.

be no more jousting. He berated them, and told them that those who had violated the agreement which the king had concluded wished him to lose his domain, for they had taken his single combat away from him.

[9462–9480] He shouted much, but succeeded little, until he could no longer keep up with them. Then he made signs to them with his arm that they should all draw back and that none of them should strike any more blows. He was anguished beyond measure. An archer shot an arrow by chance—he did not see or know about it—and it struck Eneas in the arm, wounding him. The arrow lodged in the bone, and the arm swelled up, and quickly became large. With the other hand, Eneas pulled out the shaft very harshly, but he left the iron within. The wound pained him greatly. Ascanius and the barons led him away hastily, put him to bed in his pavilion, and quickly sent after a good physician who was in the army.

[9481–9495] Turnus had observed this well, and was extremely happy when he saw that Eneas was wounded. He armed himself very quickly, mounted his horse, unfurled his banner, and said to his men that none of them should hesitate to strike the Trojans. He charged through the ranks, striking well with his lance and better with his sword, emptying many a saddle there: no one could stand against him. It would be tiresome to relate all those who were struck down, who struck them, and who died. Turnus wrought very great destruction.

[9496–9520] A Trojan, Naptanabus, addressed him, wishing to show his prowess by a little bravado.[159] "Vassal," he said, "stand back, and do not act in this manner! You think you have overcome and defeated and killed us all, because Eneas is not here! Do you think that no one remains here who will not flee before you? But you still have to deal with us. If

[159] Naptanabus is the French poet's addition, the name perhaps suggested by Neptanabus (or Nectanabus), teacher of Alexander the Great. See S. de Grave in *Eneas,* Cfmâ, II, 137.

Eneas were now dead, we would not give up the battle. If he
did not have a captain here in the company except me alone,
yet I would conquer all from you—both the woman and the
land. If Eneas were to come no more, you would not be at
peace because of that. So far as I can wield arms, I think I will
make you pay very dearly. If you are not now a master of
jousting, and do not know well how to shield yourself, vengeance will be taken very quickly for our men whom you have
killed."

[9521–9542] Naptanabus stopped talking, spurred his horse,
and charged at him, attacking him with great anger. He
struck Turnus on the gilded shield, but the lance slid off
without splitting or piercing it. The lance-head harmed nothing, and Turnus did not move from his saddle. He in turn
struck Naptanabus on his shield, completely breaking and
splintering it, and tearing the mail of the hauberk. He drove
the lance and its ensign into his body as far as the pennons,
and threw him dead from the saddle-bows. Turnus saw him
lying cold on the ground, and said, "From you I will have no
more war; by you I will never be conquered. You will leave
me all of my land; you will not have a whole foot of it, or a
half, except only that where you will lie. I have given you
livelihood in very stingy measure."

[9543–9565] While they were fighting the battle, and striking and killing one another, Eneas was in the pavilion. Ascanius and the barons wept bitterly around him; they were in
great fear for their men and for themselves. In the tent they
were feeling great sorrow, and saying that they were all dead
and captured. Iapus, a very good physician, came and looked
at the wound. He felt the iron, and probed deeply, to learn if
he might be able to draw it out, but he could in no way remove
it with forceps or iron tongs, and Eneas cried out loudly. The
physician went to his bag, took out a box, drew from it some
dittany, steeped it, and had Eneas drink the potion. When he

had swallowed it, the arrowhead disappeared, and the shoulder was immediately healed; quickly he was again all healthy.[160]

[9566–9574] Dittany is of such power and the roe an animal of such a nature, that when it is wounded, it runs directly to the dittany, its medicine. Whether it eats of the leaf or of the root, as soon as the herb has passed its throat, its illness is all cured; and when iron is in its body, it must fly out because of the dittany.

[9575–9596] Eneas was wholly cured. He armed himself in great haste, and had it announced throughout the army that they should all come to him very quickly. There was no boy or squire in the army who did not come to shoot an arrow or throw a lance. His people were in great need of his quick help, for Turnus was defeating them. They were almost wholly conquered: he had put them to flight. He expected to overcome them all, and would have, quickly, had not Eneas come with a large following and permitted them to escape to the rear. Quickly Eneas and his men made a thousand of the enemy die, and put them to flight. Then Eneas cried out: "Now lay on, noble knights. You can avenge yourselves very well indeed. They are facing defeat: take no care to spare them."

[9597–9622] Then the Trojans laid on mightily. Their enemies were fleeing, for they could not defend themselves against them. Eneas was unwilling to linger and attack those who were fleeing, but went through the swordplay, seeking to see his enemy. But Turnus moved away. He did not wish to go in the direction in which he thought he would encounter Eneas, for he saw most clearly that everything was going

[160] The French poet ascribes to a human physician the prescription which Vergil ascribes to the intercession of Venus (*Aeneid* xii. 411–29). The powers of dittany— this last of *Eneas'* marvels of flora and fauna—are, however, described in the *Aeneid*. Venus mixes the herb with ambrosia and panacea.

badly for him, and that fortune was against him. He did not know what to do, for it seemed very bad to him to flee, but he did not yet wish to die. Eneas, who wished greatly to joust with him, was unable to meet him.[161] When he saw that he could not encounter Turnus, he departed from there with a very great following and went spurring toward the city. He knew that all were outside on the battlefield, and that very few of them remained within. Of all the men of the city, there were not three hundred inside. They were all outside in the battle.

[9623–9642] Before Eneas attacked them, one group of them wished to surrender, but the others wished to defend themselves. They ran to shut the gates, and climbed up on the walls, not wishing to admit the Trojans inside. Eneas ordered the city assaulted; he had his men shoot arrows and throw spears at them, and set up ladders against the walls. Then he ordered fire to be brought, and had all the palisade ignited. They set fire to the city, and in a little while it was all in flames. Then the citizens were occupied with beating out the fire more than with doing battle or defending the city. Those outside would have entered, had it not been for the fire, which impeded them and prevented the entry. There was no more opposition, for there was nothing at all to defend.

[9643–9668] Turnus looked in that direction and saw the city in flames. He knew well that Eneas was winning and that he would not stop until he had taken the city: he had put it to fire and flame. Turnus had his followers withdraw in one direction and showed them what he wished to do, speaking to them briefly. "My lords," he said, "sons of barons, as far as fortune has permitted, each of you has aided me, and you would still do so very willingly, if you could. But I believe that the gods do not wish me to have the land and the country;

---

[161] These lines cover the episode in *Aeneid* (xii. 468–99), in which Juturna gives supernatural protection to Turnus, never letting him come near Aeneas.

they have given it all to the Trojan, and you will be dispos-sessed of it. Enough of you have died for me here. I believe that the gods do not wish that any of you do more, but that all of you should stand far back. I will do battle with Eneas, and will put my life in hazard. I wish rather to die in battle than to surrender alive, or flee."[162]

[9669–9682] They all began to weep when they heard him speak thus, but they could aid him no longer. Turnus depart-ed, spurring his horse until he came to Laurente, which was burning while the Trojans attacked it. Turnus began to call out that they should let the town be, and should not destroy or burn it. From far off they stopped and gazed. He asked them all to draw back, for he was ready to do battle; Eneas wishes to joust with him; let him come forward, and he will find him.

[9683–9700] Eneas heard what Turnus said, and was very happy and joyous over it. He ordered his men to abandon completely the assault, and the combat and the tourneying. Since Turnus was willing to do battle, he did not wish that anyone more die there for it, either of those within or of those outside: he wished to end it by himself alone. He has them all draw back to make the field very large, and lay down all their arms: they do not have to fear at all that anyone else will interfere again. Through one of the two, there will be peace. All the troops stand at a distance. Then, without further discussion, without oaths, without threats, without chal-lenges, they have recourse to their lance-heads.

[9701–9726] Turnus spurred his spirited charger and struck Eneas in front, on the breast, over the handle of the shield; but the strong hauberk held, so that the mail did not give way, and Eneas rose up. He struck Turnus below the shield. Thus they knocked each other down, but both rose very

---

[162] Hoepffner (*Arch. romanicum,* XV, 267) notes the parallel between these lines (vv. 9666–68) and Wace (*Brut,* vv. 10255–57).

quickly to their feet, drew their steel swords, and attacked each other very fiercely. Turnus struck first on the shield which Vulcan made—the god, who put great skill into it. Nothing came of the blow: it neither split the shield nor broke it. Eneas struck him in turn on the helmet with his burnished sword, knocking a quartering from it. The blow came down on the shield and made a gap in one side of it. Turnus saw this, and was much afraid. He saw well that if his opponent could recover and land another blow quickly, all would be finished with him. He could hardly avoid being afraid.

[9727–9747] They resume their fencing, Fortune doing battle with Strength. A thousand sparks fly out from the clash of the blades. Turnus delivers a solid blow which strikes Eneas on the top of the helm. It damages none of the helm, but the sword breaks in the middle, and half of it falls to the ground. At this, Turnus is deeply dismayed: since he sees that he has nothing with which to attack, he throws the other half on the ground and takes to flight through the field. He finds his way all blocked in front of him, for the open place is surrounded by people. He does not know what to do, but runs all about in flight, calling his friends by name, asking their help and aid. Not one of them moves: they have left everything to the decision of the battle.

[9748–9774] When Eneas saw him fleeing, he followed behind him at his back and addressed him in this manner: "You will never conquer by fleeing, but by giving combat and striking blows. Turn around and come forward." Then Eneas stopped and picked up his lance, which was lying there. But Turnus saw in front of him a great rock which had been placed there to border and separate the fields. He lifted it from the ground with both his hands and turned to attack the Trojan. He threw the rock with very great strength. It struck the shield next to the boss, so that the rock bounced off; but it did not break or split the shield, nor did anything come of that blow, nor did Eneas move a single foot. Then Eneas threw his lance at Turnus, flinging it with great strength. It pierced and split the shield, and struck him in the thigh, so that he fell to his knees in the sight of his followers and barons, who were crying out so loudly that all the woods echoed from it.

[9775–9793] When Eneas saw him on his knees, he went toward him with long strides. Turnus saw him, and was afraid. When he saw that he could do no more, he stretched out both his hands to Eneas and begged for mercy. "Sire," he said, "I surrender myself to you in the presence of your men and your followers. Everyone sees well that you have defeated me and conquered all with great strength: I have no defense against you. Lavine is yours: I grant her to you, and with her I give up all the land. You will never have more war from me if you let me go alive. I can ask no more of you: I will be your vassal; I surrender myself to you." Then he took off his helmet and held it out to him. Eneas had great pity on him.

[9794–9814] Turnus gave up his helmet to Eneas. While he was holding it out, Eneas saw on his finger the ring of Pallas, which Turnus had taken from him when he killed him. All his great sorrow was renewed when he recalled Pallas. All dark with anger, he sighed and said, "You have begged mercy of me, and have left and abandoned to me all this realm, and the king's daughter. I would have had pity on you, nor would you have lost life or limb; but because of this ring I remember Pallas, whom you killed: you have put very great sorrow in my heart by that. Eneas will not kill you, but Pallas avenges himself on you." With this word he jumped forward, struck Turnus immediately with the sword which Vulcan forged, and took his head: he had avenged Pallas.

[9815–9838] Turnus is dead. Everyone sees that Eneas has won. There was a marvelous outcry. The men of Troy were joyous over it, and those of the other side, sorrowful. But nevertheless it was time for them—since it so happened to them—to accept Eneas. They were thus sorrowful, but gave in appearance a countenance of great joy. The barons came to him to submit themselves. The king had him receive on the battlefield the fealty of his barons, and gave him his strongholds. There was a great crowd around him that day, and all received him as their lord. He did not then go to Laurente, but returned to his tent, and King Latinus escorted him. At the parting he named the day when he would marry Lavine: he will be king and she, queen. In their deliberations the time for the marriage was fixed at eight days hence.

[9839–9866] Lavine had heard and seen that Eneas had won, and saw that he was going away. She thought that he hardly held her dear, since he did not go to talk with her, and she was sorrowful when she saw him depart. She wept and wailed and sobbed, and said, "I mean very little to him indeed; I am entangled in a mad affair, for he has no care for me in any way. Now, through the pretext of winning me, he will have the king's land and realm. If he has all the rule, my love will mean very little to him; if he is possessed of the heritage, then he will treat me with much cruelty and will hold me unworthy of him, for he will have all the castles. I will have no one to aid me, and he will show me great haughtiness. Whether he loves me little or much, he will always show me the appearance of great pride and cruelty. He will reproach me often because I was impulsive in my love of him, and he will hold me for a lover of change. I will have haughtiness from love: he will win in the end."

[9867–9900] "Foolish Lavine, do not be angry if he wins in the day and you at night."

"Do not be angry, alas? In truth, I should have been haughty in this affair. He should have had to beg and flatter and wheedle for my love."

"Stop! Speak no more! This is immoderate. Woman is weaker by nature than man in suffering ill: she can never contain it in her heart. Woman is too bold in loving; man knows much better how to hide his heart."

"In faith, this one hides it very well, for I am nothing to him."

"But he would give no indication at all whether one meant little or much to him."

"He did not deign to come here, or even to look up at his departure. The eye is always for love and the hand is for pain: one puts one's hand where it hurts, and one turns one's eye there where one wishes love. Therefore, I say that if he had loved me, he would have turned his eyes toward me at his departure; but it was more important to him to go home. I well believe that he hardly holds me dear. Now it seems to him, since he has won, that he has gained everything through the battle, and indeed he thinks that he will have dominion without me. He will make himself king. He does not fear that I will dispute it, nor does he care how he takes the rule. Since he has escaped from the battle, he thinks he will set me aside."

[9901–9914] "What have I said? I despair too much. It would certainly not be true that the barons of this domain would receive him as their lord, if he did not wish to take me as his wife. A thousand knights would die before I were dispossessed. If he wishes to deceive me in love, and in the end to disinherit me, I have bestowed my love in a bad place. I complain little of being disinherited: I want nothing but love. If he does not make me sure of it very soon, I will have no more care for my life."

[9915–9941] The maiden wept bitterly, for she feared much that her beloved would not deign to love her. But she did not have to fear, had she known with certainty how strongly he missed her, and how he was distraught for her. During the day, indeed, he had no time, but at night he lay awake, in tears, and called on the god of love, begging him very humbly not to treat him so harshly. He tossed and lamented, then said softly between his teeth, "What have I done, sorrowful wretch, that I have set such a distant date to have my beloved and take her? I can never wait so long. The time must be much shortened, for waiting is not easy for me. An hour of one day is longer than a year! He who suffers anguish, evil, and pain, desires greatly to be cured, but I am driven mad, since my illness is of such an origin that there is only one medicine which will give me respite from it.

[9942–9968] "Love is always torturing me greatly, for it will let me have no rest. I would like much to know with certainty if she for whom I was inflamed the other day still holds firm in her love, and if she in turn knows how I love her. Love has indeed taken me with his hook, which he baited with the maiden.[163] After I first saw the damsel, I could not take my heart from her. Never was I so distraught from love. It is a very strange thing indeed: he who loves truly does not rest. I have already paid dearly for all the pleasure which I await from her. I yearn for her, and am most impatient for the beautiful maiden to help me. But by now she has repented of her love, for a woman's heart changes quickly. Nevertheless, she is not at all to blame if she hesitates to love me, for I did not give her a sufficient sign that she mattered in the least to me. Without doubt I wronged her much when I did not go to her immediately after the battle. I have wronged her, and I beg her pardon for it.

[163] Faral (*Recherches,* p. 141) refers to Ovid (*Ars amat.* iii. 425), wherein is described the lover as a fisherman: "semper tibi pendeat hamus." But the metaphor derived strength and cogency from the imagined connection between *hamus,* "a hook," and *amor,* love. Thus, Isidore of Seville (*Etymologiae* x. 5): "The word *amicus,* a friend, is derived from *hamus,* a hook, that is, a bond of love." The derivation was later taken over by Andreas Capellanus in *The Art of Courtly Love* (tr. Parry), p. 31: "Love gets its name *(amor)* from the word for hook *(amus),* which means 'to capture' or 'to be captured'. . . ." Parry cites the passage from Isidore.

[9969–9998] "She should not bear resentment, anger, or ire for long: Love has no care for long wars, but he who does wrong should seek mercy. If someone has treated another rather haughtily, then let him beg her a bit, and let her in turn pardon him, since he has begged for mercy from her. Very good indeed is the reconciliation when there has been a quarrel, and a little anger is a great promoter of love. Anger which does not last too long is a great medicine for love, and whets and excites it much. When one of the lovers has been angry, later the reconciliation avails much: it is a renewal of love. Afterward one single kiss is worth more than nine were before. If there had not been anger and ire, the love would not be so good or so fine. He who has had storms at sea is much happier on his arrival than if he had passed safely without any suffering; when he has been in fear of death, he is much pleased on coming to port.[164] Such is love: it pleases most strongly after a little resentment.

[9999–10026] "I know well that my beloved is right in being a little angry, for I acted most immoderately when I did not seek her immediately after the battle was over. I have shown her a poor love, and I know that I was wrong. Then I did worse—if I could do worse—when I set the date so far away. If it pains me and I complain of it, this is very just, for I did wrong in setting it on the eighth day. It would have seemed too long to me to wait only until tomorrow. It is very just that I repent of it, that I am ill from it, that I feel it so strongly. I have never repented of the date to which I thus agreed except once: that once has lasted ever since, and has grieved me much. It is most disagreeable to me when each day I think, 'It will not be today that I will be possessed of my love.' Then

[164] At this point *Manuscript D* begins a widely divergent ending to the romance, 319 lines in length.

I cannot keep from tears. It is very bad to wait; so much the more should I desire that the time were past, and I in possession of her.

[10027–10047] "But these days last extremely long; never were days so long. I think that there are three of them in one: this week will be worth a good three months. The heavens cannot turn, and evening is most slow in coming. The sun cannot set; there is a marvelous delay in nightfall; and then the night in turn lasts so long that it is a great vexation. When the sun has set, before it has risen again I think a thousand times that it is lost, and I fear that it will never be seen again, for it delays much, and lingers long. Then I think that I will never see that hour when it returns here above. When it returns, I am always turning to gaze and see if I will find it moving: it seems to me that it hastens very little.[165]

[10048–10078] "I was very stupid and foolish ever to agree to that delay. This illness of mine is most just, and can turn worse for me, for I have seen an opportunity change quickly. When I might have taken my love, did I then cause this delay? I never did it: it could very quickly destroy me. It is often harmful to put off a thing when it is ready, for in a short time it is quickly changed. One should do what one can do: a delay may turn quickly to disaster. I could have hastened everything, but I delayed, for no reason at all. If I were now all certain and had my will, it would not now be at all so hard for me, but instead I would be having beautiful joy. It is right that he who can have a good and lets it go should have all the shame of it. I am still waiting for what I could now have possessed, and I am saddened by it. Thus I am in great fear:

---

[165] There is no better example in *Eneas* than the above lines of the sort of amplification—so popular in medieval narrative—which consists in repeating the same thing in a number of different ways. It is this carefully contrived procedure which so frequently makes medieval romance wearisomely repetitive and verbose to modern ears. The reader will recall numerous examples in *Eneas*. Faral (*Recherches,* pp. 106–7) mentions a few among many.

I have seen fidelity in such a case fail quickly when it came to the taking. But I must suffer now, and wait: I could have done much before, I can do nothing now. I could now have been wholly at peace. A man often turns away from his own good; thus have I done, and I repent it much."

[10079–10090] Eneas was much perturbed, and desired greatly the day when he would take his love. It vexed him sorely to wait, and the time passed very slowly for him. Each of the lovers wished for it on his own part, and both were meanwhile in anguish. If the delay in uniting the two had lasted another week, one of them would have had to pay for it, or indeed it might have soon turned out badly for both.

[10091–10119] When it came to the appointed time, for which they had waited with great difficulty, the king invited his friends and summoned all his barons. He went out to meet Eneas, who was received with great joy and led to Laurente. In the sight of them all the king made him heir to his realm and his rule. He granted everything to Eneas on the day when he married his daughter. Great joy was felt there, many instruments were sounded, and there were many entertainments. Eneas was elevated to kingship and crowned with great joy, and Lavine was crowned: he was king of Italy and she, queen.[166] Never did Paris have greater joy when he had Helen in Troy than Eneas had when he had his love in Laurente. He did not think that any man in the world would ever have so much happiness. And Lavine in turn thought that surely no woman ever had such happiness except herself alone. Eneas could mention nothing which might be lacking, which she had not wholly accomplished.

[10120–10130] When the king had given him possession of her and her of him, he was overjoyed. The feast was solemnly celebrated; the wedding entertainment lasted a month. The

[166] Hoepffner (*Arch. romanicum,* XV, 254) sees in these lines (vv. 10105–8) an echo of Wace, *Brut,* vv. 63–64.

king selected a very large part of the best of his land, where Eneas chose, and granted it to him for his lifetime.[167] He gave him all his land to be lord of after his death, so that no one might wrongfully claim it from him.

[10131–10156] Eneas had the best part of Italy, and began to build a city. He made good walls there, and a strong fortress, and gave his city the name of Albe. It was very rich and very large, and its rule lasted many years. Eneas held it long. Then all the land of King Latinus came into his hands, and when Eneas in turn came to his end, Ascanius reigned after him. Then it happened just as Anchises in hell had described to Eneas, when he had shown well the kings who would come after him—just as he said they would be born. Thus they were born, one after another, as he had told his son. They were all men of very great power, and descended from heir to heir until Remus was born of their lineage, and Romulus. They were brothers, and very strong men. They founded the city of Rome, to which Romulus gave his name, for it was he who first named it.

[167] Hoepffner (*Arch. romanicum,* XV, 254) sees in vv. 10124–27 an echo of Wace, *Brut,* vv. 42–43. In vv. 10129–31 he sees an echo of *Brut,* vv. 65–66, and in vv. 10138–39, an echo of *Brut,* vv. 67–68, in addition to other parallels.

APPENDIX

Alternate Ending from *Manuscript D*[1]

Manuscript D was written toward the end of the fourteenth century, almost two centuries after the earliest manuscript of *Eneas*. It contains major alterations and additions to the text represented in the other manuscripts, almost sufficient for it to merit consideration as a separate rehandling. The most significant of these changes and additions is the ending edited by Salverda de Grave in appendices to his two editions, and translated here. In recent years at least one scholar[2] has suggested that *Manuscript D* may reflect a more primitive state of the text than *Manuscript A*. Nevertheless, it seems likely, not merely on the basis of the manuscripts, but also on the basis of tone and style, that the divergent ending is a later addition.

The author of the ending was obviously dissatisfied with the *Eneas* author's abrupt termination of the love story. In our final view of the minds of the lovers they are in agonized suspense over the delay before the wedding, and full of lovers' jealous doubts about one another. Then, suddenly they are brought together, married with great pomp, and endowed with their lands, with no opportunity for a resolution of their love, or a lovers' understanding, with not even a chance to

[1] Bibl. Nation., f. fr. 60. Cf. S. de Grave in *Eneas,* Cfmâ, I, iv-vii.
[2] Cola Minis, *Neophilologus,* XXXIII (1949), 65–85. See pp. 6–7 above. Professor Raymond Cormier has informed me of his intention to publish a partial edition of *Manuscript D.*

exchange private words of endearment. The *Eneas* author was clearly in haste at this point. Feudal pomp and ceremony had pushed aside the private concerns of the lovers.

The author of *Manuscript D* attempted to rectify this haste and to bring about a satisfactory and gracious concord between the hearts of the lovers before the formal ceremonies which consummated the romance. One can only guess at the date of the new ending, but in it, the relatively fresh, simple, and straightforward narrative of *Eneas* has become highly florid. Directness has given way to elaborate, adjective-laden cliché and mannerism. Eneas is now "Eneas li cortois," burning with "fine amor toz tens estable," and Lavine is "la belle des belles," "franche dame, gentilz pucele." Both lovers give vent to their emotions in language full of romantic *préciosité*. Rings and jewels are moralized and allegorized in the fashion of the day, and the *gaucherie* and confusions of the earlier author's lovers are resolved into a suave, sophisticated, and stylized *acordement*. The effect on the reader of these alterations is not happy, but the conclusion is an interesting illustration of the growth of cliché, and the hardening of convention.

[9997–10004] "Thus, if the beauty would love me and receive fair glances from me, and all were as I might have wished; if I feared none of the difficulties which many men have with their true loves—so it pleases the gods—then nature or reason would not have it that she would remain so always.[3]

[3] The translation of this passage is conjectural. The original lines follow:
Por ce se la belle maime
se biau samblant de moi aie
e il comme ie vousisse
saucun contraire ne cremisse
dont mult avient a finz amis
por ce sil plaist aus diex na miz

[10005–10041] "But I must remove the care which is thus in my heart, since I have caused this long delay with a lady of such noble worth that no one can imagine it. In her alone one can find more good sense, worth, solace, and moderation than in a thousand other creatures. Like a true lover I will tell her in what distress she has put me, holding me in her sweet prison; and when the desired day comes, when I am to take her, I—who am caught without hope of escape, so that I will never seek to leave her—will beg only this of her: that she pardon me the misdeed of giving her so little appearance of love, from which I believe indeed that she is sorrowing. And as love wishes and commands, for the sweet rose who has no equal in beauty, I will beg and ask and advise that she hold her heart in joy and that she be certain that I have been divided into two parts since that hour when she first cast her blue eyes on me and released the arrow, capturing me with its sweet message. Wherever my body may be, she has my heart, and indeed she should have it, for without her, I could not be in hope of joy. And my joys will then be doubled on the appointed day, when my heart and my other members will be reunited."

[10042–10061] Trembling with ardor, Eneas quickly called a messenger, to assuage his sorrows. "Malpriant," he said, "come forward. You will go to that city there before us to speak to my betrothed, the beautiful Lavine, my love. Beg her that it may not displease her that I have not had the place or the leisure to give her a sign of my love, for my heart burns in hope of the body which will return to it directly at the end of these eight days. May she know in her loyalty that as she saw my heart, she will then in turn see all of me. I have an agreement with her father to

---

en li nature ne raison
que ne maine en toute saison.

assemble all my barons, when I will take her as my love
and my spouse, with the favor of the gods.

[10062–10088] "In love of me I wish her to wear on her
tender, gentle, beautiful hand this little ring which I send her
in lasting remembrance of true love forever firm, and of a
loving and faithful heart. The ring has no ending, but is round
and firm all about, by which it signifies that love envelops the
loyal heart; it cannot in truth be broken or brought to an end
by delay. And let the beautiful Lavine know that with this
ring I send her my love, for she has my heart. During the wait
let her utter no sighs for me, feel no anguish, shed no tears,
such as lovers are wont to do, but with savory remembrance
let her bring peace to her heart in sweet desire."

"I see well your pleasure and your intent," said Malpriant.
Pray to the gods for me, for I will go there." With these words
he parted from Eneas and—to speak briefly—traveled until
he came to Lavine's city.

[10089–10114] Now Malpriant held to the road until he
came to where the beautiful Lavine was, whom Love held in
his power, and who was saying, "Gentle Eneas, if you have
forgotten me, I have not therefore forgotten you. Alas, high
gods, I pray you that in time I may hear news to make me
more joyful for you, and to assuage my sorrows." Then behold
the messenger enters the tower by the gate, bringing her what
she desires. The porter quickly asked him who he was and
what he sought.

[10115–10122] "I am from great Troy," he said; "Eneas
sends me to carry a message from him to Lavine."

The porter bowed humbly to him. "May he who sends
you," he said, "have only good, and may great joy be with you
also; you are a thousand times most welcome. You will not be
held back today either from the tower or the chamber." Without more delay he was led into the great, plaster-decorated
hall, where the noble, tender maiden was standing at a win-

dow. There she delighted much to be, for from this window she had seen Eneas receive the arrow by which she had sent the message, as we have described before.

[10123–10140] The porter greeted the beautiful girl. "Noble lady," he said, "gentle maiden, this man whom I hold by the hand I bring to you because he comes from the best man possible, a good count, of good ancestors: that is the courteous Eneas. I will return to my gate and leave the noble messenger with you." Like a wise man he quickly left the room, and the gracious, noble maiden took the messenger by the sleeve, since he had things to tell her. On his finger she saw the ring, whose like she had never seen before.

"May you be welcome," said the beauty of beauties to him. "Now tell us your news."

[10141–10178] "Lady, he said, "your friend Eneas of Troy, whose heart you have in your keeping, sends me to you."

The maiden then looked at him and answered, "What, Eneas? My friend, most sweet Eneas, you have ravished my heart from my body! Eneas, since I saw you, there where the arrow fell from that tower, it has not returned to me; my heart is thus with you."

The messenger, the courteous and worthy Malpriant, answered humbly. "Lady," he said, "as humbly as he can, Eneas prays you and begs you as his beloved not to consider it a misdeed that he gave you no other sign when you caused the arrow to be shot, nor again later, for, by reason of the perversity which often makes love troublesome, he has been continuously in doubt; the loving heart is never finished with doubting; and just as you say that he has your heart, know you that his heart is fixed within you and that he has it not at all, except as love unites it to him. And because it will never be separated from you, no matter how far away is his body, he sends you this little ring, that, just as it has no ending, it may hold together and unite his and your two hearts, joined in true love in such a way that it will be perfect forever. He makes this union with you in love without any disloyalty."

[10179–10200] Lavine looked at the ring; she held out her hand—she delayed no longer—and he presented it fairly. Love beyond measure then transported and ravished her so completely that in one outburst she kissed the ring more than a hundred times. "Sweet love," she said, "now I am at ease and filled with all joy, since I am certain of your love. Your loyal heart has healed me; I can no longer be angry about the delay or the wait. My sighs are finished, and tears can no longer flow from my eyes, since the high gods have granted me what I have prayed for from this lord: honor from him and joy in love." Then she put the ring on her finger and said, "Sweet love, I send you my heart! Sweet love, you have made it joyful! Sweet love, gentle Eneas!"

[10201–10212] Then Lavine said, "Now there is nothing more. To my lord I send all my greeting. I know well that his great loyalty will not permit him to think or do cruelty to me. I have no more anxiety about anything except to do his sweet pleasure; in this alone is all my desire. He has completely ravished me to himself; by his kindness I am his betrothed. Now may the high gods grant me grace that I may complete the rest quickly."

[10213–10238] Lavine—who was most joyful—like a true, loyal lover made in her turn a gift to her beloved of a sapphire and a diamond, set in two rings. "This sapphire which is set here," said the maiden to Malpriant, "signifies three things: royalty, chastity, and loyalty. To my lord I present the kingship and all the domain of Laurente, together with my chastity, for the loyalty which is in him. The high gods themselves, it seems to me, are all ready to do him honor; and, therefore, I send him together with the sapphire a diamond. These stones have the power to protect from all peril the lovers who loyally keep them." Then the maiden took more jewels of noble worth, and gave them generously to the messenger. And he wisely took leave of the maiden of the beautiful countenance and returned to his lord.

[10239–10262] Malpriant departed from the rich tower and started his return to his lord, who was burning with love. Much did Eneas yearn and long to hear news of her who awaited her joy from him alone. The messenger held the road until he came to where he was much desired. To speak briefly, he told everything to Eneas, that he might rejoice. This lord was not foolish or stupid; he rejoiced very greatly when he had heard Lavine's message from the messenger, and all the signification which she had given to him in her gift. "I am healed," he said. "I feel no illness, for I have received a very good cure from this. She has brought me honor, for which I should praise the high gods. Now I have only to wait to achieve my desire, that this marriage be accomplished."

[10263–10287] The bold and gentle Eneas was attentive to his duty, and made preparations nobly, as he should and could do; and on the appointed day he married the beautiful girl to whom he was betrothed, in the city of Laurente. When he had taken the noble maiden, the barons of the Latin land, followers of Lavine's father, agreed, great and lowly, to receive him as their lord after the death of the king. Eneas, who was without vice, moderate, courteous, and wise, won the love of the barons through his good sense and his bravery, so that after their lord's death he held the land peacefully, and ruled all its domains. He was its king and the beautiful Lavine, his courteous wife, was queen; and they lived in good peace for as many of their days as remained, without trouble and without the disturbance of war.

[10288–10296] Thus came the Latin land to Eneas, who held it as the first of its kings, since he had conquered Turnus. The story is finished: there is no more that remains in memory. Now may the God of heaven grant us glory with the cherubim and seraphim. Here the romance is at its end.

Explicit

BIBLIOGRAPHY

※

Editions

Baehr, R., ed. *Eneas: antikisierender Roman des 12. Jahrhunderts.* (Sammlung romanischer Übungstexte, 53.) Tübingen, 1969. [Selections totaling about 2000 verses from Salverda de Grave's Cfmâ edition, including almost the entire Lavine episode. Designed for school use. Very brief introduction, bibliography, glossary.]

Salverda de Grave, J. J., ed. *Eneas, texte critique.* (Bibliotheca Normannica, IV.) Halle, 1891. [Excellent detailed introduction; full glossary.]

Salverda de Grave, J. J., ed. *Eneas, roman du XIIè siècle.* (Classiques français du moyen âge, 44, 62.) Paris, 1925–29. [Text not critical; based on Bibl. Laurent., Florence, Plut. XLI, cod. 44, the oldest (c. 1200) and best *MS*; referred to in the notes as *Eneas,* Cfmâ.]

Eneas. In *MS* Fr. 1450, Ancien Fonds, Bibl. Nationale. Reproduced by the Modern Language Association of America in photo facsimile (MLA Collection of Photographic Facsimiles, No. 143.) New York, 1930. [The manuscript contains the following, in this order: *Troie, Eneas,* first part of *Roman de Brut, Erec et Enide, Perceval, Cliges, Lancelot,* remaining part of *Roman de Brut, Dolopathos* in a verse translation by "Herbert."]

Scholarship

Adler, A. "Eneas and Lavine: *Puer et Puella Senes," Romanische Forschungen,* LXXI (1959), 73–91. [A significant effort to discern a coherent *sen* for the whole romance. Interpretation persuasive, though sometimes rather forced.]

Angeli, G. *L' "Eneas" e i primi romanzi volgari.* (Ricciardi Documenti di filologia, 15.) Milan, 1971. [Careful and perceptive. Views *Eneas* as the most innovative product of a literary *atelier* in the employ of Henry II, a group which included Wace and the authors of *Thèbes* and *Troie.*]

Auerbach, E. *Literatursprache und Publikum in der Spätantike und im*

Mittelalter. Berne, 1958. (Available in translation: *Literary Language and its Public in Late Latin Antiquity and in the Middle Ages.* [Bollingen Series.] New York, 1965.) [Ch. III: "Camilla oder über die Wiedergeburt des Erhabenen," pp. 135–76; see esp. pp. 137 ff., 156 ff.]

Baumann, F. *Über das Verhältnis zwischen Erb- und Lehnwort aus dem Latein im altfranzösischen Eneas Roman. Ein Beitrag zur Lehnwörterfrage im Französischen.* Ph.D. dissertation. Heidelberg, 1912. [Linguistic rather than literary or historical in interest.]

Bezzola, R. *Les Origines et la formation de la littérature courtoise en occident (500–1200),* 3 pts. in 5 vols. Paris, 1944–63. [This distinguished work treats *Eneas* only briefly, in historical context; see esp. Vol. III, 280–87.]

Biller, G. *Etude sur le style des premiers romans français en vers.* Ph.D. dissertation. Göteborg, 1916. [Detailed examination of stylistic devices in *Thèbes, Eneas, Troie,* and comparison. Useful.]

Cohen, G. *Un grand romancier d'amour et d'aventure au XIIè siècle: Chrétien de Troyes et son oeuvre.* New ed. Paris, 1948. [Ch. II: "Les origines du roman courtois. La triade classique: *Thèbes, Eneas, Troie,*" pp. 31–74. A lucid synthesis of older material, without new contributions. Section on *Eneas* largely summary and commentary on Eneas–Lavine love episode.]

Cormier, R. J. "*Comunalement* and *Soltaine* in the *Eneas,*" *Romance Notes,* XIV (1972), 1–8.

—— *One Heart One Mind: The Rebirth of Virgil's Hero in Medieval French Romance.* (Romance Monographs, 3.) University, Miss., 1973. [Not published at the time of writing. By far the fullest separate interpretation of *Eneas* in any language.]

—— "The Present State of Studies on the *Roman d'Eneas,*" *Cultura Neolatina,* XXXI (1971), 7–39, [A thorough survey, with summaries and commentary. Very useful.]

—— "The Structure of the *Roman d'Eneas,*" *Classical Folia,* XXVI (1972), 107–13. [Adapted from parts of Cormier's study, *One Heart One Mind,* see above.]

Crosland, J. "*Eneas* and the *Aeneid,*" *MLR,* XXIX (1934), 282–90. [Compares *Eneas* with the *Aeneid,* to *Eneas'* great disadvantage, stressing the French poet's lack of interest in character and personality and his thorough debasement of the Latin epic: "the stalwart warrior has become the fastidious cavalier, the valiant matron has degenerated into a simpering maiden, the ingenuous youth has turned into a precocious moralizer, the religious background has disappeared and has not yet been replaced by the chivalrous ideal"—charmingly crusty and prejudiced.]

Dittrich, M. L. *Die "Eneide" Heinrichs von Veldeke. I. Quellenkritischer*

Vergleich mit dem Roman d'Eneas und Vergils Aeneis. Wiesbaden, 1966. [To be followed by a second volume. The most recent and detailed comparative study of the three works. Remorselessly thorough. Stresses Heinrich as a Christian poet, and sharply challenges the work of Frings and Schieb.]

Dressler, A. *Der Einfluss des altfranzösischen Eneas-Romanes auf die altfranzösische Literatur.* Leipzig, 1907. [Göttingen inaugural dissertation. Thorough, cautious. Despite its age, important and extremely useful.]

Duggan, J. J. "Virgilian Inspiration in the *Roman d'Enéas* and in the *Chanson de Roland,*" in *Medieval Epic to the "Epic Theater" of Brecht,* edited by R. Armato and J. Spalek (Los Angeles, 1968), pp. 9–23.

Fairley, B. *Die Eneide Heinrichs von Veldeke und der Roman d'Eneas.* Jena inaugural dissertation, 1910.

Faral, E. "Le récit du jugement de Paris dans l'*Eneas,* et ses sources," *Romania,* XLI (1912), 100–102. [Inconclusive suggestions.]

—— *Recherches sur les sources latines des contes et romans courtois du moyen âge.* Paris, 1913. [A magisterial series of studies, indispensable to the understanding not merely of *Eneas,* but of the rise of courtly romance in France. Its validity has not declined with age.]

Frappier, J. "Remarques sur la peinture de la vie et des héros antiques dans la littérature française du XIIe et du XIIIe siècle," in *L'Humanisme médiéval dans les littératures romanes du XIIe au XIVe siècle, Colloque de Strasbourg, 1962, edited by A. Fourrier (Paris, 1964), pp. 13–54. [Remarks on Eneas scattered but perceptive.]

Frederick, E. C. "The Date of the *Eneas,*" *PMLA,* L (1935), 184–96. [Denies, *contra* Hoepffner, the chronological priority of Wace's *Brut.* The *Brut* may be indebted to *Eneas,* though this is not provable.]

Frings, T., and G. Schieb. *Drei Veldeke-Studien.* Berlin, 1949.

Gogola de Leesthal, O. "Enrico Veldeke e l'Eneit," *Studi medievali,* V (1932), 382–95.

Grillo. P. R. "The Courtly Background in the *Roman d'Enéas,*" *Neuphilologische Mitteilungen,* LXIX (1968), 688–702. [Contrasts the Dido and Lavine episodes.]

Heyl, K. *Die Theorie der Minne in den ältesten Minneromanen Frankreichs.* Marburg, 1911. [Examines the development of love doctrine. Still useful for all the *romans antiques.*]

Hoepffner, E. "L'Eneas et Wace," *Archivum romanicum,* XV (1931), 248–69; XVI (1932), 162–66. [An important study. Sees in *Eneas* the strong influence of Wace's *Brut.*]

—— "Marie de France et l'*Eneas,*" *Studi medievali,* n.s., V (1932), 272–308. [Careful study of influence of *Eneas.*]

Jodogne, O. "Le Caractère des oeuvres 'antiques' dans la littérature française du XIIe et du XIIIe siècle." *L'Humanisme médiéval. . .Colloque de Strasbourg, 1962,* pp. 55–86. [*Eneas* as a stage in the establishment of the romance genre; see esp. pp. 73–79.]

Jones, R. *The Theme of Love in the Romans d'Antiquité.* (*MHRA* Dissertation Series, 5.) London, 1972. [Esp. pp. 30–42.]

Langlois, E. "Chronologie des romans de Thèbes, d'Eneas et de Troie," *Bibliothèque de l École des Chartes,* LXVI (1905), 107–20. [Establishes an order later supported and confirmed by Faral, and now generally accepted.]

Laurie, H. C. R. "*Eneas* and the Doctrine of Courtly Love," *MLR,* LXIV (1969), 283–94. [The interpretations (see also below) by Miss Laurie are learned, imaginative, allusive, richly suggestive, and indirect, sometimes to the point of obscurity. Her view of *Eneas* is consistently that of a first renewal and redirection of Ovidian and other classical themes in the radically altered context of twelfth-century humanism; *Eneas* is a faulty but worthy beginning of movements brought to perfection by Chrétien de Troyes.]

—— "*Eneas* and the *Lancelot* of Chrétien de Troyes," *Medium Aevum,* XXXVII (1968), 142–56.

—— "A New Look at the Marvellous in *Eneas* and Its Influence," *Romania,* XCI (1970), 48–74.

—— "Some Experiments in Technique in Early Courtly Romance," *ZRP,* LXXXVIII (1972), 45–68.

Levi, E. "Marie de France e il romanzo d'Eneas," *Atti de Reale Instituto Veneto di Scienze, Lettere et Arti,* LXXXI, ii (1921–22), 645–86. [Sees Marie de France as the author of *Eneas.* The view has not found acceptance.]

Macabies, A. M. "Que représente la Carthage d'Eneas?" *Revue des langues romanes,* LXXVII (1967), 145–51. [Finds typological overtones in the Carthage episode,]

Micha, A. "Eneas et Cligès," in *Mélanges de philologie romane et de littérature médiévale offerts à Ernest Hoepffner.* (Paris, 1949), pp. 237–43. [Influence.]

Minis, C. "Textkritische Studien über den *Roman d'Eneas,*" *Neophilologus,* XXXIII (1949), 65–85. [Makes use of the readings of Heinrich von Veldeke's early German translation as an instrument in analyzing the MS tradition of *Eneas.* Conclusions significantly different from those of Salverda de Grave.]

Muscatine, C. *Chaucer and the French Tradition.* Berkeley and Los Angeles, 1957. [Significant comments scattered through pp. 19–44.]

Nitze, W. "A Note on Two Virgilian Commonplaces in Twelfth Century_

Literature," in *Mélanges de linguistique et de littérature offerts à M. Alfred Jeanroy* (Paris, 1928), pp. 439–46. [The treatment in *Eneas* of Vergil's *Fama* and *varium et mutabile semper femina.*]

Otto, G. *Der Einfluss des Roman de Thèbes auf die altfranzösische Literatur.* Ph.D. dissertation. Göttingen, 1909.

Pauphilet, A. "Eneas et Enée," *Romania,* LV (1929), 195–213. [A sensitive and revealing comparison of the *Eneas* poet's treatment of the Dido episode with Vergil's treatment.]

—— *Le legs du moyen âge.* Melun, 1950. [Ch. III, "L'Antiquité et *Énéas,*" pp. 91–106, enlarges on Pauphilet's earlier study, dealing perceptively with the poet's adaptation of antiquity to his own time.]

Petullà, R. "Il *Roman d'Eneas* e l'Eneide," *Filologia medioevale e umanistica,* CII (1968), 409–31.

Raynaud de Lage, G. "Les Romans antiques et la représentation de la réalité," *Moyen âge,* LXVII (1961), 247–91.

Rottig, O. *Die Verfasserfrage des "Eneas" und des "Roman de Thèbes."* Halle, 1892.

Salverda de Grave, J. J. "Un imitateur du *Roman d'Eneas* au XIIIe siècle en France," *Studi medievali,* n.s., V (1932), 300–16.

Schieb, G. *Heinrich von Veldeke.* (Sammlung Metzler, M 42.) Stuttgart, 1965. [A terse, authoritative, informative introduction.]

Söhring, O. "Werke bildender Kunst in altfranzösischen Epen," *Romanische Forschungen,* XII (1900), 491–640. [Useful discussion of the artistic and architectural marvels in *Eneas* and the other *romans antiques.*]

Varvaro, A. "I nuovi valori del *Roman d'Eneas,*" *Filologia e letteratura,* XIII (1967), 113–41. [Thorough exploration of *Eneas* as interpreter of Vergil to the twelfth century.]

Warren, F. "*Eneas* and Thomas' *Tristan,*" *MLN,* XXVII (1912), 107–10.

—— "On the Latin Sources of 'Thèbes' and 'Eneas,' " *PMLA,* XVI (1901), 375–87.

Wilmotte, M. *Les Origines du roman en France. L'évolution du sentiment romanesque jusqu'en 1240.* Paris, 1942.

Wittkopp, W. *Die Eneide Heinrichs von Veldeke und der Roman d'Eneas.* Ph.D. dissertation. Leipzig, 1928.

Medieval Adaptation

Heinrich von Veldeke. *Eneit.* Edited by O. Behaghel. Heilbronn, 1882. [Written c. 1170–85. Heinrich's narrative is a free reworking of *Eneas,* much expanded, to 13,500 lines.]

—— *Eneide.* Edited by G. Schieb and T. Frings. 3 vols. (Deutsche Texte des Mittelalters 58, 59, 62.) Berlin, 1964–70. [Vol. 1 contains, on facing pages, an edition of the *Gotha Manuscript* (Chart. A, Nr. 584), and a critical reconstruction of the text in Heinrich's Old Limburg dialect. Vol. 2 contains extensive notes, and Vol. 3 (edited by G. Schieb with G. Kramer and E. Mayer) contains a thorough glossary. The reconstructed Old Limburg text has aroused considerable misgiving.]

Translation

Le Roman d'Eneas. Edited and with an introduction by Monica Schöler-Beinhauer. (Klassische Texte des romanischen Mittelalters in zweisprachigen Ausgaben, 9.) Munich, 1972. [Very brief introduction and bibliography. The text reproduced and translated on facing pages is that of Salverda de Grave's first (critical) edition. Not available while my translation was in progress.]

INDEX TO THE INTRODUCTION

DATE DUE

DEMCO 38-297